HOW TO GET THROUGH
YOUR STRUGGLES

or

YOU CAN WALK ON THE STORMY
WATERS OF YOUR LIFE

by ORAL ROBERTS

FIRST PUBLISHED EDITION

FIRST PRINTING	400,000 COPIES	NOVEMBER 1977
SECOND PRINTING	100,000 COPIES	DECEMBER 1977
THIRD PRINTING	100,000 COPIES	JANUARY 1978
FOURTH PRINTING	100,000 COPIES	MARCH 1978
FIFTH PRINTING	100,000 COPIES	APRIL 1978

SOME ACTUAL STRUGGLES
PEOPLE HAVE WRITTEN TO ME ABOUT

I've forgotten how to smile inside, my heart aches so.

Something has taken the heart out of me.

I pray that Jesus will fix my wings a little so I won't FALL SO HARD.

most of all for my health.

For our financial problems.

Pray for me to have enough faith to believe that God will lift up my hung-down head.

If I can't make the payment, they're going to turn my lights off.

I've felt like throwing in the towel because I feel so discouraged and unloved.

I am depressed

My husband asked me for a divorce and I am shattered.

I am a sinner so I want your prayers to move in on me like a magnet.

What I thought was a mountain, once I got to it, it had been made a plain surface.

When I write you I feel as if I'm writing to a close friend one who really cares. How I need some caring.

My life is in constant danger

Just help me get through the day...

I'm having a bout with doubt.

When we have smooth sailing, we always forget to give, to plant seed for struggles that lie ahead.

for peace of mind

For the healing of my entire body

Table of Contents

A very personal word on how to get through your struggles

Evelyn, my darling wife, was sitting with a small group at a luncheon. Someone asked her where I was.

"He's writing a book," she answered.

"What kind of book?" someone asked.

"Well, it's a little hard to explain. It's about struggles."

Instantly a young man, about thirty, spoke up. "Struggles? He's writing about struggles?"

"I'm not sure that's the name he has decided on yet but, yes, it's about struggles and how to get through them."

The young man almost jumped out of his chair. "I'll buy a copy. I need it right now."

"Well, Oral still has some work to do on the book, besides he doesn't sell his books. He gives them away."

"He doesn't have to give me a copy. If his book will tell me how to get through my struggles, I'll buy it!"

Evelyn told me she looked at this young man and thought: *How can this young man be going through struggles? He is nice looking. He is dressed well. He is with nice people. What's bothering him?*

Then she remembered. She remembered what I have

known all my life, and even more since Christ came into my life. *Everybody struggles!*

She remembered also that down deep everyone wants to get through his struggles.

To the young man she said, "This is July. My husband's book will be offered on our television programs, starting with the Christmas Special. Just write and request it and Oral will send you one free, with no obligation."

He said, "I'll sure do that." Then he added, "If I'm still around."

When Evelyn related this incident to me I sighed. I really did. I said, "Thirty years old and he is going through such struggles he would BUY my book. And if he is still around when it is offered free, he'll write for one. Thirty years old with struggles that are destroying him."

Evelyn said, "Do you think he's talking about suicide?"

I said, "Maybe. But I don't think so. I think he is just a normal, average person bound up inside with problems that he isn't solving, and he feels he may never get through his struggles. He is no different from anybody else. Every one of us has struggles. As soon as we get through one, another hits us.

"Evelyn, I'm glad you told me about this young man, because I'm going to put more in this book than I had planned. I struggle. I know that everybody struggles. I also know how to get through struggles. Not because I am so smart. I know how because I know a lot about God. I know a lot about the way people struggle. I know a lot about faith and how to release it. All the ways I have used to get through a life of nothing but struggles, I can put down in this book. And God has given me a way to write so that people can understand and relate to what I am saying."

Evelyn said, "Oral, every book you've ever written, I've read. Every one of them has reached me. It's helped me get through something that was bothering or hurting me.

You brought God to me. You showed me how. I think, however, that I'm like the young man. The struggle you and I are going through — and have been going through ever since Rebecca and Marshall's death in February — is a struggle we must get through. We've got to get to the other side of it."

"I know," I said. "I think I'll start this book with the greatest hurt we've ever experienced and tell exactly how it struck at us, the storm we were in, and finally how we began to see that we were going to make it."

She said, "Honey, I don't know how we can re-live it, all the details, the fear, the cry in our hearts, the responsibility . . ."

I said, "That's just it. Everybody is going through some struggle. Perhaps like ours, perhaps a different kind. But they are hurting, they are reaching, they are crying out inside. They would give anything to know what God has shown you and me. And that's the way I'm going to write this book — letting our hurts hang out, our mistakes and failures, our risks of faith, and our successes. And I think I'll call it, HOW TO GET THROUGH YOUR STRUGGLES."

Evelyn said, "Oh, I like that title. I can't wait until you get it written so I can read it, all of it."

I replied, "Darling, if you, my wife, feel that way, perhaps a lot of others will feel the same way."

IF YOU ARE STRUGGLING, HERE'S WHAT I AIM TO DO TO HELP YOU

All through this book I'm going to try to show you your real self and why you have to struggle so much. If you learn the WHY you'll have a better chance to find the HOW to get through. And you've got to get *through* your struggles, every one of them.

God wants you to have wholeness, health, healing, and a full measure of success. I know that.

I'm going to show you exciting things about God you

never knew before. God has revealed them to me. I am not an imitator but an initiator, an innovator. I believe God gave that ability to me as a gift to use to help people like yourself. You can get help through this gift of God in my ministry.

I'm going to show you how to get miracles. You won't make it without miracles. If you think you can, I can assure you that you won't ever, ever, get through your struggles. I tried that but after getting bumped around with no an- swers and finally with no way out, I opened up and began thinking about the possibility of miracles. I have a hard head. It was hard for God to get my attention. When He did, and I saw my need of miracles, I began to get myself open. Getting yourself open for miracles to happen TO YOU is something you can do. It will change your life.

I'm going to show you a great fact — God will always meet you at the point of your need. That I know without a shadow of doubt. GOD WILL ALWAYS MEET YOU AT THE POINT OF YOUR NEED. I'll talk to you in this book about God meeting you at the point of your need until it will be burned into your consciousness.

I'm going to show you that you have faith. Maybe a whole lot, *maybe only a little.* But you have it. I'm going to show you that FAITH IS NOT SOMETHING YOU HAVE TO GET — IT'S SOMETHING YOU ALREADY HAVE. When I first learned that, my life started changing. I quit asking for faith and started using the little that I had. I've seen it grow and grow. I know this is going to do something great for you. It will put you in position to use what you already have. You'll feel uplifted by it.

I'm going to show you how to pay more attention to your "gut feelings," your premonitions, your inner urges, and how to get that *knowing* inside you. Those are things you can't buy. God gives them to you. But you can waste and throw them away by not knowing *how* and *when* to pay attention to them. You're going to learn something very important about them and they will help you get through your struggles. I say this because I know it will happen.

I'm going to show you that in order to get through your struggles, you've got to start right. Not by starting with your reason or your thought processes or by what your five senses can do for you. Starting right is doing something utterly different from what you've been taught — even brainwashed — to do all your life. Starting right is to originate every response you make toward your struggles BY STARTING FIRST IN YOUR SPIRIT. I stumbled onto this when medically all hope was given up for me to live. I got a great miracle and I'm alive today because of it. Ever since that I've tried to understand better how to see myself as a spiritual being with a mind, living in a physical body. In other words, a whole person. Every time I've succeeded in starting with my spirit first — my inner self — I have found myself in position to receive a miracle! The thing about a miracle is, it settles the issue. It gets the job done. It gets you through! Getting through is the only thing that will ever make you successful and happy.

Then — and this may help you most — I'm going to show you how to get yourself into position to use your faith, how to know it is faith, really how to know that you know that you know!

NOW BEFORE YOU READ THE TERRIBLE STRUGGLE of Evelyn and me and our family, and how we came through it, here are two things I ask you to do.

FIRST, I ASK YOU TO TRUST ME. GO WITH ME IN THE JOURNEY I AM ABOUT TO TAKE YOU ON. TRUST ME.

As St. Paul said, "Follow me as I follow Christ" (1 Corinthians 11:1). I'm following Christ the Man, the Savior. I know I am. From this standpoint, I ask you: Trust me. I will show you THE WAY.

SECOND, I ASK YOU TO OPEN YOUR MIND TO THE HUMANNESS OF JESUS. YES, HE IS THE SON OF GOD. HE IS ALSO THE SON OF MAN. A MYSTERY? YES, BEYOND ALL HUMAN UNDERSTANDING. You can get it only by your faith. I'll show you how to do that. You'll be so much better off that you will feel you're a new person.

In this book you're going to see Jesus the man, the human being, doing human things, going through human experiences, using only the kind of faith that you and I have ourselves. No phoniness, no hocus-pocus. Something real that you can touch and that will touch you to the core of your being.

No matter where you hurt or what struggle you are going through this moment, I want you to meet Jesus, the flesh and blood person like yourself. I want you to meet Jesus the man. It may be the ONLY way you'll ever fully know Him as the Son of God Who is the Source of your total supply . . . your Savior.

Do these two things I've just mentioned and I commit something to you.

I promise you a most marvelous journey THROUGH your struggles. Your struggles will not succeed in riding you under. You will RIDE THEM UNDER. I promise you that.

Chapter One

How in the worst struggle Evelyn and I ever had, we discovered Jesus walking on the water and learned we could walk on the water too

"And Jesus went unto them,
walking upon the water" (Matthew 14:25).

February 11, 1977, was the worst struggle Evelyn and I have ever faced, the worst our family has ever faced.

A plane exploded over a Kansas wheat field and our daughter Rebecca and her husband Marshall were instantly killed.

The police, with my long-time associate Collins Steele, knocked on our door early the next morning. Evelyn opened the door then called: "Oral! Oral! Will you come in here right now?"

The sound of her voice made me drop everything and hurry to the door. Evelyn was in a state of shock and started trying to tell me but couldn't get through it.

The policeman said, "Mr. Roberts, I've come to tell you YOUR DAUGHTER AND SON-IN-LAW ARE DEAD."

I said, "Just a moment, officer. What happened?" Collins told me. The plane had exploded and Rebecca and Marshall were in it.

Someone handed me the newspaper. The headline clear

Evelyn and I faced the worst tragedy of our life when death claimed the lives of our beloved daughter and son-in-law, Rebecca and Marshall Nash, leaving their three young children without parents.

across the front page screamed the words. ORAL ROB-
ERTS' DAUGHTER KILLED.

It went on to tell of Marshall and Rebecca and two other
couples being killed.

Collins volunteered to make absolutely positive identifi-
cation and have the bodies brought to Tulsa.

Evelyn said, "Oh, the families of the other couples."

I can't tell you the terror, the grief that swept over
Evelyn and me. Evelyn and I grabbed each other. We
didn't know what to do. We weren't even fully dressed.

Then Evelyn said, "Honey, we've got to hurry and get
dressed and go over to Rebecca's house and tell the
children."

I thought of Brenda, thirteen; Marcia, eight; and little
Jon Oral, five, over there at their house waiting for their
parents to come home.

As Evelyn and I were trying to hurry and dress I thought
we would die.

Rebecca, my oldest. Rebecca was the only one of our
four children born at home. The others were born in hospitals. We lived where there was no hospital and the doctor
had delivered her at the house. I had been there with
Evelyn when that little curly-haired daughter came out of
her mother's body. I saw her and in a few moments held
her in my arms.

This was rushing through my mind. All those years of
raising her, seeing her married, then the three precious
grandchildren, Brenda her oldest, our first. I remembered
the first time Rebecca and Marshall met at age four.

Marshall was dark and part Indian like myself — so loving, so thoughtful, a young man of hard work and integrity,
full of love for God and his family. He was a young man
making his mark on Tulsa, a man with a future. He was
dead. He and Rebecca. They had gone away for a few
days and on the way home the plane had exploded.

Only a few weeks before, I had said to the people of America, "There's going to be a Breakthrough from Heaven in '77." God had spoken these words in my heart. Over and over on television and radio, in our magazines, in my letters answering people who had written me for prayer, in my sermons and my private conversations I had said, "Breakthrough from Heaven in '77."

I believed it and because I believed it and saw it, others believed it. We were all looking up.

Now it seemed the devil was mocking me. "Where is your Breakthrough from Heaven in '77?"

It seemed a voice said, "Oral Roberts, you've preached to people everywhere that there is a God, that there are miracles, that God cares and intervenes in people's lives, He comes to them in the storms of life. Now what do you have to say? What are you going to do now?"

One of my other long-time associates, Ron Smith, had arrived by this time and he drove Evelyn and me over to Rebecca and Marshall's house, about two miles away, where the three little ones were waiting, not knowing their parents were dead. I said out loud, "God, You've got to know something about this that we don't know."

Over and over I said it as Evelyn held my hand and Ron drove, with tears filling his eyes. "God, You've got to know something about this that we don't know."

It was Saturday morning and usually the children slept late. But at 7:00 when we arrived, they were eating breakfast. When we walked in I said, "Why are you up so early?"

Little eight-year-old Marcia said, "We're waiting for our Mommy and Daddy. We want to see them."

And I had to say, "Your Mommy and Daddy are not coming home. You'll have to see them in heaven."

Evelyn and I couldn't help it. We burst into tears. Brenda, the oldest, picked up a new little plaque I had prepared for my partners —

GOD IS GREATER THAN ANY PROBLEM I HAVE

She held it to her breast as the tears started flowing. The five of us wrapped our arms around each other and cried. Evelyn and I thought we were going to die.

Our daughter. Our son-in-law. Their bodies strewn over the ground, scarcely recognizable. The children suddenly orphaned.

At that moment we never thought of anybody else's children. We never thought about others having lost loved ones. We only thought about ourselves. We were hurt, bent double in our grief. Our loss was killing us. How could we make it through all this?

What would happen to the children? A new home had to be arranged. We felt everything was out of balance. Talk about a storm grabbing at us and things tearing us apart, I thought for awhile we might go down. I thought we were going to die.

For thirty years of our ministry we had told of a good God. Was He real after all? Was He good?

Well, somehow we got through the first day. We knew Marshall and Rebecca were very close to Bill and Edna Earle Nash, Marshall's brother and sister-in-law, and there had been an agreement between them that if anything ever happened to Marshall and Rebecca, Bill and Edna would take their children. There were only two years difference in their ages. Bill and Edna Earle were returning to Tulsa and I reached them by phone at the St. Louis airport. Already reports of the tragedy were on all the news services. They had heard and were crushed. Would they, could they, take the children?

"Oh, yes. We've been praying and God has impressed us to take them as our very own and raise them as Marshall and Rebecca would, in church and in God's love and ways."

They had only one daughter. She had gone to Oral Roberts University, where her father was on the Board of

Regents. And she had just married an ORU boy and left home to set up housekeeping. Bill said, "It seems right. Now we'll have three more to raise and they'll be like our very own."

SUNSETS ONLY MAKE FOR MORE SUNRISES

Later I met with Rev. and Mrs. Walter Nash, Marshall's parents, and found them strong in the Lord. This was the second of three sons they had lost within a period of two years. But their faith made their faces glow in their tears. I asked them about the children. Brother Nash said, "Brother Oral, we're in our seventies. We're facing the sunset and then the sunrise in glory. We have confidence in you to do for our grandchildren what God wants done. We'll leave it in your hands. I know Bill and Edna Earle love God. They love the children. And under the circumstances, everything will work out for good."

What Brother Nash had said in his strong faith had ministered to my own spirit. Life does have its sunsets. The sun had set for Marshall and Rebecca. But the sunrise in heaven for them was certain. Now in our struggle to get through the dark and desperate hours after the sunset, our own spirits were going to have to bring assurance there would be a sunrise for us. The curtain of grief would be pulled back and we would be able to experience the sunrise.

We joined hands and prayed. From there Evelyn and I went to Bill's house and we consecrated the new family and dedicated the new union to God. Grief and joy were mingled but we knew God was at work. The children accepted their new parents, later legalized, and today they are one beautiful family.

WITH THE HELP OF THE HOLY SPIRIT . . .

We got through all that. Already the Abundant Life Prayer Group in the Prayer Tower was swamped with telephone calls. Love was flowing into our hearts from our dear partners. Telegrams were pouring in to us, many from people we didn't know and many from people like Billy Graham, Dale Evans, President Carter. Our other children stood with us. Their own grief was almost overwhelming, for we are a close family in Christ. My associates took charge of the funeral arrangements in Mabee Center at ORU. They expected a large crowd. Members of the ORU and OREA boards came from near and far and loved us with their prayers and words of affection. It helped so much.

But on the fourth night as Evelyn and I were getting ready for bed, she said, "Oh, Oral, I'm not going to make it tonight. This is the worst night of all."

Again I thought I would die. She said, "Honey, would you take me in your arms and hold me and pray for me in the Spirit?"

"Praying in the Spirit" is what St. Paul calls praying in tongues (1 Corinthians 14:14, 15). This is part of the charismatic experience of the Holy Spirit Evelyn and I have had and have used so effectively in our private devotions. Remember that Jesus came to His disciples during a storm in the fourth watch of the night. Well, this was the worst storm that had ever come to us.

I took my darling in my arms and prayed in tongues, which I call the prayer language of the Spirit. As I prayed in the prayer language, she began to pray in the Spirit also. When we finished we prayed in our own tongue and it was the interpretation back from God for our loss. This is the first part of the interpretation we received:

> "For we wrestle not against flesh and blood, but against principalities, against powers, against the rulers of the darkness of this world ... Wherefore take unto you the whole armour of God ... and having done all to stand. Stand therefore" (Ephesians 6:12-14).

In the midst of our sorrow the Holy Spirit told us to plant a seed out of our grief by going on national television and sharing our hurt with the people.

The second part of the interpretation was:

"Go on national television in your half-hour program the next Sunday morning and while you feel the hurt and loss, tell the people how you feel and give witness to My power and to the Resurrection."

YOU NEED TO PLANT A SEED, ESPECIALLY IN YOUR GRIEF

Evelyn cried, "I can't do it. It's too soon. I'll break down and won't be able to get through it."

I said, by the power of the Holy Spirit in me, "Darling, then I'll go on by myself. We've got to go on television and plant a seed out of our grief. If we don't plant our seed now, we'll never have the miracle to get over this and it will haunt us the rest of our lives."

She said, "Why can't we wait a few months?"

I said, "This grief will destroy us. It'll destroy my ministry. It'll tear us apart. Let's not wait six months or a year, then tell the people how we felt when the storm hit. Let's do it while our hearts are being torn out of us. Let's let them see us in our humanness and our hurts just like theirs. Let's tell people how we feel."

She said, "I won't let you do it alone. I'll do it with you. I'll plant my seed, too."

My associates quickly arranged the camera set-up, put us on a simple homelike set and we started. Just like that, with no preparation, no music, no introduction — just us.

As Evelyn and I looked at the camera suddenly we were aware of all those who have lost loved ones, and with the tears streaming down our cheeks we began telling them how we felt when we lost our daughter and son-in-law.

Our hurt hung out. Our tears stung our faces. There were moments the words wouldn't come and we stumbled around some. It was a live program with a few of our associates and friends who could get in a small taping studio. Yet we felt so alone.

Near the end of the half-hour I began to feel the upward swell of the Spirit, our miracle already starting to come from the seed we were planting out of our need. I heard myself telling that we knew Marshall and Rebecca were real Christians, that they had come to Christ in their youth and had lived for Him. "But," I said, "if they weren't Christians, in the brief moments of the plane crash a good God would have given them time to call on His name. And all you who have lost loved ones and don't know they are saved and are in heaven with our Lord, how do you know there wasn't that moment before their death that the Holy Spirit opened their hearts and they came to Christ? None of us knows how far God's mercy extends. But we know it extends further than man's."

I added, "On the cross one of the men crucified with Jesus, a thief, had in the last moment cried, 'Lord, remember me when thou comest into thy kingdom,' and Jesus did!"

We ended it on the Resurrection and it seemed that heaven came down and shone across the earth. We could feel it.

When the cameras were turned off, Evelyn and I stood up and hugged each other. We had planted our seed of faith. The studio was flooded with love from our associates and regents. And suddenly we knew our miracle was happening. WE WERE WALKING ON THE WATER!

God had taken the grief in His great hands and was pulling it out of our hearts. We said to our associates, "We're going to resume our lives. We're going on with this ministry. There is a God. He is good and He is real to us as never before. He is more real to us through the homegoing of Rebecca and Marshall than we ever could have known. We know they are in heaven and someday we are going there. There will be a Breakthrough from Heaven in '77. I still believe it."

When we finished taping, the small audience of associates, the ORU Regents, and other friends all crowded around us. There was one more word Evelyn and I felt in our hearts:

"There's going to be a Resurrection from the dead . . ."

Already we feel that Resurrection. It's all over us and in us. Through it we're going to be able to help people better than ever. We are walking on the water in our struggle and they are going to see that they can walk on theirs, too.

LIFE'S CHALLENGES

And that's how this book came to be written. Because we hurt, because we planted a seed, because our miracle has been happening, this book couldn't be held back. I had to write it.

NOW I WANT YOU TO READ *ALL* OF MATTHEW 14:22 THROUGH VERSE 36. Because from this moment on I want to make this portion of Scripture more real to you than the very breath of your nostrils. I want it to live in you until you, too, can learn to "walk on the water" in the worst storms of your life.

HERE IS MATTHEW 14:22-36.

"And straightway Jesus constrained his disciples to get into a ship, and to go before him unto the other side, while he sent the multitudes away. And when he had sent the multitudes away, he went up into a mountain apart to pray: and when the evening was come, he was there alone. But the ship was now in the midst of the sea, tossed with waves: for the wind was contrary. And in the fourth watch of the night Jesus went unto them, walking on the sea. And when the disciples saw him walking on the sea, they were troubled, saying, It is a spirit; and they cried out for fear. But straightway Jesus spake unto them, saying, Be of good cheer; it is I; be not afraid. And Peter answered him and said, Lord, if it be thou, bid me come unto thee on the water. And he said, Come. And when Peter was come down out of the ship,

*he walked on the water, to go to Jesus. But when he
saw the wind boisterous, he was afraid; and beginning to
sink, he cried, saying, Lord, save me. And immediately
Jesus stretched forth his hand, and caught him, and said
unto him, O thou of little faith, wherefore didst thou
doubt? And when they were come into the ship, the
wind ceased. Then they that were in the ship came and
worshipped him, saying, Of a truth thou art the Son of
God. And when they were gone over, they came into
the land of Gennesaret. And when the men of that place
had knowledge of him, they sent out into all that country round about, and brought unto him all that were
diseased; and besought him that they might only touch
the hem of his garment: AND AS MANY AS TOUCHED
WERE MADE PERFECTLY WHOLE."*

Now at the end of Chapter 1, as at the end of each
chapter, are some very deep challenges, life's questions we
all have to answer. Please do exactly as I tell you . . . and
test yourself. It's going to help you.

NOW ASK YOURSELF . . .

LIFE'S QUESTION: How can ➤ **GOD'S WAY**
I get through the worst storm   SAY IT: I CAN LEARN TO
of my life without going   WALK ON THE WATER AS
under?   JESUS DID.

LIFE'S QUESTION: How can ➤ **GOD'S WAY**
I find hope when night falls   SAY IT: I CAN FACE THE
and the storm rages?   NIGHT AND THE STORM
                                   KNOWING THAT SUNSETS
                                   ONLY MAKE FOR MORE SUN-
                                   RISES.

LIFE'S QUESTION: How can ➤ **GOD'S WAY**
I deal with the death of a   SAY IT: I HAVE HOPE – THE
loved one?   BLESSED HOPE OF THE
                                   RESURRECTION!!

LIFE'S QUESTION: When → GOD'S WAY
tragedy strikes, how can I go   SAY IT: EVEN IN TRAGEDY I
on living?   CAN GO ON LIVING BECAUSE
                                 I KNOW. THERE'S GOING TO
                                 BE A BREAKTHROUGH FROM
                                 HEAVEN FOR ME! I BELIEVE
                                 IT!

LIFE'S QUESTION: What can → GOD'S WAY
I do when my problems so   SAY IT: I CAN GO TO GOD
overwhelm me I feel helpless   FOR HELP AND HOPE BE-
and hopeless?   CAUSE I KNOW HE IS GREAT-
                                 ER THAN ANY PROBLEM OR
                                 NEED I HAVE. HE WILL SEE
                                 ME THROUGH ANY STORM I
                                 FACE.

LIFE'S QUESTION: What can → GOD'S WAY
I do when I want to keep   SAY IT: I CAN SAY, "GOD
asking "Why?"   KNOWS SOMETHING ABOUT
                                 THIS THAT I DON'T KNOW."

LIFE'S QUESTION: What can → GOD'S WAY
I say when the worst hap-   SAY IT: I CAN LOOK THE
pens and the devil mocks me   WORLD IN THE EYE AND SAY,
and people say, "Where is   "GOD WILL COME TO ME
your God now?"   WALKING ON THE WATER.
                                 HE IS ALWAYS THERE WHEN
                                 I NEED HIM THE MOST."

LIFE'S QUESTION: How can → GOD'S WAY
I make it through terrible loss SAY IT: I CAN OVERCOME
and hurt?   HURT AND LOSS BY PLANT-
                                 ING A SEED OF FAITH AND
                                 EXPECTING A MIRACLE.

LIFE'S QUESTION: In this → GOD'S WAY
terrible storm I can't help but SAY IT: EVEN WHEN THE
wonder — is God real? Is He   WORST STORM OF MY LIFE IS
a good God after all?   RAGING, I KNOW THERE IS A
                                 GOD, HE IS GOOD, AND HE IS
                                 REAL TO ME AS NEVER BE-
                                 FORE.

LIFE'S QUESTION: Can anything take away the grief that is literally breaking my heart and destroying my life? → **GOD'S WAY** SAY IT: GOD CAN TAKE THE GRIEF IN HIS GREAT HANDS AND PULL IT OUT OF MY HEART AS I PLANT A SEED OF FAITH.

PUTTING IT ALL TOGETHER FOR MYSELF

I CAN LEARN TO WALK ON THE WATER AS JESUS DID.

* * * * * *

I CAN FACE THE NIGHT AND THE STORM KNOWING THAT SUNSETS ONLY MAKE FOR MORE SUNRISES.

* * * * * *

I HAVE HOPE — THE BLESSED HOPE OF THE RESURRECTION!!

* * * * * *

EVEN IN TRAGEDY I CAN GO ON LIVING BECAUSE I KNOW THERE'S GOING TO BE A BREAKTHROUGH FROM HEAVEN FOR ME! I BELIEVE IT!

* * * * * *

I CAN GO TO GOD FOR HELP AND HOPE BECAUSE I KNOW HE IS GREATER THAN ANY PROBLEM OR NEED I HAVE. HE WILL SEE ME THROUGH ANY STORM I FACE.

* * * * * *

I CAN SAY, "GOD KNOWS SOMETHING ABOUT THIS THAT I DON'T KNOW."

* * * * * *

I CAN LOOK THE WORLD IN THE EYE AND SAY, "GOD WILL COME TO ME WALKING ON THE WATER. HE IS ALWAYS THERE WHEN I NEED HIM THE MOST!"

I CAN OVERCOME HURT AND LOSS BY PLANTING
A SEED OF FAITH AND EXPECTING A MIRACLE.
EVEN WHEN THE WORST STORM OF MY LIFE IS
RAGING, I KNOW THERE IS A GOD, HE IS GOOD,
AND HE IS REAL TO ME AS NEVER BEFORE.

******

GOD CAN TAKE THE GRIEF IN HIS GREAT HANDS
AND PULL IT OUT OF MY HEART AS I PLANT A
SEED OF FAITH.

******

Now with these powerful facts — God's ways — in your
mind it would be a good idea to go back and read the
chapter again. Why don't you?

Chapter Two

When you are doing what you think is right, why do you have to go through storms and struggles? Why?

"And straightway Jesus constrained his disciples to get into a ship, and to go before him unto the other side . . . . But the ship was now in the midst of the sea, tossed with waves; for the wind was contrary" (Matthew 14:22,24).

Can you imagine it? Jesus' own hand-picked disciples, the ones closest to Him, sent on a journey in which a storm would strike them? A storm of tossing waves, contrary winds, and fearful hearts? Well, let me tell you the hardest thing in the world for me, and I believe for anyone else. It's to be doing what I believe is right, when a storm hits me so hard it stuns me nearly out of my senses. Every time this happens to me I find myself asking:

WHY HAS THIS HAPPENED TO ME?

I have said enough WHYS to last me a lifetime. Yet I keep on asking them. You no doubt do, too. But let me tell you something else. I'm not the only one who asks why. You're not the only one. The twelve disciples of Jesus asked why too.

The storm on the Sea of Galilee tore them up. Its suddenness and danger almost tore their emotions apart. They couldn't understand the storm hitting them. After all, they were doing what they were supposed to be doing.

They hadn't blasphemed God.

They hadn't killed anybody.

They hadn't done ANYTHING to cause that death-dealing storm to strike their boat and suddenly plunge them into a situation where they were absolutely helpless. And hopeless.

They were doing what they thought Jesus wanted them to do. They were taking the boat and going ahead of Him to the other side of the Sea of Galilee. He had prevailed upon them to do it.

NO ONE DID ANYTHING WRONG

Of course, Jesus knew something about this journey they didn't know. He was sending them to a place they ought to be. It was necessary that they arrive, that they have a goal. For the success of their lives it was terribly important to them, too, to ARRIVE ON THE OTHER SIDE.

Although it was always dangerous to be on the Sea of Galilee, which is 600 feet below sea level and subject to quick, violent storms, the twelve disciples were doing the right thing. Jesus had said, "Go." So even though it was night, which greatly increased the danger, they went on their way.

Not only were the disciples doing the right thing, Jesus Himself was doing the thing He felt was right for *Him*. He had some praying to do in a quiet place in one of the mountains nearby. And just as nighttime increased the danger for the twelve disciples, it also increased the danger of Jesus being in the mountains alone.

Jesus as a man, whom the Father sent to be a human being like us, felt the need to communicate with the Father

— to talk, to listen, to give, to receive. It was the time and place for Him, as a man, to pray. It was the time and place for Him, as a man, to communicate with God and for God to communicate with Him in His humanness on this earth.

Neither the twelve nor Jesus did anything wrong. They were all doing the things they felt were right for them.

THEN WHY DID THE STORM STRIKE?

Can you understand that? What kind of God would let that happen?

Well, one day as this was pressing in upon my mind, I decided to ask God about it. I said, "Jesus, let me ask You a question." I felt Him responding in my spirit and I continued.

"Why did You command these disciples of Yours, men who were trying to obey You, to do something that would allow the worst storm of their lives to hit them? Why did You permit this awful struggle?"

Are you concerned about it, Oral?

"Am I concerned? I am more than concerned. I'm baffled. I'm hurt. A lot of people feel the same way. You see, Jesus, this hits home. I want to know why it happened to them. And, I want to know why it happens to me. What have I done? And what did they do? Everybody I know asks the same questions."

Oral, you have studied My Word, the Holy Scripture, haven't you?

"Many times through many years, from Genesis to Revelation, over and over."

Have you noticed the two threads that run through the Bible?

"I think so. But would You help me see them more clearly?"

The two threads running through the Bible and all of life on earth are, first, God seeking to bless and guide man

— that's you too, you know — whom He created in His own likeness; and second, the devil seeking to change you from the way God made you so he can lead you astray and destroy you. These are the two threads. Everything hangs on them, Oral.

I BEGAN TO SEE THE WHY

As I thought back through the Scriptures from the very beginning as God describes it, and as I continued listening to Jesus I began to see the WHY of all the whys I had ever asked. The answer started coming. And in the midst of my storm, the inner light shone and a better understanding dawned concerning the two threads running through the Bible and through our lives. So think about what I'm going to share with you. You need to know it. Because it will really help you understand THE WHY of your having to go through struggles.

SOMETHING HAS GONE WRONG IN THIS WORLD GOD CREATED

Something has gone wrong from the way this world began. That something has turned good into bad. It's the same thing that happens when a child is born. He's started out right in all the good things of life. Then suddenly he falls into wrong hands. He listens. He hears the part that sounds so great, so desirable. But he misses the part that is so bad. He says, "I believe I'll just take this way for my life. My parents won't understand but I know how to take care of myself. I can handle it."

The parents reach out to him. They tell him this is not the way.

And after a while he wakes up. He discovers the good teaching he had was not so bad. He's hurting now because he's gotten into something over his head. It's bad. It's bad!

Then begins the struggle for us to get him back, and for him to find the right way for himself.

What I have described happened to me. I was the boy who listened to the wrong voices and got on the wrong road. In the struggle to get back, death rode the waves of my life and I almost went under.

If you can understand what I'm saying, you can understand how things started in the beginning, and then went wrong.

A TIME I DIDN'T BELIEVE

There was a time I didn't believe in the Creation story in Genesis. It meant nothing to me. So I began studying all the other theories. I found some things that appeared to be truth. But in every theory something was lacking. Something was missing.

I discovered in myself I was more than just a mind or an intellect. I was more than just a physical body reacting to life with the five senses of sight, hearing, taste, touch, and smell.

I learned the hard way that I had an inner self. And I wanted to know what that was. I finally realized the only place I could find out the *whole truth* was not in the various theories of evolution I had been studying. It began in the first book of the Bible — Genesis, which means *beginnings*.

GOD MADE MAN DIFFERENT

I read that wondrous story and something in me told me it was true. It was God Who, in the beginning, created the world and everything in it. But His masterpiece was man. God had made him different from any other creature. He wasn't different physically, for his body was made from the dust, the chemicals, of the earth. He had an animal body. My own body confirmed this in the instincts it had felt that influenced me to do many wrong things before my salvation.

God made man different spiritually. He breathed into man's nostrils and man became something different from all

How I, as a boy loved my parents — and that love grew even deeper with every year. This is one of the last pictures taken with Mamma and Papa and me.

other animals, something special beyond all telling. "MAN BECAME A LIVING SOUL" (Genesis 2:7).

When I read that, it really got hold of me. I began to feel inside me there IS a God. I saw God had to have a special love for man. He made him different from the animals. He gave him a SOUL. And He not only gave him a soul, he became soul. I saw that man is a spiritual being created in God's own likeness, living in a physical body, possessing a mind with which to think and reason. I saw that man is a spiritual being with gifts from God so great I stood in awe. I stood in awe to think these gifts were in me for I realized I, too, was a human being. Let's think about these God-given gifts. It's very important to you to know about them and how they can work in your life, in your struggles.

THE GIFT OF COMMUNICATION

The first man and woman God made were able to talk with God, their Creator, easily and naturally, with no inhibitions, no fears, no awe. They talked in a normal way with the loving God Who had given them their life, their identity, their personality, their body, their intellect, and above all their inner self — their SPIRIT. They were able to make a whole-man response to God, the Creator.

And God talked with them too, easily and naturally. There was no threat in His voice, no condemnation, no judgment . . . just love. He made a whole-God response to man and woman, the masterpiece of His creation.

He had made them in His own spiritual likeness and therefore they were good. EVERYTHING WAS GOOD. Everything could communicate.

What beauty and harmony there was in this kind of communication! How we need it today — and can have it.

I can remember as a little boy growing up how I loved my father! How I adored my mother! How I could feel their love!

Papa would put me on his lap and talk to me so easily and so naturally.

And Mamma would often talk to me. She told me about my birth. She told me how she had promised me to God. She told me the stuttering with which I had been born would one day be healed by God. She told me I would be normal. She told me God would speak to me. And both Papa and Mamma told me I would preach the Gospel.

It was strange that I could talk with Papa and Mamma without stuttering. With others I stuttered. What was the difference? I think it was the loving relationship between us. There was no fear, no inhibition. There was love and understanding and acceptance. We could communicate.

Because of this gift of communication between me and my parents, I was able to see with something from within me that God loved me and there was good ahead. It was the worst mistake of my young life to allow other people's reaction to my stuttering to warp my personality and give me a terrible inferiority complex. I thought I would never amount to anything. I rebelled against my parents, against God, and fled from home. Communication was broken and I lived to see it haunt me — and nearly destroy me.

THE GIFT OF POWER AND DOMINION

In the beginning God handed man a gift of power over every living thing, including the earth. The earth and all other creatures would be responsive to him. Man simply "took dominion" and it happened. Some think this was the beginning of science. I have come to know that science, used under God, can harness this universe for our good. If wrongly used, science can create monstrous things to destroy all of God's creation on this earth. Science must never be allowed to control us. We must control and guide it!

Through the gift of power and dominion, man had the potential to discover every good thing on the earth, to bring it into harmony with himself, with God, and with others. The incomparable things of nature — energy, precious metals, food, medicine — are things that still astonish and delight us. At the same time man has the potential to fail to discover these things or to misuse them, bringing on himself poverty, hunger, discrimination, bitterness, even war.

THE GIFT OF CHOICE

As I read the Genesis story, I saw how God had endowed man with the power of choice. I thought, "God, why did you give man the power of choice? Why did you give him this awesome privilege, the incomparable power to choose? Why?"

I felt the Lord speaking to me again.

Oral, I gave man the gift of choice. But I also gave him guidelines. I gave him choice WITH responsibility.

"Lord, didn't You take an awful chance in giving man the power to choose — the power to say yes or no to You, his Creator?"

Yes. I took the chance that man would choose to reject My love as well as to accept it. I made myself vulnerable. But love is always vulnerable. It's an act of faith. It risks everything.

"What do You mean, Lord?"

I didn't want man to be a robot. Nor did I want him to be just an animal, like a horse into whose mouth a bit may be placed and who can be forced to be subservient. I didn't want to force man to love Me back against his will. I wanted him to love Me because he WANTED to love Me. I wanted it to be a voluntary act of his own choice. Only in this way could I be his true God and he My true man.

"Is this why you permitted the devil to tempt him in the Garden of Eden?"

What I did was to place before him the potential of choosing good or bad. The good was to eat of the Tree of

Life which, if he had chosen, would have enabled him to live forever in the perfect state in which I created him. The bad was to eat of the Tree of the Knowledge of good and evil which, if chosen, would take away his immortality and bring him into a state of death, or a separation from the perfect state in which he was created.

"The devil told him a lie, didn't he? The devil caused him to doubt You and Your intention for him. Isn't that right?"

The devil didn't make man do anything. He doesn't have that power. The power of choice is in man alone. The devil merely offered the temptation. Man had the power of choice. He could choose to eat of the Tree of Life as I told him. He could choose to eat of the Tree of Knowledge as Satan told him. It was within the power of man himself to choose. By giving man this power of choice, neither I nor the devil could force him.

"Lord, what was so bad about man choosing to eat of the Tree of Knowledge instead of the Tree of Life?"

The Tree of Knowledge of good and evil was a symbol I used. I could have set apart something else. And the devil would have used it also to tempt man. But the Tree of Knowledge was the more important because it tempted man to choose to let Me be God or to be god to himself.

"What do You mean, Lord?"

I made man a spirit, to reflect My likeness. Since I made him a spiritual being, I clothed him with a mind and a body. My intent for him was that he respond to Me and live through his spirit first. I made him that way. The devil was cunning. As the fallen archangel, Lucifer, coming in the form of a serpent, which at the time was a beautiful creature very different from serpents today, the devil appealed to man's mind and to his five senses rather than to his spirit. You see, the devil, having tried to become God and failed, was now trying to get back at Me, the Creator, through man,

My greatest creation. The battle over man is between the devil and Me. So the devil saw that if he could get man to choose his own knowledge over the knowledge and wisdom of God, it would be the first step toward reducing man from a spiritual being to a mere physical being responding to life on the level of his intellect and physical senses alone. I had told man if he chose this path he would die, that is, he would separate himself as a spiritual being from Me, he would elevate his mind above his spirit and find himself in worlds of problems that knowledge alone could not handle. Because he used his gift of choice in accepting the devil's temptation, he lost the most precious gift of all.

"What did he lose that was so precious?"

He lost his relationship with Me, his closeness with Me, his communication with Me, his understanding of Me, his love for Me, the proper function of himself as a soul. He lost the power of his spirit — his real self — to respond with joy and love to Me, to life, and to his fellow beings. He couldn't communicate easily and naturally anymore. When he lost the power of true communication, suddenly he was all tied up inside. By trying to be a little god, strutting around as a know-it-all, he became NOT what I made him, but instead he became a fearful, frustrated being, trying to cover up the fact that the knowledge he had was not enough. Through choosing the devil's way instead of Mine, he lost his immortality. He became mortal. That means now he would have to die. He felt naked and defenseless. It made him frightened of Me. His environment changed from an Eden to an unconquered and frightening earth. It scared him. He was scared of everything — of Me, of himself, of his environment, of what was going to happen to him. In his fear he began to cover up, trying to hide the self he had become, the position he was now in. I began seeking to find him the way he was as I made him. And I am still seeking to find him.

"Is this why You sent Your Son to be a man, a human being like we are, to come down here and suffer in man's place, even going to the cross to die?"

When the devil succeeded in getting man to wrongly use his power of choice, I promised a Redeemer from the off-spring of the woman. The Redeemer would be a man whom I indwelt in my fullness, really, the Second Adam. The first Adam was created and chose to fall from his first estate. The Second Adam was born of woman and chose, by His obedi-ence to Me, to take man's place in his fallen condition and go to the cross to die in his place so He could redeem and restore him to My likeness; so that man, in choosing to be redeemed by the Savior, would find all the gifts returned. The gift of communication would return and we would be close again. We would communicate with each other easily and naturally. The gift of power and dominion would return and as we used that power together, the universe would open up its secrets of life to man. The gift of the power of choice would still be in effect and man would learn how to choose responsibly. Once again he could be made a whole man.

A MAGIC MOMENT OF REVELATION

I thought long and deeply about what God had said. I knew it was true. Still, there were questions.

I said, "God, what about the constant struggles facing me, facing everyone? Why do they come? Why is there no let-up?"

When God answered, a second thing was revealed. It was like a magic moment when I began to grasp it. He said to me:

I am trying to get man to the OTHER SIDE! Because man chose to run his own life through his mental and physi-cal senses instead of through his spirit, even the elements have been changed. Everything is upset and out of order. By man's inability to handle life's situations through his intel-

lect, he has brought upon himself wars, murder, violence, perversion, a terrible darkness over his inner self. Sickness strikes him. Death overtakes him. Everywhere he turns he faces problems and needs he can't cope with.

He has poisoned the earth and the atmosphere by too often taking the wrong kind of dominion, a kind that leaves God out. He has poisoned his mind and body by denying his spirit its proper place in his life. He has put his spirit down and put his mind in charge. This is a reversal of the order in which I made him to function as a whole person. Because man chose to respond through his intellect and five senses rather than his spirit first, there are storms and struggles in the way of getting to the other side. ANY DIRECTION HE TAKES — GOOD OR BAD — HE RUNS INTO STORMS, INTO STRUGGLES THAT SEEK TO DESTROY HIM.

After that I, Oral Roberts, began to "see" in a different way. Instead of opening my physical eyes, I opened the eyes of my spirit. What God was saying was beyond my mind's ability to grasp or the ability of my five senses to see, hear, touch, taste or smell. But my spirit got it easily and naturally. I am sure you will get it, too.

GOD IS TRYING TO GET ME TO THE OTHER SIDE

Then I began to understand why I, like the twelve disciples, have to go through violent storms, through constant and hard struggles. God is trying to get me to the other side. He is trying to do something good with my life. He wants me to live on top of my struggles instead of letting my struggles stay on top of me.

YOU ARE A LIVING SOUL

The only way God can do this for me — or for you — is to get us to understand we are a spirit. We have a body. But even *it* is to be considered the temple of God in which our spirit lives (1 Corinthians 6:19,20). We have a mind and we become what we think (Proverbs 23:7). But the spirit God breathed into man is what caused him to "become a living soul" (Genesis 2:7).

I, Oral Roberts, am a living soul. I asked God to redeem me from the fall of man, to restore His image and likeness in my spirit. He did, by giving me a new birth. I was born again! Then He began teaching me the value of my body and mind in making them subservient to my spirit. He began teaching me to respond first through my spirit, then through my mind and body. In this way I can make a whole-man response to life — and to all my struggles. Struggles that are always seeking to destroy me.

THE WHOLE-MAN RESPONSE

I can candidly tell you that whatever success I have had can be traced back to the time when I first began to learn to respond to life first with my spirit, with my inner self. I can also admit every failure I've had has been when my response originated in my mind or in my senses, instead of in my spirit. If I tried to reason it out, I failed. If I tried only to hear it or touch it or smell it or taste it or see it, I failed. Each time I was left baffled and pointed in the wrong direction. I felt only frustration and fear.

An example of a whole-man response was the statement I made about Rebecca and Marshall's tragic death. As Evelyn and I were on our way to tell Brenda, Marcia and Jon Oral that their parents had been killed, eight words came from deep within me. GOD KNOWS SOMETHING ABOUT THIS WE DON'T KNOW! It came out of my spirit, not out of my mind or my five senses. From that moment of responding through my spirit, I was on my way to getting through that awful struggle.

Despite the storm we were in, despite the way this awful struggle was tossing us like the waves tossed the boat on the

After the death of Marshall and Rebecca my inner man told me, "God knows something about this we don't know."

Sea of Galilee, Evelyn and I, by responding through our spirits, have been able to walk on the water as Peter did.

Evelyn and I do not consider ourselves special. Our struggles are terribly real, often devastating, and are ever upon us as we strive to go to the other side. The important thing we have learned is to originate our response to our struggles FIRST IN OUR SPIRIT. This is when the knowing comes inside that we as human beings can walk on the water.

This is why I am excited about your ability to walk on the water of your struggles. I tingle inside as I see you reaching down inside yourself and gathering up that inner knowledge and power and starting to WALK UPON THE WATER!

NOW ASK YOURSELF...

LIFE'S QUESTION: When I ➤ am doing what I think is right, why do I have to go through storms and struggles?

GOD'S WAY
SAY IT: I HAVE TO GO THROUGH VIOLENT STORMS AND CONSTANT STRUGGLES BECAUSE GOD IS TRYING TO GET ME TO THE OTHER SIDE. HE IS TRYING TO DO SOMETHING GOOD WITH MY LIFE.

LIFE'S QUESTION: Is God ➤ really concerned about the problems and struggles I face?

GOD'S WAY
SAY IT: GOD CARES MORE ABOUT ME THAN I CAN POSSIBLY IMAGINE OR THINK.

LIFE'S QUESTION: Why do ➤ the struggles never let up?

GOD'S WAY
SAY IT: A BATTLE IS RAGING. WHILE THE DEVIL IS SEEKING TO DESTROY ME, GOD IS SEEKING TO BLESS ME.

LIFE'S QUESTION: Is my life ➤ really important?

GOD'S WAY
SAY IT: I AM GOD'S MASTERPIECE . . . UNIQUE AND IRREPLACEABLE.

LIFE'S QUESTION: Why does ➤ **GOD'S WAY**
God allow the devil to tempt   SAY IT: GOD DID NOT MAKE
me?   ME TO BE A ROBOT. I HAVE
                                THE POWER OF CHOICE. I
                                CAN CHOOSE BETWEEN
                                GOOD AND EVIL.

LIFE'S QUESTION: How can ➤ **GOD'S WAY**
I live on top of my struggles   SAY IT: I CAN WALK ON THE
that are getting me down and   TROUBLED WATERS OF MY
keeping me down?   LIFE AND NOT GO UNDER
                                WHEN I LEARN TO RESPOND
                                TO LIFE FIRST THROUGH MY
                                SPIRIT, THEN THROUGH MY
                                MIND AND MY FIVE PHYSI-
                                CAL SENSES.

LIFE'S QUESTION: How can ➤ **GOD'S WAY**
I understand God and com-   SAY IT: I WILL OPEN THE
municate with Him?   EYES OF MY SPIRIT BEYOND
                                THE ABILITY OF MY MIND
                                AND SENSES TO GRASP. MY
                                SPIRIT WILL GET IT AND I
                                WILL START COMMUNICAT-
                                ING WITH GOD EASILY AND
                                NATURALLY.

PUTTING IT ALL TOGETHER FOR MYSELF

I HAVE TO GO THROUGH VIOLENT STORMS AND
CONSTANT STRUGGLES BECAUSE GOD IS TRYING
TO GET ME TO THE OTHER SIDE. HE IS TRYING
TO DO SOMETHING GOOD WITH MY LIFE.

※ ※ ※ ※ ※ ※

GOD CARES MORE ABOUT ME THAN I CAN POS-
SIBLY IMAGINE OR THINK.

※ ※ ※ ※ ※ ※

A BATTLE IS RAGING. WHILE THE DEVIL IS SEEK-
ING TO DESTROY ME, GOD IS SEEKING TO BLESS
ME.

I AM GOD'S MASTERPIECE ... UNIQUE AND IRRE-PLACEABLE.

* * * * * *

GOD DID NOT MAKE ME TO BE A ROBOT. I HAVE THE POWER OF CHOICE. I CAN CHOOSE BETWEEN GOOD AND EVIL.

* * * * * *

I CAN WALK ON THE TROUBLED WATERS OF MY LIFE AND NOT GO UNDER WHEN I LEARN TO RE-SPOND TO LIFE FIRST THROUGH MY SPIRIT, THEN THROUGH MY MIND AND MY FIVE PHYSICAL SENSES.

* * * * * *

I WILL OPEN THE EYES OF MY SPIRIT BEYOND THE ABILITY OF MY MIND AND SENSES TO GRASP. MY SPIRIT WILL GET IT. AND I WILL COMMUNICATE WITH GOD EASILY AND NATURALLY.

* * * * * *

I CAN START WALKING ON THE WATER TODAY — AND I WILL.

Chapter Three

In the midst of your struggles— how you can put God to the test and get results!

"And in the fourth watch of the night Jesus went unto them, walking on the sea. And when the disciples saw him walking on the sea, they were troubled, saying, It is a spirit; and they cried out for fear. But straightway Jesus spake unto them, saying, Be of good cheer; it is I; be not afraid. And Peter answered him and said, LORD, IF IT BE THOU, bid me come unto thee on the water. And he said, Come. And when Peter was come down out of the ship, he walked on the water, to go to Jesus" (Matthew 14:25-29).

How can you know God will come to you in every struggle you face? How can you know He will come and help you through your struggles?

Many times I've said, "Lord, are You going to help me?"

Then when I felt something of His presence I thought, "O God, is it really You trying to help me?"

WE GIVE GOD A HARD TIME

You see, God has a hard time with us, just as He had a hard time getting the disciples to recognize Him when He came to them on the water and to accept His help.

Jesus came to the disciples in the storm. He came walking on the water, subduing the tossing waves, making it a *liquid floor beneath His feet.* No one had ever walked on the water before. No one had ever handled a struggle like this before.

WE SEE HIM...BUT WE DON'T

The disciples saw Jesus walking on the water. They saw Him with their own eyes.

It was both good news and bad news. It was good news in that *He came to them* on the very waters that were trying to suck them under. It was bad news in that they saw Him *only* with their physical sight, rather than with their spirit first.

Suddenly the disciples were in double jeopardy. They were in jeopardy because they were struggling with a storm they couldn't get through. They were in double jeopardy because, by trying to see Jesus with their physical eyes instead of with their spirit, they didn't see the REAL Jesus. It troubled and agitated them so much they cried, "It's a spirit!"

Seeing, but not seeing, caused them to cry out for fear.

What were these twelve men afraid of? They were afraid it wasn't Jesus after all. They were afraid that what they saw was a ghost.

Many times in my struggles what I saw with my eyes or heard with my ears made me say, "It's not real. It's not happening." But it was happening. And it was devastating me. I've done the same as the disciples — thinking "it is not Jesus at all" and I've gotten scared to death. Haven't you?

WE HEAR HIM...BUT WE DON'T

Jesus got closer and closer to the disciples. And standing firmly on the water, He lifted His voice and sent words of hope to the fear-stricken men.

"Be of good cheer," He said. But they were out of cheer. They were so low that if they had died you would have had to jack them up to bury them. They were so down they would have had to reach up to touch bottom.

Jesus said, "Cheer up!" But they didn't see or feel anything to cheer up about. The thought never even crossed their mind that Jesus was there and He could take them out of the storm and through the struggle. It just didn't occur to them.

I remember very well the couple who came to one of my crusades in Oklahoma City. Bob was suffering from an inoperable brain tumor. And he quietly began to prepare himself to go down in his storm. Listen to it in his own words.

Dear Brother Roberts:

I should have known that my wife Mary was beginning to recognize the telltale signs that I had a brain tumor. While I was worrying about keeping it from her, she was worrying and wondering how to tell me. Our doctor had confided to her that at the rate my brain was deteriorating, it would only be a matter of time before she would have to commit me to a mental institution. Being aware of what we accepted as inevitable, we began to prepare for the storm to swallow us up. I started preparing Mary to take care of things when I was gone. At that time she didn't even know how to balance the family checkbook or any of these things. But she realized, as I did, that she had to learn.

Later, Mary said, "You don't know how many times I begged God to let you have a brain hemorrhage and die suddenly just to get it over with. To watch someone I loved so dearly waste away to nothing was more than I could bear."

One Sunday I was at home trying to get some rest when the doorbell rang. It was a friend from the church. And he didn't waste any time. "Bob, do you believe Jesus Christ can heal?" I said, "Well, certainly, I believe it." Then he said, "But do you believe He can heal *you?*" That question made quite a difference. "Well, I don't know about that . . ." I believed He could, but I didn't know if He wanted to. He didn't argue. He just gave me the books and magazines he'd brought over and asked me to read them.

I picked the books up. They were Oral Roberts' books on healing and several copies of his ABUNDANT LIFE magazine. I started to read them. And as I read I prayed for God to give me a personal faith for healing and to reveal the Scriptures about healing to me. And something started to come through to me.

There was a chapter in one of the books that really hit home. It answered the big question in my mind. It outlined seven steps to healing. The first was to KNOW God wants to heal you. Once that was settled in my mind, the rest came fairly easy.

I started praying. My prayers were simple. But He answered. I received this "knowing" and I went to church the following Sunday morning and said to my friend who had given me the books, "I'm coming forward tonight to be healed." He grabbed his head and said, "Oh, my! What have I done now?" But I knew he was thrilled.

I went to church that night. Our pastor asked me to lead in prayer. I said, "Pastor, my head is so foggy I don't think I can, but I'll try." I well remember how faltering my words were. I started:

"God, You know I don't feel right. I've got
  cobwebs in my brain; You will have to help me ... "

And He did help me — from there on I knew my miracle of healing was on the way.

Oral Roberts was in Oklahoma City at this same time. And we made arrangements to go there on the following Tuesday night. I felt my healing had already started, but I still wanted to go.

When we arrived at the meeting I was so excited that I was trembling inside. When my time for prayer came I stood before Brother Roberts and he reached out and laid his hands on my head. Then he drew his hands back almost as though he'd been shocked. He said, "WHY, BROTHER, YOU'VE ALREADY BEEN HEALED." It was really a great thrill to witness the Holy Spirit working through him. Then

I told him I wanted the anointing of the Holy Spirit upon my life. He laid hands on me and prayed that I would receive not only the anointing of the Holy Spirit, but everything that God had for me. I felt the power of God go through me from the top of my head to the soles of my feet. I walked away from that crusade and returned to my job the next day a new man. I never had another headache, dizzy spell, or anything. I got through that terrible storm and struggle. I continually thank God for giving me back my life.

Jesus got this man through his struggle. And He wanted to get the disciples through their struggle. Even though He was a human being like they were, even though He was in the storm Himself, He had faith and His faith was working.

A man said to me once, "You know, it's hard for me to think of Jesus as a human being like me. It seems sacrilegious. The Bible says He is the Son of God."

I replied, "That's right. The Bible teaches us Jesus is the Son of God. I believe He is the Son of God. He is my personal Lord and Savior. But did you know Jesus' favorite and most often used description of Himself was 'Son of man'? That He called Himself 'Son of man' some 80 times in the New Testament?"

The man said, "I never heard that before. Tell me more." I did. And I'll tell you because if you never learn that Jesus became a man, to sit where you sit, to feel what you feel, you may never know Him as the mighty Son of God to deliver you and take you through your struggles.

THE PROOF OF JESUS

Jesus said something very personal to the disciples as He walked toward their boat. He said, "It is I." He said it to cheer them up, to take away their fear.

And almost impetuously, Peter shouted back at Jesus, "Lord, if it IS You, tell me to come to You on the water."

Some people talk about how daring Peter was, but I

don't think so. Which was more daring, to stay in a boat being battered to pieces and go down with it, or to put Jesus to the test and bring Him into the NOW of your struggle? Which is more daring?

Peter saw he had a choice. He could believe or not believe. He had the power of choice to do something about his struggle with the storm. He could choose to stay in it or to get through it. You have that same power of choice. So do I. So does everyone. To choose — that's the important thing.

A STORM OF TUBERCULOSIS

When I lay dying with tuberculosis I had a choice to make. One choice was given me by the pastor of the church I had joined, who ended his prayer for me by saying, "Son, be patient." Well, if I had been patient, I would be dead today.

Another choice was given me by the doctors. My parents wisely put me under the care of three top physicians. They gave me different kinds of medicine and advice. There were no so-called miracle drugs then, like they have today, so effective against tuberculosis.

The sanatorium for tuberculosis was next. The doctors got my parents to sign to place me there. At that time you went to the sanatorium to die. I chose to go only as a last resort.

Another choice was given me by God through my mother. Mamma had said, "Pray, son, pray." I said, "Mamma, I don't know how to pray." Papa said, "Oral, ask God to save your soul so if you die you will go to heaven." But I didn't want to go to heaven. Not then, anyway. I wanted to live ... live ... live ...

Then my sister Jewel came in one day, leaned over me and said seven magic words, "Oral, God is going to heal you."

Shortly my oldest brother Elmer came to see me. He

said "Oral, I'm taking you to a meeting where a man of God is praying for the sick and many are getting healed."

I had chosen not to be patient in my illness. I had chosen not to go to the sanatorium at that time. And now I had a new choice. What proof did I have that Jewel's seven words would be real to me? What proof did I have that healing prayers would help me? What proof? What evidence?

My choice was no different than that of the disciples or of the impetuous Peter. No doubt they were advising each other to do this, to do that. They were shouting at each other. They were accusing each other. What they needed was proof that it was all right to jump from the boat upon the same waters that were destroying it and them. They needed proof that the raging waters would hold them up better than their man-made boat. They needed evidence that He Who said, "It is I," was really the Jesus they knew. They needed evidence that when He said, "Cheer up," He would give them something to cheer up about. That's what you need too, isn't it?

IT'S ALL RIGHT TO ASK FOR PROOF

Have you ever felt guilty about asking God to prove Himself to you, about asking for evidence for your faith? Is it all right to ask for proof?

God says, "Prove me" (Malachi 3:10).

And Peter showed us how. He said, "Lord, if it is really You, if You are really out there on TOP of the troubled waters, then TELL ME TO COME TO YOU, WALKING ON THE WATER."

Now that's saying it like you feel!

Jesus welcomed Peter's test of Him. Does that surprise you? It does a lot of folks. At one time it shook me up to see *anyone* who had the audacity to test God — much less me.

We owe a lot to Peter for asking for proof. "Lord, if it

is You, tell me to come to You on the water."

Peter knew if he could get the answer to that question, everything could work out. And he knew if he didn't, he wouldn't make it. And that's what getting through your struggles is all about — knowing Jesus well enough that you can hear the inner voice telling you to come to Him walking on the water — and to know you are going to make it.

HOW DO YOU GET YOUR PROOF?

How did Peter get his proof? How can I? How can you?

Peter got his proof by going right after the truth. He wasn't bashful or intimidated or inhibited. When he shouted at Jesus, what he really said was:

Jesus, You are telling us it is You walking on the water. You are telling us not to be afraid, but to cheer up because it is REALLY You coming to us. Jesus, You are saying that You are the same man we've walked and talked with. You're the same Jesus, the same Person. Well, if You are, we know You. We've heard hints that You are the Son of God. We've got to know more about that. But we know You are a man, clothed in flesh as we are. You've told us that You, as a human, use nothing that is not also available to us if we have faith as a grain of seed, that nothing is impossible to us when we use our faith. We can move mountains. And, Jesus, if in Your humanness You can use Your faith and walk on these stormy waters, then tell me to come to You. Tell me that I, in my humanness, can use my faith and come to You walking on the water. I can get through my struggle with this storm. I can get to the other side.

Remember, this all happened BEFORE the revelation came to Peter when he declared, "Thou art the Christ, the Son of the living God" (Matthew 16:16).

Right now, in testing Jesus, he was asking Him if He felt what he was feeling. He was asking if He hurt the way he hurt. Peter was asking if Jesus had really come to the point of his need.

Peter said, "Yes, Lord! If it's You, tell ME to come."

Without a moment's hesitation, Jesus said, "Come!" He was giving the proof, supplying the evidence, answering the test of an honest heart.

"But," you may ask just as I did, "when Jesus told Peter to COME, what was He really saying? What does it mean to me in the struggle I'm facing right now?"

Here's what I believe Jesus is saying: *Yes, Peter! I am the same Jesus, the same man. I am using my faith in the Father, the same faith anyone who believes in Me has and can use. In My humanness I am believing God and He is responding to My spirit, My faith. The waters are being made a bridge. I'm on top of My problem, not under it. Yes, COME!*

I assure you Jesus is saying these same words to me, to you — to every human being. And I'm excited about it. Aren't you?

WHAT IF I FAIL?

Instead of making a leap of faith, Peter could have said, "What if I'm seeing things and hearing things?" He could have said, "What if I try to walk on the water and fail?"

That's exactly what happened to me when as a young minister I was trying to change from the status quo and bring healing to the people as Jesus did. I was trying to understand how to obey God and get into this ministry which is helping so many today. My ministry is seeing the miracles of God now but it wasn't very effective then. It simply was not working! How miserable and defeated I felt.

There I was in 1947, in Enid, Oklahoma, pastoring a small church, having terribly small results. I was also attending college, carrying a full load of sixteen academic hours each semester. I had a family to support and precious little with which to support them. I had so little time to do all these things. Then one day everything blew up. No matter what I did, nothing seemed to work out for me. The

In 1947 I began to walk on the water towards Jesus when I held my first mass healing service in the Education Building in Enid, Oklahoma.

storm was all around me. How hard I worked! But I felt I might be sucked under.

Then that same Presence came to me that had come to Peter. I didn't know it was Jesus any more than Peter did. I was desperately wondering if God knew Oral Roberts existed, if He knew where I was and what was happening to me. I wanted to be valuable to myself, to other people — to *be* something, to accomplish something with my life.

At the very time I was hidden away in that small city, following the daily routine, just hoping I would get through one more day, *Jesus was walking on the water toward me.* Yes, toward me!

Like Peter, I thought I heard God's voice. It was INSIDE me. But it was not very clear.

God sent people across my path whom I thought had something. I wanted what they had. But it still seemed that all I really had was struggle, troubles, questions. I kept thinking, "What about me? Me?"

GOD GAVE ME A DREAM

Then I dreamed a dream, the same dream every night for months. It would awaken me. It seemed God let me see people as He sees them, and hear them as He hears them. What I saw and heard almost took my breath away. I saw that everybody is sick in some way — with problems, illnesses, bad relationships, fears, frustrations, lack of faith, living in troubled waters. I saw everyone really struggling. I heard them. They were crying inside, "Why has this happened to me? What have I done to deserve it?"

This dream shook me up. It took me back to my conversion and healing twelve years before when God had said I was to take His healing power to my generation. But during those twelve years God had been strangely silent about the calling He had given me. Now I began to feel I was indeed to have a healing ministry and it was to start

In my dream I saw people in their desperate needs and hurts, and I knew that God had called me to pray for the healing of their lives.

soon. It scared me to death but at the same time it put me to thinking.

I thought about going to the people, going to them in their hurts, illnesses, sins, blasted hopes, their stormy lives, praying for them to be healed. Then I woke up to what I was thinking. I said, "God, what if I fail?"

What if I fail? Nobody likes to fail.

Then from the depths of my spirit I heard these words, "You've already done that!"

What an eye opener! It was a revelation from God. I had already failed. Therefore, by going to the people and using my faith to pray for them to be healed, I had only one way to go. And that was UP. Jesus was telling me, as He had told Peter, "Come!"

Let me tell you, in 1947 when scarcely anybody was in the healing ministry of our Lord, it meant something for me to launch forth right in the midst of the struggle I was in.

YOU ARE NO DIFFERENT

How does all this relate to you and to your struggles? You are no different than Peter. He was a human being. If there ever was a real human being with all the highs and lows a person can have in this life, Peter was that man.

Also, you are no different than I am. I get a little concerned when another human being walks up to me and says, "Are you THE Oral Roberts? The one on television? Man, it's got to be great to be on television, to build a university, to get people healed. I wish . . ."

I don't always answer the way I feel. I feel like saying, "Yes, I'm Oral Roberts. I'm the one who gets scared, who makes all kinds of mistakes, who gets to start with nothing on all these things you admire so much and that look so easy. Yes, I'm Oral Roberts, the one who hurts, who gets sick and has to go to hospitals, who has accidents, who runs out of money, who sometimes doesn't know what to do next."

But they wouldn't like to hear that. It seems to me they either want to put me down as a nothing or to try to make me a superhuman. Well, I'm neither. I'm a human being exactly like you are. I'm struggling, trying to hear the inner voice, seeking to respond to life first through my spirit. Really, I'm trying to get my faith up to walk on the water.

I remember one time after we had finished making a television special on location. Evelyn went down to the laundromat to do my shirts and underclothes. After they were dried, she went to a grocery store so we could have something to snack on in our room. A woman saw her and followed in the background. As Evelyn was getting into the rented car, she rushed up and said, "Oh, Mrs. Roberts! You wash clothes and go to the grocery store just like the rest of us. I didn't expect . . ."

Later when Evelyn shared this with me she said, "If she only knew how human we really are." I agreed one hundred percent.

I know beyond the shadow of any doubt that the times we walk on the water we struggle to do it. We struggle to get the proof of our own faith that Jesus is telling us to come, that the water will hold us up, that it will be a liquid floor beneath *our* feet, that *we* will make it.

When we don't make it we hurt like anyone else. If there is any difference, it is that WE REFUSE TO GIVE UP. Like Peter, when he got the proof he asked for and started walking on the water, we feel we can do it too.

Based on my experience with thousands in virtually every walk of life, and with virtually every conceivable problem, I know that in the midst of your struggles, you CAN put Jesus to the test. He WILL give you proof. You CAN act on the evidence that He gives you and get results.

You can trust Jesus!

NOW ASK YOURSELF...

LIFE'S QUESTION: Jesus said → GOD'S WAY
to cheer up, but why should   SAY IT: I CAN CHEER UP BE-
I? I don't see or feel anything CAUSE JESUS IS COMING TO
to cheer up about.   ME WALKING ON THE WATER
                               AND HE IS GOING TO SHOW
                               ME HOW TO WALK ON THE
                               TROUBLED WATERS OF MY
                               LIFE.

LIFE'S QUESTION: How can → GOD'S WAY
I test God?   SAY IT: I CAN SAY, "GOD, IF
                               YOU ARE REALLY WHO YOU
                               SAY YOU ARE, THEN TELL ME
                               TO COME TO YOU. BID ME
                               TO WALK ON THE WATER."
                               AND HE WILL!

LIFE'S QUESTION: Why is → GOD'S WAY
putting God to the test so   SAY IT: IT'S IMPORTANT
important?   THAT I PUT GOD TO THE
                               TEST BECAUSE HE WILL GIVE
                               ME PROOF. I CAN ACT ON
                               THE EVIDENCE HE GIVES ME
                               AND GET RESULTS!

LIFE'S QUESTION: How can → GOD'S WAY
I walk on the water?   SAY IT: I CAN WALK ON THE
                               WATER BY BELIEVING GOD.
                               MY FAITH PUT INTO ACTION
                               IS A BRIDGE OVER THE
                               TROUBLED WATERS.

LIFE'S QUESTION: What if I → GOD'S WAY
try to walk on the water and   SAY IT: I HAVE FAILED AL-
fail?   READY. I HAVE ONLY ONE
                               WAY TO GO — AND THAT'S UP!

LIFE'S QUESTION: Do I have → GOD'S WAY
to stay in a boat that is being SAY IT: I HAVE A CHOICE. I
battered to pieces and go   CAN BELIEVE OR NOT BE-
down with it?   LIEVE. I HAVE THE POWER
                               TO DO SOMETHING ABOUT
                               MY STRUGGLE WITH THE
                               STORM. I CAN CHOOSE TO
                               STAY IN IT OR GET THROUGH
                               IT. I CAN CHOOSE NOT TO
                               GIVE IN TO MY PROBLEMS.

LIFE'S QUESTION: Is it OK ➤ GOD'S WAY
for me to ask God to prove   SAY IT: GOD WELCOMES
Himself to me?   HAVING ME PUT HIM TO THE
                              TEST. HE GLADLY SUPPLIES
                              THE EVIDENCE FOR AN HON-
                              EST HEART.

PUTTING IT ALL TOGETHER FOR MYSELF

I CAN CHEER UP BECAUSE JESUS IS COMING TO
ME WALKING ON THE WATER AND HE IS GOING
TO SHOW ME HOW TO WALK ON THE TROUBLED
WATERS OF MY LIFE.

* * * * * *

GOD WELCOMES HAVING ME PUT HIM TO THE
TEST. HE GLADLY SUPPLIES THE EVIDENCE FOR
AN HONEST HEART.

* * * * * *

I CAN SAY, "GOD, IF YOU ARE REALLY WHO YOU
SAY YOU ARE, THEN TELL ME TO COME TO YOU.
BID ME TO WALK ON THE WATER." AND HE WILL!

* * * * * *

IT'S IMPORTANT THAT I PUT GOD TO THE TEST
BECAUSE HE WILL GIVE ME PROOF. I CAN ACT ON
THE EVIDENCE HE GIVES ME AND GET RESULTS!

* * * * * *

I CAN WALK ON THE WATER BY BELIEVING GOD.
MY FAITH PUT INTO ACTION IS A BRIDGE OVER
THE TROUBLED WATERS.

* * * * * *

I HAVE FAILED ALREADY. I HAVE ONLY ONE WAY
TO GO — AND THAT'S UP!

* * * * * *

I HAVE A CHOICE. I CAN BELIEVE OR NOT BE-
LIEVE. I HAVE THE POWER TO DO SOMETHING
ABOUT MY STRUGGLE WITH THE STORM. I CAN
CHOOSE TO STAY IN IT OR GET THROUGH IT. I
CAN CHOOSE NOT TO GIVE IN TO MY PROBLEMS.

Chapter Four

When you don't know where Jesus is, remember— He knows where YOU are

"And He saw them toiling in . . . the night" (Mark 6:48).

"I'm going through an identity crisis," a friend wrote me. He said, "O God, if only I knew You know who I am, that I exist and that You hear me when I pray. If I could know You know who I am and where I am, O God, if I only knew."

He and I began to exchange letters. It took many letters to fill this void in his thinking. He would write and say, "Oral Roberts, you come across on television and in your letters that you know God knows you exist. You don't seem to feel alone — ever!"

WE SOMETIMES FORGET GOD KNOWS

Little did he realize what an identity problem I've had, the many times I've had no feeling at all that God knew I existed or ever even thought about me. He didn't know about the times in my life when I wasn't sure there is a God; or if there *is* a God, does He know who I am or where I am?

He didn't know about the times in my childhood I was so paralyzed with fear and stuttered so badly I couldn't even tell my school teacher my name.

Relatives, friends, teachers, playmates, all said the same thing about this young barefoot boy, on the right, in the wrinkled coveralls: "Oral will never amount to anything. He can't even talk."

He didn't know about the times relatives would say, "Oral will never amount to anything; Oral can't even talk."

He didn't know about the times when some of my relatives and my playmates would tease and tantalize me to talk, and then mock me and make fun of me.

He didn't know how I felt standing on the back porch looking out across the hills wondering if I would ever amount to anything, anything at all.

All this man could see of me on television and in my replies to his letters was that somehow I had in his mind reached the position that I finally know there is a God . . . that I know Him personally . . . that I have experienced His healing power in my entire being . . . and that I am able through my faith to help people even when they are most desperate.

But, oh, those agonizing times I didn't know, and didn't think God knew. And the times now that I seem to forget!

JESUS KNOWS WHERE YOU ARE

One day he wrote, "I heard you talking on your television program about Peter in the storm, how he felt all alone and feared he wasn't going to make it."

He reminded me I had pointed out something very important. While Peter felt he was all alone in the raging sea and hadn't the slightest idea where Jesus was — JESUS KNEW WHERE PETER WAS ALL THE TIME.

He said, "Brother Roberts, the Lord spoke to my heart so clearly, *'YOU MAY NOT ALWAYS KNOW WHERE I AM when you feel surrounded by the storms of your life. You may feel I'm not near. BUT I KNOW WHERE YOU ARE.* I know where you are all the time.'"

He added, "That's the important thing. God knows where I am."

I wrote back, "I know exactly how you feel. I used to read in the Bible where Jesus said that He saw the sparrow fall, and was acquainted with all our grief.

"One day it seemed Jesus was so close I could touch Him. I could hear His voice inside me:

'If I see the sparrow falling, I know exactly where YOU are in your stumbling, doubting, your searching for Me. I will bring you out of this storm into a great calmness. And when you come out you will be better than when you went in. You will come out knowing that you know I AM GOD TO YOU.' "

I added, "That experience was very important to me and it has been repeated many times since. It has helped me have this knowing inside that I have most of the time."

JESUS KNEW WHERE PETER WAS

Peter, in the worst storm of his life, didn't know where Jesus was. But Jesus knew where Peter was. And that changed everything.

Also, in the fierceness of that storm Peter couldn't recognize Jesus' voice. But Jesus could recognize Peter's voice. And that made all the difference in the world.

In Peter's fear Jesus didn't look like Peter expected Him to look. Jesus seemed to be a ghost. But that was because Peter's spirit didn't recognize Him. It was the real Jesus, with a real voice, with the right words. And He was coming closer every second. That's when things began to look up for Peter.

But before this, Peter, like many of us, didn't recognize Jesus. He wasn't expecting Jesus to come to him or answer him in the way He did. Peter no doubt had a thought in the back of his mind that Jesus could do something about his situation if he were *in* the boat. He knew that was possible because Jesus was in their boat in another storm and spoke peace to the angry waves, saying, "Peace be still," and calmed the sea.

Up to this moment Peter had done all he could do to get through the storm. Now Jesus was coming to do what only He could do. The trouble was Peter was afraid to let Jesus do what He could do. He felt that not even Jesus could handle the storm. There wasn't enough faith in the world to pull them through. Peter felt no hope and that's the worst feeling in the world.

LEARN TO THINK ABOUT A NEW OPPORTUNITY

About the time it seemed the waves would suck their little boat under, a new opportunity opened up. Because of God's great love, a miracle was coming toward the disciples. It was Jesus coming to do what He could do.

And right in the middle of this deadly storm — the disciples thinking it was the end, and Jesus walking to them on the waters, scaring them out of their wits at the sight of what they thought was a ghost — there is another glimpse into *Jesus' humanness.* I think He was testing them. The Scripture says, ". . . He would have passed by . . . ."

True, the storm was real, the waves were about to dash the little boat to pieces, the disciples knew their lives were at stake. But in the very midst of their desperation, Jesus acts as if He would walk on by. I can almost see the twinkle in Jesus' eye as he waited to see if the twelve would reach out to Him for help or accept their own reasoning that He was nothing but a ghostlike figure on the water.

That's just like a father and his children. I remember when our children were little. Occasionally, while playing, they would encounter a problem that was just overwhelming to them and they would fuss and fume and work and sweat and maybe even cry a little. In a second I could fix it for them if they would only ask. Sometimes they would even refuse my help. But I would stand by, waiting for them to recognize that I really could help them. Then when they could see it was totally beyond what they could do, I would start to pass on by. And then they would really cry out! "Daddy, fix this for us!" But I had to wait for them to cry out and be willing to accept my help.

Before God can meet your need you've got to recognize you have a need. Before you can expect a miracle you've got to recognize you need a miracle, that only a miracle will do.

EXPECT YOUR MIRACLE OR IT WILL PASS YOU BY

For months God has inspired me to tell people, "A miracle is coming toward you or past you every day. Don't let it pass you by. Expect your miracle. Reach out and take it!"

That night as Jesus walked on the water to His disciples, coming toward them and at the same time making as though He would pass them by, He gave a perfect example of this. I personally urge you to understand that miracles are coming toward you or past you every day. You can choose. Don't let them pass you by! Choose to reach out and take them! God wants you to have a miracle!

A few months ago I received an amazing letter from Mrs. Warren Kelly. It will show you what God can do even when it may seem your miracle has passed you by.

> My husband lay in the hospital. His fever had climbed to 104°. It wouldn't go down. Tests and more tests had been taken but still there was no diagnosis. We were scared. Warren is 6'5" and normally slender, but in just a short time his weight had dropped to 140 pounds.
>
> It was a long drive home from the hospital. And alone in the car I began to sob. Why had all this happened? Eight weeks before, Warren had injured his back and had to stay in bed for six weeks. We'd even gone on welfare. Then back at work for two weeks and he'd come down with this. Still sobbing I cried out:
>
> > God, You know I love Warren to the depths of my soul. I've waited all my life for a man

> like this, but *if it's Your will that he be
> taken, I turn it all over to You.*

The tears blurred my vision. I don't know how I saw to
drive home, but when I got there I suddenly thought of
the Prayer Tower at Oral Roberts University. I didn't
know anything about it, only what I'd seen in a copy of
ABUNDANT LIFE magazine my mother had sent to me.
As I looked at the date on the magazine, I didn't know
how I'd happened to keep it or why — it was over a year
old. Should I call? — I'll try . . . The lady on the phone
listened as I poured out my pain. Then she asked, "Is
your husband a Christian?"

"He believes there's a God," I said.

"Has he confessed Christ as his Savior and Lord?"

"No," I answered.

"Then we'll pray about that too," she promised. "Now
you start looking for your miracle to happen today."

When I went to the hospital the next day the doctors gave
us a diagnosis of rheumatic fever and liver enlargement,
and they began treatment. Three days later I brought
Warren home. That night we were so happy just to be
together again. Suddenly Warren started throwing questions at me:

"What's the difference between God and Jesus?"

"What is the Holy Spirit?"

"How do you know the Bible is right?"

I felt as if I were on a witness stand, and was grateful for
my Sunday school experiences to help answer him.

Finally after many questions and answers and more conversation, I fell asleep. During the night while I slept
Warren invited Jesus to be his Lord and Savior.

The next morning when he told me I was ecstatic! Just
weeks before, this was the man who had said to me, "Stop
trying to shove God down my throat! I don't want to hear
any more about it!"

When we went back to the doctor for a checkup, he told
us there was no heart damage and the liver was back to
normal! Wow!

We were up to our necks in bills and when Warren went back to work the promised raises never came and the working conditions were terribly dangerous. I was out of work too. Then we heard about the miracles God sends through Seed-Faith and just turned our messed up checkbook over to the Lord. We started looking for another miracle.

Within a week we got a call from the University of Michigan. I couldn't believe that they wanted an interview with Warren. When we'd taken Warren's application in, they told us they seldom hired electricians from outside the university, they weren't hiring now, and that they threw all applications away after six months. This was over seven months later! Warren got the job, with double the salary he had been making, and benefits besides. I was hired as a secretary for the university the same day. A short time later my husband received the baptism in the Holy Spirit. Oh! I could go on and on, but the most important thing is that Jesus cares about you in your storms. It overwhelms us to think how much He loves us. Also we know — not think, but *know* — that Seed-Faith living works. Every problem is just another opportunity to the Living Christ. We *can't* outgive Jesus!

Thank you so much, Brother Roberts, for showing us these things through your ministry and teaching. Praise the Lord!

LEARN TO DO WHAT YOU CAN DO

As the Kellys discovered, there is something you must *do*. And there was something the twelve men aboard that sinking boat had to do. They had to do what they could do. They had to make a response, no matter how hesitant they were to do it or how strange it seemed to them to do it.

There was a Presence on top of the water that was trying to help them. It was the most important Presence they — or you — would ever know. It was their way out. It was no longer a dead-end street. It was an opening in their storm for them to walk through their troubled waters. It was hope. It was help.

This Presence was more than an "it." This Presence was a PERSON! Jesus! It was He Who knew where they were even when they didn't know where He was. It was the One Who knew they existed when they didn't even know He did.

And this very same thing is happening to you in your troubled waters, and to me.

Jesus knows you exist.

Jesus knows where you are.

Jesus is coming toward you with a miracle.

Jesus, at the same time, may seem to be passing you by.

What this means to you is, you must do what YOU can do. Then you must not be afraid to let Jesus do what HE can do. You just can't keep thinking or saying, "If there is a God, why doesn't He do something?"

You must turn that around. "There is a God. I must do what I can do. Then I must let God do for me what He can do."

WHAT CAN YOU DO?

One thing you can do is what Peter did. And that is to stop waiting for others to do something and do it yourself!

Peter thought he saw the Presence there on the raging water. He thought he heard the words, "Be of good cheer. It is I. Be not afraid." He thought just maybe it could be Jesus. He thought just maybe Jesus knew he existed. He thought just maybe Jesus knew where he was. Peter thought it strongly enough that he did something.

Peter acted on that thought. He did the most important thing you or I can ever do. He did something. He said, "Lord, if it is You, tell me to come to You walking on the water." He was saying, "Jesus, be real to me."

That was doing something. That was doing what he could do. That was doing what he could do, then expecting Jesus to do what He could do! You see it, don't you: do what you can do then expect Jesus to do what He can do! That adds up to a miracle happening — to you.

THINGS HAVE TO BE MADE TO HAPPEN

Things like this don't happen of and by themselves. I've learned that the hard way.

My marriage to my darling wife Evelyn had to be made to happen.

It started like a coincidence. But neither Evelyn nor I think there is anything coincidental in the life of a Christian.

I sat down in the only empty seat in the little church orchestra. Next to me was a girl I had never met. I had hurried so I wouldn't be late and I breathlessly leaned over and said, "Is my hair combed?"

"Oh, yes," she replied, slightly embarrassed.

She went to her room that night and wrote in her diary, "I have met my future husband." Later she said, "When he's my husband, I'll see that his hair is combed." She's done a pretty good job of it too.

But of course I didn't know this. In the following year my parents moved to her town, Westville, Oklahoma. But she had left for Texas to teach school. Nearly everybody I met in that little town told me about Evelyn Lutman. I met her family and suddenly felt an urge to send her a little pamphlet I had written. She wrote right back. And we started a correspondence.

Meanwhile I asked questions about Evelyn Lutman. What I learned from people who knew her was everything I, as a young preacher, wanted in a wife.

I sent her a letter saying, "Wouldn't it be strange if we fell in love and got married." Back came a letter saying, "Listen, Oral Roberts, if you think I'm going to marry a preacher and have a houseful of children, you better think again."

Immediately she was sorry and wrote an apology. Meanwhile, I had answered by saying, "Just forget it. I wouldn't marry you anyway."

Months after I saw Evelyn in the church orchestra, I drove down to Texas to see her.
My mother was with me.

Well, her second letter caused me to write and apologize too. We resumed our writing. We fell in love through our letters.

Months later I drove down to see her. My mother was with me. She wanted to see the girl her baby boy liked so much.

As I drove up into the school yard the students said, "Oh, Miss Evelyn, your boyfriend is here."

She blushed, but invited us into one of her classes. She said she was so nervous with me back there watching her every move. However, she didn't let it show.

When school let out I said, "Would you mind playing that piano over there?"

She said, "Why do you want me to do that?"

"Oh, just because," I replied.

You see, that was part of my test of God providing the right wife and helper — right for me, and her. I needed a wife who, among other things, could play the piano. She played it beautifully.

She had written a full year before, "Tonight I have found my future husband." What she didn't know when she finished playing the piano was, I felt in my heart, "I have found my future wife."

It was a little thing, but big in the things that had to be done to make our marriage happen. It's a marriage that has grown in love and accomplishments through the years. We are more in love now than ever before — after 39 years!

Things have to be made to happen. For Jesus to walk on the water and get Peter to walk on it, it had to be made to happen. For Peter to get out of his fear and into faith so he could walk on the water, things had to be made to happen.

Wishing wouldn't do it. Just praying wouldn't do it. Peter had to do something. Jesus had to do something.

Peter had already put Jesus to the test by saying, "Lord,

Things have to be made to happen. My marriage to my darling wife Evelyn had to be made to happen. After 39 years of sharing the same struggles, we are more in love now than ever before!

if it's really You, tell me to come to You walking on the water!"

With a daring statement like that, you can see that Peter was ready for his miracle from Jesus. Are you ready for yours?

NOW ASK YOURSELF . . .

LIFE'S QUESTION: What can ➤ **GOD'S WAY**
I do when I feel all alone and SAY IT: I MAY NOT ALWAYS
I haven't the slightest idea KNOW WHERE GOD IS, BUT
where God is? HE ALWAYS KNOWS WHERE
I AM . . . AND THAT'S WHAT
COUNTS!

LIFE'S QUESTION: How can ➤ **GOD'S WAY**
I know that God knows who SAY IT: IF GOD SEES THE
I am? How can I know He SPARROW FALLING, THEN HE
hears my prayers? KNOWS EXACTLY WHERE I
AM. HE IS GOING TO BRING
ME OUT OF THIS STORM
WITH GREAT CALMNESS, AND
I WILL COME OUT OF IT
BETTER THAN I WENT IN.

LIFE'S QUESTION: There's no ➤ **GOD'S WAY**
possible way out of the situ- SAY IT: WHEN I'VE DONE
ation I'm in. It's a dead-end ALL I CAN DO, I CAN EXPECT
street. Now what? GOD TO DO WHAT HE CAN
DO. I CAN EXPECT HIM TO
DO THE IMPOSSIBLE . . . TO
MAKE A WAY WHERE THERE
IS NO WAY!

LIFE'S QUESTION: When ➤ **GOD'S WAY**
God is passing out miracles SAY IT: THERE IS SOME-
why does He always seem to THING I MUST DO. I MUST
pass me by? REACH OUT AND TAKE MY
MIRACLE WHEN IT COMES
OR ELSE IT WILL PASS ME BY.

LIFE'S QUESTION: If God ➤ **GOD'S WAY**
really cares about my strug- SAY IT: GOD WANTS TO HELP
gles, why doesn't He help . . . HE REALLY DOES CARE
me? Why doesn't He do FOR ME. HE IS SIMPLY WAIT-
something? ING FOR ME TO CRY OUT
AND ACCEPT HIS HELP.

LIFE'S QUESTION: What can → GOD'S WAY
  I do about my problems?   SAY IT: I CAN STOP WAITING
                              AROUND FOR SOMETHING TO
                              HAPPEN AND I CAN MAKE
                              SOMETHING HAPPEN. I CAN
                              ACT!

LIFE'S QUESTION: How can → GOD'S WAY
  I get out of fear into faith?   SAY IT: WISHING WON'T DO
  How can I walk on the water? IT. JUST PRAYING WON'T DO
                              IT EITHER. I HAVE TO DO
                              SOMETHING. I WILL PUT MY
                              FAITH INTO ACTION!

PUTTING IT ALL TOGETHER FOR MYSELF

I MAY NOT ALWAYS KNOW WHERE GOD IS, BUT HE ALWAYS KNOWS WHERE I AM . . . AND THAT'S WHAT COUNTS!

※ ※ ※ ※ ※ ※

IF GOD SEES THE SPARROW FALLING, THEN HE KNOWS EXACTLY WHERE I AM. HE IS GOING TO BRING ME OUT OF THIS STORM WITH GREAT CALMNESS, AND I WILL COME OUT OF IT BETTER THAN I WENT IN.

※ ※ ※ ※ ※ ※

WHEN I'VE DONE ALL I CAN DO, I CAN EXPECT GOD TO DO WHAT HE CAN DO. I CAN EXPECT HIM TO DO THE IMPOSSIBLE . . . TO MAKE A WAY WHERE THERE IS NO WAY!

※ ※ ※ ※ ※ ※

THERE IS SOMETHING I MUST DO. I MUST REACH OUT AND TAKE MY MIRACLE WHEN IT COMES OR ELSE IT WILL PASS ME BY.

※ ※ ※ ※ ※ ※

GOD WANTS TO HELP . . . HE REALLY DOES CARE FOR ME. HE IS SIMPLY WAITING FOR ME TO CRY OUT AND ACCEPT HIS HELP.

I CAN STOP WAITING AROUND FOR SOMETHING TO HAPPEN AND I CAN MAKE SOMETHING HAPPEN. I CAN ACT!

******

WISHING WON'T DO IT. JUST PRAYING WON'T DO IT EITHER. I HAVE TO DO SOMETHING. I WILL PUT MY FAITH INTO ACTION!

Chapter Five

How to watch for God
'to appear to you'
on the troubled waters of your struggling

"Be of good cheer, it is I, be not afraid" (Matthew 14:27).

The *first step* in getting through the struggles of your life is to practice doing what you can do. Get it thoroughly grounded in your thinking that —

GOD EXPECTS YOU TO DO WHAT YOU CAN DO

The *next step* is to be aware when things start getting out of control. Watch for danger signals. As you reach the extent of what you can do, then you are at a point of need. IT IS AT THIS POINT OF NEED THAT GOD WILL APPEAR TO YOU — without fail. He will appear, to do what only He can do and that means a miracle is about to appear to you.

Do you believe this? Will you try to *practice* believing it? This is a practice I've engaged in for many years, continually reminding myself that God always appears to me at the point of *my* need — and to other people at the point of *their* need. Over and over I remind myself of this.

GOD EXPECTS YOU TO EXPECT HIM TO APPEAR TO YOU AT THE POINT OF YOUR NEED

Your point of need is not the only time God may appear in some form of help to you. He is sovereign. He can — and does — appear as He wills. There are times in your life when you feel an urgency to reach out to God. And you are apt to think that it is YOU searching after Him. But He says: "You have not chosen me ... I have chosen you" (John 15:16). He wants you far more than you can ever dream.

GOD IS RIGHT THERE WITH YOU IN THE MIDDLE OF YOUR STORM

Here are three things to say to yourself —

- God expects me to do what I can do.
- God expects me to expect Him to appear to me at the point of my need.
- God is right here with me in the midst of my storm to give me my miracle.

When you remember these things and put them to work, you will recognize Jesus has come to you in your most desperate moments — He is here right now at the point of your need.

Listen to this letter from two of my partners from South Carolina. When they had done all they could do, they looked for Jesus. And they received a miracle.

Dear Oral Roberts:

I believe in the power of prayer and miracle healing!

Our two-year-old child awoke during the night last Thursday and was having trouble breathing. She had a fever and was vomiting. My husband and I immediately realized that our child was extremely ill, and my husband called our doctor. The doctor could hear her labored breathing and gasping for air over the telephone, and we were in the next room! He said she was having spasms. He did not want to give her medication. He suggested that we use a vaporizer — which we did not even have. We boiled water in the kitchen and turned on the showers in the bathrooms — a very poor substitute for a vaporizer. She still could not breathe normally. We did not know what to do, but *pray!* My husband suggested we use our bottle of anointing oil you sent us as a point of contact to release our faith in God. We read three Scripture passages, anointed our child's forehead, and held each other as we prayed. Our child wanted to sing "Jesus Loves Me" even as she continued gasping for air. By the time she had sung the first verse, and *part* of the chorus, she was breathing much more easily and had fallen asleep. Our child's fever was so high that we could feel the heat from her little body. Within a *few* minutes, she didn't feel too warm at all!

My husband and I were silent — we were speechless! We could feel the presence of God right in our room.

The next morning, I carried our child to our doctor, and he told me he had expected us to call him again for help. He did not think the "vaporizer" would relieve her labored breathing!

We know God touched our child, and we are so very thankful!

Jesus met this couple in their night of desperation just as He had appeared to Peter and the others at their most desperate moment.

TWO EXPRESSIONS OF JESUS

In a matter of minutes there were two definite expressions of Jesus upon the troubled waters. The first was when they *saw* Him walking to them on the water. True, they did not recognize Him completely but they knew there was something there that was out of the ordinary. At first they thought it was some magical something — a ghost. But they knew it was something. WHATEVER it was, they were no longer alone!

The second expression was when they heard Jesus talking to them, talking personally to them while they were in the storm! Yes, Jesus talks . . . and He always says the right things.

Jesus said, "Be of good cheer. It is I. Be not afraid."

Those were words worth hearing. It really was Jesus. He was telling them to cheer up because it was He walking on the water to help them. They didn't have to be lonely and hopeless any longer. What a feeling it is not to be lonely and hopeless. To see and hear and feel inside you that Jesus is coming directly toward you in your struggle with the perfect miracle. It's got to cheer you up.

YOU CAN TALK TO JESUS IN THE MIDST OF THE STORM

Then Jesus and Peter spoke to each other. It was a relatively short conversation. Have you ever noticed there's not always time for a lot of words in a storm? But you don't need a lot of words.

YOU NEED A MIRACLE!

YOU NEED TO BE ABLE TO WALK ON TOP
OF THE STORM RIGHT INTO THE
SAFETY OF THE ARMS OF JESUS.

And you can, just like Peter did.

I received a powerful testimony from a partner in Canada not long ago. She had been told by her doctors that they were certain she had a brain tumor. They wanted to run some tests and she was terribly frightened. As she lay on the examination table with all the equipment above her, she said simply, "Jesus, if You're with me right now, just stay with me." She was going through something and she didn't have time for any more than that. But Jesus honored her faith. The next tests were negative. And she was filled with a feeling of peace and cheer nothing could destroy. She says she hasn't had a headache since. She went through her storm to Jesus.

Jesus, Son of God, Son of man, is the One who can bring

His good cheer into any cheerless situation you have. The storm may be raging all around you and inside you. You may be looking at things at face value, and see nothing to be cheerful about. But remember to look for Jesus in the storm. For He is there and He will come walking to you on the waters of your troubles and speaking words of cheer. His words are usually simple. His sentences are short — but HIS WORDS ARE SPIRIT AND THEY ARE LIFE! And He is in the very NOW of your life to start giving you the miracle you need. I *know* that. I believe you are getting to know it too. Don't discount any part of anything special that appears to you. BEING SPECIAL IS GOD'S SPECIALTY. He delights in being SPECIAL to you and in making you SPECIAL too.

A MIRACLE PARTNERSHIP

These are moments when you must choose to expect God to do what He can do. Don't be afraid to do it. I promise you when you do what you can do and then expect God to do what He can do, you will form a new partnership between yourself and God — a miracle partnership where you will get on top of this problem instead of having it stay on top of you until it destroys you.

> You will walk on it.
> It will be a miracle.
> This miracle will happen to YOU.
> And you will arrive.
> You will make it.
> The thrill will make you a new person, one who has faced the worst, successfully gone through it, and looked back upon it with a powerful new partnership with God!

This is a partnership that will be even greater over the rest of your life, with its other storms and problems, than getting through the storm you're in right now. For you will have learned if you walk on the water in your storms once, you can do it again and again.

YOUR FORMULA FOR SUCCESS

When you get a miracle, it tells you something. It tells ·you it is only the beginning of miracles. You get into a relationship with Jesus of doing what you can do, then expecting Him to do what He can do . . . for the rest of your life.

Now HERE IS YOUR FORMULA FOR SUCCESS. It is infallible. It never will fail you. It will always work. By following this formula you will arrive and keep on arriving. You will make it and keep on making it.

Here it is:

> I will do what I can do.
> Then I will expect God to do what He can do.
>
> I will not ask God to do what I can do.
> I will not try to do what only He can do.
>
> I will get a new relationship with God as my miracle partner and we will do what we can do together.
>
> I will expect the good from what I can do.
>
> I will expect the miracles that God can do.
> I will expect a miracle!

I WILL EXPECT MIRACLE AFTER MIRACLE!

NOW ASK YOURSELF . . .

LIFE'S QUESTION: What can ➤ **GOD'S WAY**
I do when things start getting out of control?
SAY IT: I CAN TELL GOD MY NEED AND HE WILL COME TO ME AT THE POINT OF MY NEED ALWAYS.

LIFE'S QUESTION: Where can ➤ **GOD'S WAY**
I find God?
SAY IT: GOD IS RIGHT WITH ME – NOW – IN THE MIDST OF MY STORM.

LIFE'S QUESTION: What does ➤ **GOD'S WAY**
God expect me to do when I   SAY IT: GOD EXPECTS ME TO
run into troubled waters?   DO WHAT I CAN DO AND TO
                              EXPECT HIM TO DO WHAT I
                              CAN'T DO.

LIFE'S QUESTION: What can ➤ **GOD'S WAY**
I expect God to do?   SAY IT: I CAN EXPECT GOD
                              TO GIVE ME THE MIRACLE I
                              NEED. I LOOK FOR HIM. AND
                              I LISTEN TO HIM.

LIFE'S QUESTION: How can ➤ **GOD'S WAY**
I keep from falling into the SAY IT: I WILL LOOK TO GOD
same fear and worry each time IN MY NEED AND I WILL
storms hit?   FORM A MIRACLE PARTNER-
                              SHIP WITH HIM THAT WILL
                              LAST FOR THE REST OF MY
                              LIFE!

LIFE'S QUESTION: How can ➤ **GOD'S WAY**
I stay on top of my troubles? SAY IT: JESUS IS MY FORMULA
                              FOR SUCCESS. HE WILL SHOW
                              ME HOW TO WALK ON TOP
                              OF MY TROUBLES TODAY.
                              AND FOREVER!

PUTTING IT ALL TOGETHER FOR MYSELF

I CAN TELL GOD MY NEED AND HE WILL COME
TO ME AT THE POINT OF MY NEED ALWAYS.

* * * * * *

GOD IS RIGHT WITH ME – NOW! – IN THE MIDST
OF MY STORM.

* * * * * *

GOD EXPECTS ME TO DO WHAT I CAN DO AND TO
EXPECT HIM TO DO WHAT I CAN'T DO.

* * * * * *

I CAN EXPECT GOD TO GIVE ME THE MIRACLE I
NEED. I LOOK FOR HIM. AND I LISTEN TO HIM.

I WILL LOOK TO GOD IN MY NEED AND I WILL
FORM A MIRACLE PARTNERSHIP WITH HIM THAT
WILL LAST FOR THE REST OF MY LIFE!

* * * * * *

JESUS IS MY FORMULA FOR SUCCESS. HE WILL
SHOW ME HOW TO WALK ON TOP OF MY TROU-
BLES TODAY AND FOREVER!

Chapter Six

How not to become discouraged over the 'little faith' you have . . . how you can make it 'great faith'

"O, thou of little faith, wherefore didst thou doubt?" (Matthew 14:31).

When Peter and Jesus got into the boat a great calm came over the waters — and they arrived on the other side.

What Jesus had told them to do — go to the other side — had happened. How glad they were!

PETER'S LITTLE FAITH

But just moments earlier, while he was walking on the water, Peter's faith had faltered. He began to sink and Jesus had had to pull him up. When He did, He said, *"O thou of little faith, wherefore didst thou doubt?"*

I used to think that was a put-down. Then it occurred to me that Peter's little faith had worked a miracle never before done in history. He had actually been able to go to Jesus and WALK ON THE WATER!

I think, in a way, Jesus was really complimenting Peter, and implying that the others who didn't walk on the water with Peter could have, even though they too had only a little faith.

I think Jesus was saying to Peter:

> *Little faith is not so bad. It's more than no faith. Your little faith got you to walking on the water to come to Me. When you doubted, your little faith caused you to pray, 'Lord, save me.' And I reached down and pulled you back up on the water. Through your little faith we walked together as partners back to the boat. Through your little faith a calm came and you arrived. You reached your goal.*

JESUS SAW GREAT FAITH ONLY TWICE

Only twice in Jesus' ministry with hundreds of thousands did He encounter a person who had great faith. One was a man who said Jesus had authority above all authority, and if He would only speak the word his dying servant would be healed. Jesus said, "I have not found so great faith, no, not in Israel" (Matthew 8:10).

The other was a mother whose demented child caused her to come to Jesus for help. To get to Jesus she had to go through these same twelve disciples I'm talking about here. They told her to go home. She refused to take no for an answer. When she finally reached Jesus He told her the healing she sought for her child was "bread for His children" only. She, a person who had not opened herself to God, had no right to take bread from His children. "True," she said. "But, Lord, even the master's little lap dog gets the crumbs from the table. The children share their bread with it — and it's only a dog."

Then she said, "Lord, if you'll give me only a crumb, my daughter will be healed."

Jesus said, *"O woman great is thy faith: be it unto thee even as thou wilt."* And her daughter was healed (Matthew 15:21-28).

This man and this woman are the only ones according to Jesus who showed *great faith*. Apparently all the others

One man planted seed a step at a time until he had helped build the Golden Gate Bridge — that's what faith can do!

had less than great faith. Peter had, at this time, only a little faith. I don't know exactly why, but in a way I'm glad Peter had only a little faith. It encourages me.

FAITH IS LIKE GOLD

In your struggles you may have great faith. More than likely, however, you have little faith. I want to remind you the key word is not great, or little. The key word is *faith*.

Gold is gold. Whether you have much or little,

it's still gold.

Let me tell you a fascinating story of how a little faith exploded into great faith and resulted in the building of the most beautiful bridge in the world — the Golden Gate Bridge.

Last summer ('77) I was in San Francisco taping our Fall Television Prime Time Special. The Lennon Sisters were our guest stars, along with Richard, the World Action Singers, and Reflection.

There were so many fascinating spots to tape from, locations as beautiful as anywhere in the world — the cable cars, the Fishermen's Wharf, the Japanese Tea Gardens, Chinatown, and the world-famous Golden Gate Bridge, among others.

Well, just before I left Tulsa Dr. Warren Hultgren, pastor of Tulsa's First Baptist Church, a long-time personal friend, sent me a story about the Golden Gate Bridge and hoped I might use the information in our Special, which I did.

Here is the story:

Joseph Strauss, a young Jewish engineer, dreamed of being the best engineer in the world. And one day he stood in San Francisco and looked out at the wide San Francisco Bay and saw the old slow ferries and said, "Somebody should build a bridge over San Francisco Bay."

And he said, "I will be that man."

So he dreamed that great dream and made his designs

and his scale models, but then couldn't arrange his financing because the Great Depression hit in the early '30s. Then he heard of a man, A. P. Giannini, an immigrant Italian who had founded a bank for the little people of San Francisco, and who as a young man had dreamed of building the greatest bank in the world.

And there came that inevitable moment when Joseph Strauss had to call on higher powers in the person of A. P. Giannini, who started his bank to help the little people cross their bridges of bills piling up and no place to borrow because the big banks would not listen.

The prospect of building Golden Gate Bridge in Depression times revived old memories for Giannini. His bank was now strong, his influence powerful. Planting his seed in getting help for engineer Strauss would shorten the distance for hundreds of thousands, later millions. It would bring people together. Also when ships came in from the Pacific, the sailors would see a living miracle. They would be inspired. The same would happen to millions of others who drove over it, or saw it in other ways.

This great bridge came into effect.

The line of that story that stood out to me was, "Someone should build a bridge over San Francisco Bay." That was a compelling thought to young Joseph Strauss and he set about doing what he could do.

When I see this great bridge and think about how impossible the engineering and building must have been, it is almost as unbelievable as Jesus becoming the bridge over the troubled waters 2,000 years ago. It reminds me that what looks so unbelievable can become believable because IT HAPPENS.

At the end of the San Francisco Television Special Richard sang a beautiful little song, "Got Any Rivers."*

---

*© 1945. Singspiration, Inc.

Got any rivers you think are uncrossable,
Got any mountains you can't tunnel through,
My God specializes in things thought impossible,
And He can do what no other power can do.
Got any problems you think are unsolvable,
Well, Jesus can do what no other power can do.

What this song really says is FAITH IS FAITH. If it's great faith or if it's little faith, it's still FAITH!

I can think of very few times I felt I had great faith. Most of my faith has been small, just enough to take a step at a time toward God. Joseph Strauss looked and planted seed a step at a time until he built the Golden Gate Bridge over San Francisco Bay. You just need enough faith to plant a seed, however small, and expect God to multiply it into something big. Doing it that way is the story of the success I've had — and am having. I've used a lot of little faith a lot of times.

YOUR FAITH MAY BE MIXED WITH DOUBT

"O ye of little faith . . . why did you doubt?"

Here Jesus told Peter he had faith — a little faith, but still it was faith. He asked him why he had doubted when he HAD that faith.

In other words, "Peter, why did you mix what faith you had — enough to walk on the water — with doubt, which caused you to start to sink? Why?"

I don't see any anger from Jesus here, no condemnation. I see a simple statement recognizing Peter's faith — and a question wondering why he had mixed the faith he had with doubt.

I think Jesus was asking Peter why he had first responded with his spirit, and then had allowed his five senses to take over and kill the spiritual response.

Remember, FAITH is the Spirit of God supernaturally emptying your spirit of doubt so you can believe and do wonders. Doubt is your five senses taking over your spirit's proper role and making you scared to death to keep on believing. All Peter had to do was to keep on using the little faith he had. That's all.

His little faith, like a little gold, was still faith. Remember that. Remember, it went a long way! It went so far as to enable him to do exactly what Jesus was doing — to walk on the water to get through his struggle.

IF YOU ARE WAITING FOR 100% FAITH, YOU MAY NEVER START

I started this ministry with such little faith. As I look back I wonder how I got anywhere at all. Right after I began my ministry in 1947, I got the courage to board a plane and fly to a small church in a distant state. They had sent me word they needed me to pray for their sick. I had only enough faith to go. I didn't know whether I would be successful or not. Making the decision to go greatly affected both Evelyn and me.

Evelyn said, "When I drove Oral from Enid over to Tulsa and put him on that plane, the very first he had ridden, and watched it disappear into the skies, I cried and cried. I didn't know if I'd ever see him again. I didn't know if anyone would be healed or not when he prayed for them. As I drove the 130 miles back to Enid, I prayed as I had never prayed before. I knew our past was as good as behind us as far as pastoring our little church was concerned. And I surely didn't know what the future held ... "

Well, she wasn't the only one wondering. To tell the truth, when I got on that plane I was scared. I hoped God would heal someone in Newman, Georgia. Thank God, it never occurred to me to hope everyone would be healed. I knew it was better to face the struggle in my heart and continue the small beginning I had made in the healing ministry by going where they at least wanted me. I felt Jesus' urging in my spirit to go. I don't think I would have gotten on that plane in 1947 had I had the big faith people seem to think you must have before you attempt to do anything.

Three weeks later when Evelyn met me at the Tulsa airport, she took one look and knew my faith, my little faith had worked for somebody. All the way back to Enid we cried and laughed with joy as I shared with her about the long healing lines — about outgrowing the little local church and having to go to the city auditorium for the final service. I told her about that last day in the city auditorium.

It was packed and the place was electric with expectation. Suddenly a man who hadn't walked in years caught my attention. Right in the middle of my sermon I fastened my gaze on him and seeing he was in a state of expectation shouted, "Brother, stand on your feet and walk! In the name of Jesus, do it . . . now!" And he did it! He did it! At first he struggled for a moment there in his wheelchair. It seemed the whole service stopped as we all focused our attention on him. He moved just a little at first. Then it seemed something powerful swept through him. And in a second he was standing. Everbody, including me, burst into tears of joy.

I said, "Evelyn, I'll never forget how after I had told him to stand and walk, I got scared he wouldn't. But God had honored the fact I had enough faith to make that first move of my spirit to His Spirit to believe he could have a miracle."

I had just a "little faith" when I took that first trip, but my faith had grown some when I returned!

FAITH CAN GROW

I like to think I have more faith now than I did when I started this ministry in 1947. However, it's still the same kind of faith. It was little faith in 1947. It's both a little faith and a little bigger faith now. But both kinds are the faith of God in my heart waiting to be released. Every time I accomplish anything I know I have released some more faith, I know I have walked on the water again.

Don't be discouraged over what little faith you have any more than the gold prospector when he finds only a little of that precious stuff. The prospector knows a little gold dust means there's a lot more where that came from — that's what keeps him going.

What will keep you going when the storms keep striking at you and your loved ones? That little faith you have. Just a tiny, tiny little bit of it. It means there's a lot more in you. Peter, a person with a little faith, walked on the water — and don't you or I ever forget it! Let's not ever forget he did this magnificent thing with only a little faith. And even it was mixed with doubt!

Don't you think we have a pretty great God who accepts what we have and does wonders with it?

GOD HAS GIVEN EVERY HUMAN BEING A PART OF HIS OWN GREAT FAITH

The Bible says, "God hath dealt to every man the measure of faith" (Romans 12:3). It doesn't say great faith, middle-size faith or little faith. It just says He has given the measure of faith to every person. To me that's great. We each have the measure of God's own faith implanted in our spirit.

I can't impress upon you or myself too much the importance of the fact that it's not the size of the measure of faith you have that is so important — but that, like Peter, you start using whatever faith you have, even if it's not completely free of doubt. The water can still be walked on, even with the faith you may feel is so small. Miracles can still happen to you if you will believe with what faith you have to believe with.

I USED MY LITTLE FAITH WHEN I ANSWERED MY FIRST LETTER

As I talk to you about little faith many thoughts come to

my mind. One of them goes back again to 1947, the very start of this ministry. I'd begun to pray for people to be saved and to be healed. I'd begun to preach "GOD IS A GOOD GOD." And somehow the news spread out across America. And I got a letter from out of state. In fact, the first week eight people wrote me.

But I remember that first letter best. Evelyn and I opened it and read it. It was from a woman who was very ill — not only ill in her body, but she had all kinds of problems. She poured out her heart to me. Well, not ever having received a letter like that and not ever having been asked to help someone with such dreadful needs, I almost wilted. I said to Evelyn, "What do you think I should do? How can I help someone who is as desperate as she is — and so far away?"

Evelyn said, "Oral, what do you feel in your heart for her?"

I said, "I'll tell you what I feel. I feel God can help her. I believe God can do anything!"

"Well, why don't you tell her that?"

"I feel like praying for her," I added.

Evelyn said, "Why don't you pray, and tell her you have prayed for her."

Now that's all the faith I had. So I sat down and wrote her that I was praying for her and I was believing God to heal her.

She turned right around and wrote me back another letter. I remember that letter because of a certain thing — as she said in it:

> "Oh, Mr. Roberts, when I got your letter and read it, it suddenly dawned on me that you are the first person who ever told me that you were praying for me. You are the first one who ever said God could heal me . . ."

Then she went on to tell me since she had gotten the

letter she had begun to improve. Everything was better.

But the main thought to me was, at least I had a little faith — enough to write and tell her I was praying for her and that God could do anything.

A MINISTRY THROUGH THE MAIL

I have been writing back to people who write me ever since. Only now it's a lot of letters, not a few. But it works just the same. People are still getting help. Some are hearing for the first time that God cares about them and wants to heal them, that He can make a way where there is no way.

I often say on our television program, "Just writing that letter helps you release your faith. You get something off your chest, out of your heart. You feel better even before your letter reaches me."

Not long ago I heard from a partner from Illinois telling me what happened when she and her husband wrote me with a prayer request. She said, "As I dropped the letter in the box, I released my faith. Brother Roberts, I claimed a miracle in my life. My negative attitude has gone, hopefully not to return." I hadn't received her letter yet. But God had honored her faith already.

I invite people to write to me, with the promise that I will write back. I tell my partners, "When I write you back I put my heart in that letter. They are my words, my thoughts, my prayers, my hope, my love, my faith — and my expectation for a miracle for your life."

LETTING MY FAITH LOOSE — RIGHT INTO THE LENS!

It's strange about the TV cameras. They used to scare me terribly. With all the bright lights in my face, the camera people moving around, and the hurried activity, I found it almost impossible to concentrate upon people. Every little thing bothered me — a strange sound, the crew speaking softly over their intercoms to the director, the stage manager pointing to the camera I was to use.

One day I had it out in my spirit. "Look, Oral Roberts, you are not going to let your sight or hearing or feeling keep you from reaching out to the people watching you on their TV set. They are struggling and you can give them a new hope in God."

My spirit responded. Now it amazes me, as well as the people in the studio who are there during the tapings, that I can look right at the camera lens and, suddenly, with my spirit see another human being. I can feel this person. I can talk only to him, not to the millions tuned in, but to him or her. I feel we are close, we are together, we are one in our spirits.

Every time we make a TV program I feel closer to the person watching me on his TV set. He feels this too for he writes, "Brother Roberts, you are talking only to me."

Evelyn told me about a woman here in Tulsa who had lost her husband. When Evelyn saw her she wanted to share the woman's grief. But the woman said, "It's all right, Evelyn, I watched your television program Sunday morning and Oral looked right at me and told me he knew what I was going through and was praying for me. I'm so glad he knew all about my loss. He made me feel so much better when he talked straight to my heart, giving me words from the Lord to strengthen me."

Then Evelyn said the woman looked straight at her, with a radiance on her face, and said, "Evelyn, it's going to be all right. I'm going to make it."

Now I had not known her by name. I hadn't known personally of her loss when I made that TV program. There was no way I could have known. But the Lord knew. The Lord was in me. As I felt Him in my spirit, I felt the people who had suffered loss. So when I looked at the camera I saw a person with a great loss. I didn't see the person's size or color of her eyes, or even the loss as it happened. But I saw a human being hurting. Jesus in me reached out to this woman. She knew I was talking to *her*.

MIRACLES ARE COMING TOWARD YOU OR PAST YOU

And that's the way Jesus comes to you. He's there when you need Him in the way you need Him the most. You just have to move toward Him with the little faith you have. And He will be there to meet you. It's true. You can believe it.

Because people can sense I'm talking directly to them in their need, little faith often grows into the ability to walk on the water of struggle.

What a release of faith I received from a woman who wrote me about a crippled leg and who had now reached the point where she didn't know if she would ever have the use of it again. Many different medical and surgical procedures had been tried on it. She was a person who believed, as I believe, both in medicine and prayer. But somehow the leg would not respond to anything. You know how you feel when you get sick and seemingly you're not able to get well, particularly if it's a crippled limb. Well, one day, she sent me a letter. I answered it and said, "Miracles are coming toward you or past you every day." And every time she'd write me, I'd include that phrase — miracles are coming toward you or past you every day. On the telecast I would say it. I said it everywhere. Then I got this letter. She said:

Dear Oral Roberts:

I was sitting there watching your telecast when you came to your prayer time. My husband and I were holding hands as you asked us to and praying with you, and God whispered in my heart, "*Your miracle is here, your miracle is here.* Receive it. Receive it."

I turned to my husband. I said, "Honey, my miracle is here. Brother Roberts is talking just to me. My miracle is here and I don't want to let it pass me by. What must I do?"

And he said, "*Do* SOMETHING!"

When I felt in my heart God saying, "Your miracle is here, don't let it pass you by," I said, "Honey, I'm going to stretch this leg out. I'm going to stretch it out." All that while I was praying and asking God to heal.

Then I said, "Husband, help me." And I stood up. I STOOD UP. And I raised my limb and stood on it. I took a step, another step, and I could feel my leg getting strong again.

Her little faith was released and became the walking on the water of her struggle. It had turned into great faith!

I've discovered in dealing with people who need healing that they need to start *doing* something. She started moving that limb.

Most of the time we have to start with just a small step. But as we get closer to Jesus, our steps become surer. We become more confident. And we finally discover we CAN walk on the water. We CAN go to Jesus.

Speaking of going to Jesus, it's amazing how His words can leap out at you and put you on the right track again. As I was completing the writing of this chapter, I received a letter from a partner in Benton, Arkansas. She says:

Dear Brother Roberts:

Thank you for writing me. It was an extra bonus since I only expected the books I requested. I read them both and intend to pass them on.

My most pressing problem was arthritis, which was about to put me in a wheelchair. My family doctor told me it was old-fashioned rheumatism and nothing could be done for it except pain killers. After a while, that made me bleed under the skin if I bumped myself so I left it off and became very depressed. I lost confidence in my doctor, and the pain wore my nerves down.

After I started reading your book, THREE MOST IM-PORTANT STEPS TO YOUR BETTER HEALTH AND MIRACLE LIVING, I came across the Bible quotation, *"They that are sick need a physician."* It jumped right out at me. I stopped and thought about that, and it gave me the idea to call a specialist, an orthopedist. I did. He made two small x-rays and found five pieces of bone about the size of lima beans. He said those had been getting into the joint as I walked, and caused the pain. He suggested surgery, and I had it February 22. Now I am exercising, walking much better, and soon hope to lay aside the crutches. I am 65 years old. I have to say right here, "Thank You, Lord, for healing me and thank You for Oral Roberts who spends his life pointing the way."

This woman discovered Jesus appearing to her through His words, "They that are sick need a physician," AND by following through with an orthopedic surgeon. When she says, "Thank You, Lord, for healing me," she is saying the delivery system God used to heal her was all a part of God. God had appeared to her in that fashion and she was grateful.

Well, I am grateful too.

NOW ASK YOURSELF...

LIFE'S QUESTION: How can I make my little faith into great faith?
➤ **GOD'S WAY**
SAY IT: I WILL KEEP ON USING A LOT OF MY LITTLE FAITH A LOT OF TIMES, AND THAT'S ALL IT TAKES TO GET ME THROUGH.

LIFE'S QUESTION: How can I keep from doubting?
➤ **GOD'S WAY**
SAY IT: I WILL MOVE IN MY SPIRIT, I WILL USE MY LITTLE FAITH, AND I WILL NOT LET MY FIVE SENSES TAKE OVER MY SPIRIT.

LIFE'S QUESTION: What will keep me going when troubles keep striking at me and my family?
➤ **GOD'S WAY**
SAY IT: MY LITTLE FAITH WILL KEEP ME GOING BE-CAUSE THERE'S A LOT MORE GROWING IN ME.

LIFE'S QUESTION: If my healing comes through a physician or surgeon, is that God healing me?
➤ **GOD'S WAY**
SAY IT: WHETHER MY HEAL-ING COMES THROUGH A PHYSICIAN OR PRAYER OR THROUGH BOTH, IT IS GOD WHO HEALS ME.

LIFE'S QUESTION: How much ➤ GOD'S WAY
faith do I need to begin?   SAY IT: I HAVE ENOUGH
FAITH TO BEGIN AND THAT'S
ALL I NEED.

LIFE'S QUESTION: What can ➤ GOD'S WAY
I do with such a little faith?   SAY IT: I WILL BELIEVE WITH
WHAT FAITH I HAVE TO BE-
LIEVE WITH. AND MIRACLES
WILL HAPPEN TO ME.

LIFE'S QUESTION: How can ➤ GOD'S WAY
I do what needs to be done   SAY IT: I CAN BELIEVE THAT
to get the miracle I need   MY MIRACLE IS HERE. MY
right now?   MIRACLE IS HERE!

PUTTING IT ALL TOGETHER FOR MYSELF

I WILL KEEP ON USING A LOT OF MY LITTLE FAITH
A LOT OF TIMES AND THAT'S ALL IT TAKES TO GET
ME THROUGH.   ✶✶✶✶✶✶

I WILL MOVE IN MY SPIRIT, I WILL USE MY LITTLE
FAITH, AND I WILL NOT LET MY FIVE SENSES
TAKE OVER MY SPIRIT.   ✶✶✶✶✶✶

I HAVE ENOUGH FAITH TO BEGIN AND THAT'S
ALL I NEED.   ✶✶✶✶✶✶

MY LITTLE FAITH WILL KEEP ME GOING BECAUSE
THERE'S A LOT MORE GROWING IN ME.
✶✶✶✶✶✶

I WILL BELIEVE WITH WHAT FAITH I HAVE TO
BELIEVE WITH, AND MIRACLES WILL HAPPEN
TO ME!   ✶✶✶✶✶✶

I CAN BELIEVE THAT MY MIRACLE IS HERE. MY
MIRACLE IS HERE!
✶✶✶✶✶✶

WHETHER MY HEALING COMES THROUGH A PHY-
SICIAN OR PRAYER, OR THROUGH BOTH, IT IS GOD
WHO HEALS ME.

Chapter Seven

How obedience to God will help you with your fears and struggles— and keep on helping you

> *"And he constrained (commanded) his disciples to*
> *. . . go . . . to the other side"* (Matthew 14:22).

My mother always said two things to me. The first was, "Oral, always obey God." The other was, "Oral, keep little in your own eyes and God will use you to bless the world."

I believe Mamma had a God-given insight into the ways of God with a person and also an instinctive insight into a person's nature, including mine.

"ALWAYS OBEY GOD." Mamma knew obedience was the most important thing. Jesus held obedience before the twelve disciples at all times. He never let up on obedience. In commanding them to go across the sea in the evening, the most dangerous time in crossing the Sea of Galilee, and to go without His *physical* presence on board, He was testing their obedience. He was also testing their ego. Was their ego bigger than their obedience to Jesus? Or was their obedience something they would build their whole lives around. That's a big question you've got to ask yourself — and settle!

The second thing was:

"ORAL, KEEP LITTLE IN YOUR OWN EYES." Apparently Mamma had struggled with her own ego and learned it is best to stay humble before God.

Obeying God and *staying little in my own eyes* are constant struggles for me. Sometimes I am very aware I am in obedience in giving my total loyalty to Jesus. At other times I struggle to obey, to keep humble in my own sight. Success has a way of momentarily throwing me off stride spiritually. The temptation is to think:

> I'm walking on the water.
> I've got it made now.
> I'll never fail again.
> I've got myself under God's control now.

It isn't long, however, until something comes up and hits me with such force I find myself like Peter as he floundered in the water, crying, "Lord, save me!"

LET'S SHARE ABOUT YOUR OBEDIENCE FIRST

There were two fears the disciples faced that evening. *First,* they were scared of the storm. They knew it could wipe them out. And *second,* they were scared of Jesus. They didn't recognize Him in a posture they had never seen Him in before — walking on water.

FEARS I HAD

When I received Jesus' command to take His healing power to my generation, like Peter and the others, I got on board and started. Everything seemed normal, no problems. But the very first month I began holding healing services I ran into storms and struggles that scared me out of my wits. There were several things that were terrifying. It began with other ministers misunderstanding my motives.

> "Why are you trying to be different from
> the rest of us?"

"Who do you think you are to believe God
works through you to heal the sick?"

When the big crowds started coming, some pastors would
question:

"What does Oral Roberts have that I don't have?"

"Why does he draw big crowds when after years of
faithful ministry only two or three hundred come
to hear me?"

I remember that first year a pastor of a large church
asked me to come there for two weeks. The church sanctuary
seated over one thousand and hadn't been filled in years, if
ever. Well, it filled right up and overflowed into the vesti-
bules and the basement. People even sat in the aisles. They
came early and stayed late. Front seats were at a premium.

I thought the pastor would be delighted. But his first
question should have put me on guard. He said, "Brother
Roberts, are your miracles real?"

I didn't think about the reason he asked. Innocently I
answered, "Well, I don't have any miracles. God works
through me and when He does, it's real, very real." I added,
"Just watch and you'll see for yourself."

By the third night he had gotten sullen. I was so busy
preaching and praying for people I didn't notice. But his
people noticed. As it drew closer to Sunday, I saw that a
sharp division had developed. The people were excited
about my ministry but so disappointed about their pastor's
reaction, a committee was appointed to talk to him.

Sunday morning I preached to an overflow crowd. The
pastor and his wife invited me to dinner. During the meal
he was extremely cold. Finally I said, "Look, I didn't know
you before you asked me to come. Obviously you are
unhappy. About what, I don't know, unless you think I am
hurting you. I think in tonight's meeting I will just quietly

announce I am not going to complete the second week. I will not implicate you but I think I should go."

I didn't know what the church committee had told him. It must have struck him pretty hard. Tears filled his eyes. "Look, I've been pastor here for over fifteen years," he said. "This is the first time my people have reacted against me. If you leave now it will finish me. Please stay the second week."

I agreed but it was a hard week for me. He put on a big front but his attitude was like a cold blast of air toward me.

Years passed. Just before he died he sent a messenger to ask my forgiveness and tell me he regretted his actions. I gladly sent my word that I had forgiven him, also that the experience had been a good one for me.

But the day I closed that meeting, fear gripped my heart. Was this to be the reaction of pastors everywhere I went? Not every pastor did this, but it happened often enough that I finally went on my own. I invited any pastors in the area who wished to cooperate. And the benefits most of them received from new members going to their churches pretty well solved the problem.

THE PRESS ATTACKS ME

Another fear I developed was of the news media. Seldom was there an objective article written about our crusades. They said I was divisive — I divided a town, the churches. In short, I was a fraud.

The first question asked me by a newsman upon my arrival in 1956 for a crusade in Australia was, "Mr. Roberts, are you a fraud?" He did this while my team and I were engulfed by a thousand people who welcomed us at the airport. I said, "No, sir, I am not. I am a man trying to obey God." The next morning's headline clear across the top of the front page was "ROBERTS SAYS, 'I'M NO FRAUD'."

In Australia the pastors and people received me with some of the largest crowds of my ministry. But the press tried to destroy me. Finally they managed to create very real problems. Hoodlums ran down the aisles screaming, cursing, trying to make the people leave, doing everything they could to break up the meetings. As I preached they would run up and spit on me, shove me, yell obscenities at me, try to drown out my voice. They literally grabbed people to prevent them from coming forward for salvation or for healing prayers. Each day the newspapers reported their activities and actually encouraged them. Then a headline ran: "MOB TO BURN ROBERTS' TENT TOMORROW NIGHT."

The insurance people told my associates they would have to cancel their coverage of our large equipment. The American Embassy told them I might be killed and advised the closing of the meeting.

Early the next morning my associates awakened me, put me in a car, and had me on a plane out of the country before the press discovered it. They exulted that they had run me out of the country.

My men had to buy space in the Australian press to tell our side of the story because they would not quote us in their news reports.

SEED-FAITH OF GORDON POWELL

But it was because of one man that the whole story was told accurately. The leading pastor of Australia was also a well-known radio personality. And he believed very strongly in what we were doing. He chided the press and the nation and alerted the people to what actually had happened.

Nearly twenty years later, Reverend Gordon Powell was asked to come to America and pastor the famous old church at Quaker Hill in upper New York where Lowell Thomas, Sr., Norman Vincent Peale, and others attend. Lowell asked me to preach there after he was a guest on our Alaska TV Special, saying Reverend Powell wanted me very much.

I felt in my spirit I should go. The church was packed and overflowing. Reverend Powell gave me a great introduction. Before my sermon I recounted the Australian incident and the press coverage that broke up the meetings, and told of Gordon Powell single-handedly turning the country around concerning my ministry, after my departure. "Now," I said, "I am here preaching in his church. I am here able to tell of a great lesson I've learned. Although fear gripped me in Australia, I want to say the seed Gordon Powell planted for me twenty years ago is coming to harvest here today. And I've discovered if you obey God neither the press or anything else can destroy you." There was spontaneous applause all over the place. I'll never forget that service at Quaker Hill. But the thing I remember best is the Seed-Faith of Gordon Powell.

THE PRESS CHANGES

The attitude of the press changed toward me almost abruptly several years ago. But not before they had nearly scared me to death. I was never worried about myself. My concern was that they might cripple my ministry which I looked upon as the most sacred thing I'd ever known. I knew in spite of myself I was helping people because the Holy Spirit was using my obedience, and my desire to touch neither the gold nor the glory — in other words, my effort to stay little in my own eyes.

YOU CAN LEARN TO OBEY IN SPITE OF YOUR FEAR

In thirty years of this ministry, I've never totally been without fear —

Fear of people dying as I prayed for them.

Fear of trying to build God a university.

Fear I couldn't do it.

Fear people would think building ORU would
take me out of the healing ministry.

Fear of the University not staying grounded on
God's authority and the Holy Spirit.

Fear of dealing with educators and students
when I had no background to do it.

Fear of the students not understanding
the founding purpose of ORU.

Fear of not having funds to build new buildings,
to operate the school, to make payrolls.

Fear of building a medical school that aims to
unify spiritual and medical healing.

Fear of building the CITY OF FAITH medical and
research center, a unique new health care
center on the ORU campus.

I even feared sometimes that the voice I heard wasn't
God's voice at all, that it was a figment of my imagination.
He would speak in my heart and tell me every step to take.
I would tell what God had said and people would look at
me like I had taken leave of my senses.

Time and again I would pour out my heart to Evelyn.
She would say, "Are you sure God spoke to you?"

"Absolutely sure."

"Then OBEY GOD. Do it and He will do the rest."

Some of my associates would say, "Brother Roberts, we
are with you."

When I would say, "Why?"

They would answer, "Your works speak for themselves.
Every time you've said God spoke to you to do something,
it has happened. We can't argue with your track record."

As I said earlier, the two fears of Peter and the disciples that night were *the fear of the storm itself* — troubled waters upsetting their lives even though they were obeying what Jesus had told them to do, and *the fear of seeing Jesus do what no man had ever done — walk on water.* Those two things had a terrible impact upon them.

NOW LET'S SHARE ABOUT YOUR EGO

I said my mother often told me to keep little in my own eyes. And in Peter's situation that meant exactly what it does to you and me. By being big in his own eyes, thinking he knew better than Jesus did, by building up his ego, he never would have used his faith to jump from the sinking boat onto the troubled waters. He never would have obeyed Jesus' command to "Come."

Peter could have said:

> "Fellas, the storm is bad but we can handle it. We can take care of ourselves.

> "That voice we heard was just our imagination.

> "Why should we leave this boat we are familiar with and trust in a ghost who looks like it's walking on the water? Let's don't trade what we know for what we don't know.

> "Well, it sounds like Jesus' voice. And I know if it is Jesus He is using something that is also available to me, His follower. But it's just too scary. I can't do it.

> "Me walk on the water? Even if it is Jesus walking on the water while we're about to go under, I can't do it. After all, I'm only a human being."

GIVE YOUR EGO TO JESUS

Peter could have said all that. But instead he did what

you and I have done at times and need to do even more. HE TOOK HIS EGO AND LET JESUS HAVE IT. He took his fears and put them under his faith. He said, "This is Jesus in His human skin, exactly the same kind of skin I'm wearing. It's Jesus using the same faith God has put in every heart, including mine. If I stay on this boat that's going under I'll go under too. But if I make a leap of faith to go to Jesus, I can walk on the water."

THE PROBLEM OF FAILURE

Peter reached the decision that he had failed to make it on the boat. His only chance lay in (1) Jesus' word, "Come," and, (2) the use of what little faith he had to leap upon the raging waters.

It was like I was when I said, "Lord, what if I fail?" And He replied, "You've already done that," leaving me with only one way to go — UP, so Peter had failed and had only one way to go: jump and expect a miracle.

Peter understood that in a moment. He made his leap of faith and started walking. But Peter's faith somehow diminished. He started to sink. And right then he learned a valuable lesson. He learnned it's one thing to obey and another to keep on obeying. It's one thing to get out of the troubled water and another to keep on getting out.

There seems to be no single act of obedience or faith that solves it all. When Peter leaped out of the boat it solved his first act of walking on the water. He did walk on the water. But he hit a snag. His faith began to fail him and down he went. That's what happens to us too. Whatever healing we receive, we get sick again. Whatever success we have, we fail again. However high we reach, we fall again. It seems we are on stairsteps. We climb, then stumble and fall back a step or two, maybe all the way back. We have to get up and climb again, always reaching toward that top step.

There is no single act of obedience or faith that solves it all, but we can always go to God in prayer.

Now Peter didn't make a perfect walk on the water. And Jesus asked him why he had doubted. But there's something Jesus didn't do. He didn't turn His back on Peter in his failure to walk on the water as well as He had. He didn't fail to hear Peter's frantic three-word prayer: "Lord, save me."

NOW ASK YOURSELF...

LIFE'S QUESTION: How can I get God's help in my problems?

→ **GOD'S WAY**
SAY IT: I WILL OBEY GOD AND HE WILL BLESS ME FOR MY OBEDIENCE.

LIFE'S QUESTION: How can I stand up against my critics?

→ **GOD'S WAY**
SAY IT: I WILL REMEMBER THAT NO ONE AND NOTHING CAN PREVAIL AGAINST ME BECAUSE I AM OBEYING GOD.

LIFE'S QUESTION: How can I overcome my fears?

→ **GOD'S WAY**
SAY IT: I WILL GIVE MY EGO TO JESUS AND PUT MY FEARS UNDER MY FAITH.

LIFE'S QUESTION: What if I fail?

→ **GOD'S WAY**
SAY IT: I HAVE ALREADY FAILED AND THERE IS ONLY ONE WAY TO GO – UP!

LIFE'S QUESTION: How can I keep from stumbling and falling?

→ **GOD'S WAY**
SAY IT: I WILL KEEP ON OBEYING GOD. I WILL KEEP ON LEARNING, AND I WILL KEEP MY EYES ON JESUS.

LIFE'S QUESTION: What can I do when I don't know where Jesus is?

→ **GOD'S WAY**
SAY IT: I WILL REMEMBER JESUS CARES ABOUT ME AND HE ALWAYS KNOWS WHERE I AM!

PUTTING IT ALL TOGETHER FOR MYSELF

I WILL OBEY GOD AND HE WILL BLESS ME FOR MY OBEDIENCE.

* * * * * *

I WILL REMEMBER THAT NO ONE AND NOTHING CAN PREVAIL AGAINST ME BECAUSE I AM OBEYING GOD.

* * * * * *

I WILL GIVE MY EGO TO JESUS AND PUT MY FEARS UNDER MY FAITH.

* * * * * *

I HAVE ALREADY FAILED AND THERE IS ONLY ONE WAY TO GO – UP!

* * * * * *

I WILL KEEP ON OBEYING GOD, I WILL KEEP ON LEARNING, AND I WILL KEEP MY EYES ON JESUS.

* * * * * *

I WILL REMEMBER JESUS CARES ABOUT ME AND HE ALWAYS KNOWS WHERE I AM!

Chapter Eight

How to capture a magic moment in your struggles

"And Peter walked on the water to go to Jesus"
(Matthew 14:29).

When Peter stepped over the side of the boat in the raging storm and his foot touched the first wave lashing against it, the Bible says: "HE WALKED ON THE WATER . . . ." He captured a magic moment.

You've known magic moments if you'll only stop and think back.

It's a magic moment when somehow during a situation that is engulfing you, you reach out with your faith and touch that Power that spins the universe and something miraculous starts happening to change things for you.

It's a magic moment when one word from God passes your intellect and explodes in your spirit, opening your spiritual eyes so you can see Jesus in the midst of your storm.

PETER'S MAGIC MOMENT

If you cannot recall a magic moment in all of your life — get ready. Because you can experience one just like Peter did.

One moment Peter's hands were being torn from the

oars of the boat as it pitched in the violent waves. He was crying, "I'm not going to make it! I can't hold the oars any longer . . . we're going under!"

The next moment those things didn't matter. Because he discovered he could enter a magic moment. He put his shoulders back and by the force of his will he raised his spirit up, and by an act of his little faith, he was saying:

"That's Jesus out there in the midst of this storm.

That's *His* voice calling *me* to come.

I can leave this sinking boat and get on something more solid and sure by going on the water to Jesus.

I'm going to make it!"

MAGIC MOMENTS ARE FOR YOU

That was a magic moment. And that's what God is all about: magic moments. Magic moments are for me and for you. They're possible for everyone. Dorothy Akuffo captured a magic moment. She was going through a storm we can all identify with. Let me share her letter with you.

Brother Roberts, you might remember my writing to you about two weeks ago telling you about the depression into which I had fallen. When I realized my bills were piling up and I had nowhere to turn, panic gripped me.

That Saturday morning when I finally dropped off to sleep after lying awake all night, it was as if someone tapped me on the shoulder and prompted me to reach up and tune in to your radio program. As I listened to your message about Seed-Faith and miracles, my heart rose with excitement. God continued to speak to me through the letters read by your dear wife Evelyn and the songs by Richard and the World Action Singers. My whole attitude and outlook changed! The depression left, not just for the rest of the day. It has never returned!

Before listening to your program, I had already planned to visit my creditors and request more time to repay them, then stop by the drugstore and purchase a supply of tranquilizers for the coming week. But as the gloom and desperation left, an inner peace came over me. Deep down I felt a voice urging me to change my plans, to just take it easy and relax the rest of the day. Before I knew it I had paper and pen in hand, writing to my creditors, explaining my problem and promising to repay them shortly. Then I wrote to you, Brother Roberts, and planted a seed for a miracle. Immediately a heavy burden was lifted from my shoulders and I didn't have a care in the world.

The following Monday I received a letter from my lawyer saying that he had an amount of money for me, which was more than enough to cover all my bills. What a return!

Her problems disappeared when she realized the possibility of a magic moment, when she acted in faith.

Now I'm not talking about magic in the way the world looks at magic. This is no make-believe pie-in-the-sky. It is not mere wishing. I'm talking about magic moments that happen because of an act of faith. I'm talking about a leap of faith that brings the miraculous power of God right into the sloshing around we're doing in the water that is getting ready to swamp us.

God is all about miracles!

> Hearing and answering prayer is God coming
> to you in the urgency of your need . . .

> God subduing the raging storm . . .

> God commanding the roaring waves to lie down
> and be calm . . .

> God enabling you to find a way when there
> seems to be no way.

That's God helping you get through your struggles. I believe it, and I want you to believe it.

How is the magic moment you need made possible? Is it

something that will happen only once in your lifetime? Is it a will-o'-the-wisp chance? Or is there a reason behind it, a cause that is sure and eternal? Can you count on it happening again and again?

A magic moment is made possible by your doing what Peter did, a specific act, by using the little faith you have to walk on the water. You may feel you have only a small amount of faith. Well, the main thing is to be specific about the faith you have, no matter how small. Put it to work. Do it! I promise you . . . you will walk on the water and GET THROUGH YOUR STRUGGLES. There is a way, God made it, and you can find it.

PLANTING SEED FOR OTHERS

When Peter stepped out of that boat, he wasn't trying to pull any stunt — "See how great I am? I can walk on water!" No!

It was a human experience of dependency on
God, his Source, the Root System of his life.

It was planting a seed of faith for himself
and the eleven others in the same boat.

It was looking at Jesus, believing His reality
was more powerful, more solid, than the
water itself.

It was putting Jesus at the center of his
thoughts and his actions.

It was expecting a miracle.

It's been many years now, but it is indelibly etched in my mind the day my oldest brother Elmer strode into my room, picked me up as a 17-year-old boy dying with tuberculosis, and carried me to a meeting where a man of God prayed with authority in his voice for my healing. Elmer felt my need. He saw the storm that was about to take my

life and walked on the water to Jesus, thereby planting a
seed that gave me faith for my healing.

The seed Elmer planted that day came to harvest for
him in February 1977. Elmer wasn't a Christian when he
carried me to be prayed for. Although he had not made a
commitment of his own life to God, he had a deep concern
for God to help me. The day after Marshall and Rebecca
were killed, Elmer came to my house. And he asked me to
pray for him. He had never done that in all the years of
my ministry. I had almost given up hope that 42 years after
he had carried me to be prayed for, and I was healed, that
he would want to test God for himself. In all those years
after my conversion and healing, after hearing me preach,
and believing in me like few brothers ever believe in each
other, Elmer had never, to my knowledge, made a personal
move in faith toward God.

Papa and Mamma died without seeing their oldest son
believe God for himself. So many times they would say,
"Oral, remember to pray for Elmer."

Courteous, respectful, wanting me to carry on a loving
healing ministry, Elmer was a great brother. He just didn't
seem to feel a need for himself.

Word had reached me that he had had surgery. He
hadn't told me. Others of my family when ill asked for my
prayers but Elmer had gone under the knife asking for
nothing from me. He who had taken me to be healed by
the power of God seemed oblivious of the power of prayer
for himself.

The next news I had was that the operation was unsuc-
cessful. There was no reason it should not have been successful. Later he went back for repairs, again failure. "Mr.
Roberts," they said, "you've got to live with it."

Months passed. No further word. Then the death in
the family. Loved ones and friends filled our home. Elmer
walked in. He looked at me. He felt my hurt.

After a few minutes he motioned me to go into the bedroom where we could be alone. We stood there. He looked at me. A tear ran down his cheek. Then down both. He had always found it hard to cry. I had never seen him shed tears, ever. Not that he didn't feel deeply or hurt; he simply was a man who couldn't cry.

Putting his arms around me and laying his head on my shoulder he cried and shook. Then he asked me to do something I had thought he might never ask for. "Help me," he said.

"They've missed on me. I'm in bad shape. Put your hand down here on me and pray. Ask God . . . . " and his voice broke.

What a prayer we had there in the bedroom. Elmer and Jesus met, we all three met. And my brother walked on the water of his need.

What caused my brother to finally ask me to pray for him, to ask Jesus to help him? A need. A need he had never had before. Jesus had been close to Elmer all his life, as He is to every person. Elmer discovered, however, that Jesus always comes to a person at the point of his need.

Only his need? No, Jesus is there in all our experiences, including all the good things. There is a different way, however, that we may be aware of Jesus and that's when we have a need.

Elmer had picked me up as a 17-year-old boy, dying with tuberculosis, and carried me for prayer. He felt my need and acted on it, telling me of a man of God in a nearby town who was praying for the sick, and that when I got there God would give me back my life.

But regardless of his own needs for over 60 years he had never felt them deeply enough to pray or to ask for prayer. The moment the need was great enough, and in the atmosphere of my daughter (his niece) dying, Elmer my brother said, "Help me. Pray for me."

And Jesus was there.

Jesus is at the point of everyone's need, including Elmer's. All Elmer had to do was open his heart and let his inner self see and hear and smell and taste and touch JESUS. He received the benefit from a seed he had planted forty-two years earlier. He learned to walk on the water toward Jesus and start to get the miracle he needed most.

YOUR MAGIC MOMENT IS YOUR WALK TO JESUS

You see, it's not to WHAT you are walking, but to WHOM. It's not a thing but a Person — the Person of the Lord Jesus Christ. The magic moment I'm talking about is the walk to Him! He's the One really running things. Nothing is going to upset Him, destroy Him, banish Him or remove Him from the sight of your spirit. Nothing is going to take away your ability to see Him with your inner self. Nothing can keep you from walking on the water but you . . . yourself holding back what little faith you have!

WHAT MY YEARS OF WALKING ON THE WATER HAVE TAUGHT ME

In all the tough things that have happened in the years of this worldwide ministry of taking God's healing power to my generation —

the years of traveling over the continents;

keeping in health so I can continue my work;

facing the multitudes of sick, demon-possessed, beaten down, defeated;

being continually consumed with the urge to touch people at the point of their need with my faith;

the threat of failure;

the spector of my own mistakes;

building something for God that will be solid and will survive all storms and contrary winds;

the impossibility of depending on any human source;

being called upon by God to build Him a university, starting with nothing but my own faith;

knowing that all I do must not be built for myself but given as seed in the lives of countless others;

the call to unify the different delivery systems of God's healing power, both medical and spiritual;

putting it all together in taking God's healing power ιο my generation, the generation of man —

in all the tough assignments from which there has been no escape for me, I have discovered there is only one way to walk on the water. And that is to be continually in the process and rhythm of going to Jesus — of keeping Him at the center of my thoughts — of believing He is always the answer — of knowing He can do anything — of giving Him my best then asking Him for His best.

JESUS IS IN THE EYE OF THE STORM

The great poet, Edwin Markham, said:

"At the heart of the cyclone tearing
there is a place of central calm . . ."

This place of central calm is right in the EYE OF THE STORM, a place in the exact center of the storm where there is perfect safety. That's where Jesus is and the storm can't touch Him because He went through it and won. He's signaling for you to step out of the sinking ship and into the confidence of going to the other side with Him.

Off the coasts of Florida, I'm told, U. S. Navy planes fly directly into the teeth of a hurricane, into the eye of the storm, and there in perfect safety they measure its strength and direction, and radio the information to shore so the people can take the necessary precautions.

This is where Jesus is — right in the eye of every storm of your life. And you can go where He is. You can learn to do what He is doing. And you can capture your magic moments.

The most beautiful truth is that Jesus is at the point of your every need. He is reachable. In fact, He is saying:

> "Leave your uncertainty and doubt and fear and come with your childlike faith to Me. Come in your humanness to Me and walk where I walked while I was a man with the same feelings you have. *Come,* because I am touched by the feelings of your weaknesses and torments. *Come,* because I am still walking on the water, and you can still walk on it with Me."

That means so much to you. Because when He says, "Come", and you obey, you capture another magic moment.

CAPTURING A MAGIC MOMENT
EVEN WHEN YOU HAVE TO START WITH NOTHING

I wish I could adequately share with you exactly how it feels to start a university with the same ingredient God used when He made the earth — nothing — and to start every building with *nothing* but a seed of faith, often a very small seed. Many times a few of my associates and I have emptied our billfolds so we could plant a seed to begin a building costing several million dollars. When we had counted the money, all of it together would be only two or three hundred dollars — a seed so small in comparison to the total cost that if Christ hadn't said, "Your faith . . . as a seed . . . will move mountains and nothing shall be impossible unto you" (Matthew 17:20), I wouldn't have dared to do something that looked so foolish.

The day we started Mabee Center, on the ORU campus, seven of us literally emptied our billfolds and laid the

We were scared to death to start this project, but firm in our faith that a seed planted contains a harvest greater than itself — and God helped us build the fabulous Mabee Center on the Oral Roberts University campus.

money on the table. There was a total of $232. It was our
seed that we planted out of our need and for a *desired* result.
Then we started digging the hole for the foundation of a
building costing *eleven million dollars.*

We were scared to death to do it. On the other hand,
firm in our faith that a seed — however small — when planted
contains a harvest greater than itself, we walked on the water
"to go to Jesus." He began multiplying our seed sown. We
were able to build and complete this fabulous building.
Mabee Center is the home of the nationally known ORU
basketball team. It is also used for other public and civic
events, as well as being the center where we tape our TV
programs, teach telecommunications to our students, and
house our Laymen's Seminars. Over one million people
attend events in Mabee Center each year. The ORU com-
mencements are conducted in it each May. Great spiritual
events often pack it out. The seed of $232, prayer, and
hard work made Mabee Center a reality. Today it is paid
for in full. Another magic moment.

Then there was the day we broke ground for the Medical
and Dental Schools at Oral Roberts University. We had only
the shovels in our hands and a few dollars, each raised to
the Lord. We did it because we as human beings were in a
storm. What was the storm? Well, we had become aware
of the *hole in medicine* by itself to heal, and the *hole in
prayer* by itself to heal. We knew they had to be joined
under one great program of healing, merging them as delivery systems of God's healing power. And then we could
approach the healing of the sick the way God intended —
filling people's need of a physician as Jesus said in *Matthew
9:12.* And combining that with the powerful prayer of faith
as stated in *James 5:16.*

If we had stayed in the storm of prayer alone or medicine
alone, there might never be a healing for the totality of man's
needs. The storm could suck us under. To get out of that

What a glorious day it was when we stepped out in faith to build the Medical Building. We broke ground on January 24, 1976, my fifty-eighth birthday.

storm we had to walk on the water. To walk on the water we had to go to Jesus.

I'M WILLING TO PLANT MY SEED

As I write about this my eyes fill with tears, my heart jumps, the adrenalin flows. For I can see that walking on the water to Jesus is the way to calm the waves that could destroy us by leaving our healing to either medicine or prayer. It's not an either/or question. Total healing will come by unifying God's powers both from the medicine of His earth and the skilled persons to administer it, and from the vast power of prayer administered compassionately and wisely to all who will receive it. To achieve that, to get out of the storm, I'm willing to plant my seed, to make my leap of faith, to walk on the water to my Lord. To me, going to Him is better than risking my life and the lives of this generation by staying in the boat battered by the storm of dividing God's healing power.

IF I CAN CAPTURE MAGIC MOMENTS, SO CAN YOU

I feel, along with many others, I am capturing a magic moment. But not by accident, not by throwing up my hands in despair, not by believing it can't be done, not by believing I'm not going to make it, not by thinking Jesus is a ghost and what I see and feel in my spirit is unreal, not by clinging to the status quo of either/or.

Then how?

By rising up in the inner man and getting out of my intellect long enough to get into my spirit and into God's Spirit, and trusting God's Spirit to unite powerfully with mine and bring me into a knowing that I CAN do it —

I, Oral Roberts,

the former stuttering boy they all laughed at;

the former tuberculosis patient they all
    said was going to die;

the former rebel against God and all things spiritual;

the most unlikely person on earth upon whom
    God would bestow even one magic moment;

a man who finally saw that obedience to God
    is better than disobedience;

a man willing to be laughed at, ridiculed,
    opposed, shot at, hindered by my own
    inability and mistakes;

a man willing to be mocked by the brainy ones;

a man willing to be assaulted by the devil and
    his temptations to leave God out of my life
    and dreams, to become ill myself in the
    midst of trying to bring healing to others;

a man willing to attempt to build God a university
    based on His authority and the Holy Spirit;

a man willing to build a prayer tower right
    in the center of an academic campus;

a man willing to bring together a Spirit-filled
    faculty and bring forth a new kind of education
    — whole man education for mind, spirit, and body;

a man who gets scared, who is subject to accidents;

a man who gets irritable and hard to live with;

a man who can climb the highest mountain and
    excel with the joy of the Lord;

a man who can fall off the mountain and land
    in the lowest valley;

God called me because I am a human being willing to obey

Him, because I know when I attempt to walk on the water, Jesus will be at the other end of that walk. It is by reaching Him that I capture my magic moments. It is by reaching Him you will capture yours.

NOW ASK YOURSELF...

LIFE'S QUESTION: What does ➤ **GOD'S WAY**
magic moment mean to me?   SAY IT: IT IS A MAGIC MO-
                                  MENT WHEN I REACH OUT
                                  IN FAITH AND TOUCH GOD
                                  DURING ONE OF MY LIFE'S
                                  STORMS SO HE CAN CHANGE
                                  THINGS! GOD DELIVERS A
                                  MIRACLE TO ME!

LIFE'S QUESTION: What ➤ **GOD'S WAY**
basis do I have to believe that   SAY IT: THE SAME LORD WHO
my magic moment will come?   LIFTED PETER OUT OF THE
                                  RAGING WAVES AND LET HIM
                                  WALK ON WATER CAN AND
                                  WILL SAVE ME FROM GOING
                                  UNDER.

LIFE'S QUESTION: Then how ➤ **GOD'S WAY**
can I experience a magic mo-   SAY IT: GOD WILL CAUSE
ment in my life?   THE MAGIC MOMENT TO
                                  HAPPEN AS SOON AS I DO
                                  MY PART, A SPECIFIC ACT. I
                                  WILL PUT MY FAITH TO
                                  WORK LIKE PETER DID!

LIFE'S QUESTION: Where is ➤ **GOD'S WAY**
God when I am facing life's   SAY IT: JESUS CHRIST OF
storms?   NAZARETH IS THE EYE OF
                                  EVERY STORM — THE CEN-
                                  TRAL CALM. SINCE JESUS
                                  STANDS BESIDE ME IN THE
                                  STORM, HE PROVIDES A
                                  SHELTER OF PERFECT
                                  SAFETY.

LIFE'S QUESTION: Will I → **GOD'S WAY**
know my magic moment is   SAY IT: I WILL TAKE A LEAP
coming?   OF FAITH, PLANT MY SEED
                           AND EXPECT GOD TO WORK.
                           THEN, I CAN BE SURE THAT
                           MY MAGIC MOMENT IS ON
                           THE WAY THAT VERY DAY!

LIFE'S QUESTION: If I tried → **GOD'S WAY**
to overcome my struggles by   SAY IT: ONLY BY RELYING ON
myself, couldn't I walk safely GOD AS MY SOURCE AND DE-
on the water of the storm?   PENDING ON HIS POWER AM
                              I ABLE TO WALK SAFELY
                              ACROSS TROUBLED WATERS.
                              WITHOUT JESUS I WOULD
                              SINK OR DROWN!

LIFE'S QUESTION: What's the → **GOD'S WAY**
most important thing for me   SAY IT: NO MATTER HOW
to remember when I'm wait-   BAD THINGS GET, I WILL
ing on my magic moment?   FOCUS MY EYES ON JESUS SO
                               HE CAN LEAD ME OUT OF
                               MY STORM!

PUTTING IT ALL TOGETHER FOR MYSELF

IT IS A MAGIC MOMENT WHEN I REACH OUT IN
FAITH AND TOUCH GOD DURING ONE OF MY
LIFE'S STORMS SO HE CAN CHANGE THINGS. GOD
DELIVERS A MIRACLE TO ME!

✿ ✿ ✿ ✿ ✿

THE SAME LORD WHO LIFTED PETER OUT OF
THE RAGING WAVES AND LET HIM WALK ON THE
WATER CAN AND WILL SAVE ME FROM GOING
UNDER.

✿ ✿ ✿ ✿ ✿

GOD WILL CAUSE MY MAGIC MOMENT TO HAPPEN
AS SOON AS I DO MY PART, A SPECIFIC ACT. I WILL
PUT MY FAITH TO WORK LIKE PETER DID!

JESUS CHRIST OF NAZARETH IS IN THE EYE OF
EVERY STORM – THE CENTRAL CALM. SINCE JESUS
STANDS BESIDE ME IN MY STORM, HE PROVIDES
A SHELTER OF PERFECT SAFETY.

❋ ❋ ❋ ❋ ❋ ❋

I WILL TAKE A LEAP OF FAITH, PLANT MY SEED
AND EXPECT GOD TO WORK. THEN I CAN BE SURE
THAT MY MAGIC MOMENT IS ON THE WAY THAT
VERY DAY!

❋ ❋ ❋ ❋ ❋ ❋

ONLY BY RELYING ON GOD AS MY SOURCE AND
DEPENDING ON HIS POWER AM I ABLE TO WALK
SAFELY ACROSS TROUBLED WATERS. WITHOUT
JESUS I WOULD SINK AND DROWN!

❋ ❋ ❋ ❋ ❋ ❋

NO MATTER HOW BAD THINGS GET, I WILL FOCUS
MY EYES ON JESUS SO HE CAN LEAD ME OUT OF
MY STORM.

Chapter Nine

How getting your eyes on Jesus will help you overcome the fears that would swamp your life

"*... They cried out for fear*" (Matthew 14:26).

Fear is different than faith. It originates from your five senses, not your inner self. It is impossible for you to realistically see it, hear it, smell it, taste it, or touch it. Real life is always just beyond the reach of your five senses.

Jesus said, "Ye know not what manner of spirit ye are of" (Luke 9:55). Your five senses within themselves aren't able to let you really know yourself. Neither through your physical senses can you really know Jesus. You have to get into your spirit. Your spirit includes your will.

Jesus also said, "They that worship God must worship him in spirit ... " (John 4:24).

In SPIRIT. That means the only way you can worship God is in your spirit (what some call your sixth sense). The Holy Spirit joining your spirit enables you to use your physical senses and make a whole-man response to God — and to man and your environment.

YOU CAN SEE GOD

Because you worship God with your spirit you can see

God. Not with your physical eyes. You can see Him with the inner sight, the inner knowing of your spirit. That's where I see and hear and smell and taste and touch the reality of Jesus — in my inner self, my spirit. It's being tuned in to a special wavelength in which you actually communicate with God. This wavelength is your spirit and the Spirit of God acting together at the same time. It is your will making your five senses subject to your spirit. In this way you know in your inner self that Jesus is pleased with what you are doing.

Let me share a story that has had a profound effect on my life. It's about a little boy who had a tremendous gift to play the piano. In fact, he outstripped all of his teachers; and finally his parents, who were poor, weren't able to provide any further training for him. They naturally wanted their child to have the best. And when they learned of an old maestro, a music master who was retired, they took the child to him and said, "Would you take him?"

The old man didn't really want to be bothered. But the parents said, "Well, would you just let him play for a couple of moments?"

And after he had heard the boy play the piano for just seconds, he smiled and said, "Ah, yes, I'll take him." For months the old maestro taught the little boy what music really is — a readable transcript of life. It's not just playing an instrument. It's telling about life through that instrument.

The old man taught the boy how to play great pieces of music. If it was about war, he taught him to play so that people could hear the planes diving, the bombs bursting, the screams of the dying. If it was about little children playing, he taught him to play so that they could hear the children laugh and jump and cry. And whatever the boy played, the maestro wanted the people not only to hear the music but to feel and smell and taste and touch life itself.

Then one day, the old man said, "Son, you're ready for your debut." They rented a great hall and the crowd filled it because they'd already heard about the boy. When the boy sat down and began to play, a magic hush came over the audience. As he played piece after piece, no one moved around. He had perfect attention. When he finished, the whole place erupted in pandemonium. Women cried and men yelled. The people all wanted to touch him. But not once did the young pianist ever look at his audience, except by a glance. He kept raising his head looking up to the balcony. The old white-haired maestro was there. He was nodding his head and saying, "You're on the right track, son, you're on the right track. Just keep it up."

Keeping his eyes on the maestro, the one who had taught him how to become a truly great pianist, meant more to that boy than anything else. It gave him the quiet confidence in his inner self that the master was pleased that his music was coming alive in the people. It gave him direction, inspiration, an anchor for his whole self . . . to be all he was meant to be.

What it means is that Jesus is our Master. He is our Source of all we can become. He holds us steady and on course. He inspires us from within so that our five senses come alive in the proper way. When I keep my eyes on Jesus I can *see* Him in my spirit nodding His head at me. I can *hear* Him say, "Oral, you're on the right track. Just keep it up."

People constantly ask, "Why am I so afraid?" The answer is, "Like most other people, you may be conducting your life by the direction your brain gets from what your eyes, ears, nose, tongue, and hands tell you, instead of allowing your spirit to tell you what to do."

St. Paul says, "God hath not given us the spirit of fear; but of power, and of love, and of a sound mind" (2 Timothy 1:7).

God does not give you fear. You get fear by allowing your senses to dim the inner light that reveals the God-given gifts of power, love, and a sound mind.

GOD HAS GIVEN YOU FAITH

Another question I'm often asked is, "How can I get faith?" I've discovered that faith is not something you get. It's something you already have. St. Paul says, "God hath given to every man the measure of faith" (Romans 12:3). It was a magic moment in my life when I quit begging God to give me faith . . . and started releasing the faith I already had.

What is faith? Faith is an inborn knowing. Every child demonstrates it. A child knows there is God. A child sees from inside. *A child learns fear* from being taught to rely absolutely on what he sees, hears, smells, tastes, and touches.

I heard a powerful testimony the other day that will bring alive what I'm saying. A woman's young son had come in after a day's play. He was hot and had sand and grass all over him. So she sent him to take a shower. Suddenly she heard a loud crash. The youngster had fallen through the glass doors of the shower somehow and his legs were cut very badly. The mother started screaming and crying. She was afraid the boy would bleed to death. She was helpless with panic and fear.

It was the little boy who said, "Don't worry, Mother, Jesus will take care of me." That child was looking from the inside, from his spirit. He wasn't paying any attention to the blood flowing out of his body or the shattered glass lying all around. "Jesus will take care of me." And that did something to the mother. Suddenly she was all right. She prayed for the child, wrapped his legs in towels, and took him to the hospital. And he's just fine today. And it's because the woman was able to get back into her spirit through the inner seeing of her son, a child who knew everything was going to be OK!

WALKING ON THE WATER HAS CALMED MANY TERRIBLE WAVES

I've done that thousands of times, just as in the tragic loss of Marshall and Rebecca. I came out of what my five senses reacted to and came into a determined cultivation of what I KNEW. I prayed in the Spirit and I KNEW God was there. I KNEW Evelyn and I should plant a seed out of our need. I KNEW we shouldn't make our grief private and let it eat at us daily. Instead we should openly share our hurt and our faith with others on the broadest scale possible. And the next day we went before the television cameras to share our grief and to let our partners know we still KNEW God was real and was a good God.

It was through planting this seed of faith and getting the harvest of our release that we were able to undertake another impossible task. We got the tragic news on Saturday morning. The following weekend — Thursday through Sunday — an ORU "Family Seminar" had been scheduled for Evelyn and me to lead. Four thousand faculty, staff, and students, and the Board of Regents of the University, were suspending their busy schedules for us to share the Holy Spirit and the Miracle of Seed-Faith with them.

Evelyn's greatest fear had been that she could not bare her feelings on television and let out her hurts. My fear was different. My fear was that five days later I might not be able to stand up before four thousand people and preach a living personal faith in a good God. The terrible, unexpected deaths put me in a position to let my five senses tell me I couldn't do it. I thought I couldn't stand to *hear* what some would be saying. I could *smell* the reaction. The taste I had had for the seminar was so thrilling, and now it was gone. And touching! How could I touch anyone? I needed to be touched myself.

I said, "I can't do it."

GIVING AWAY FROM YOURSELF

A faithful associate quietly said, "Brother Roberts, the needs of these four thousand are very real. They have been getting ready for you to minister to them. They need you. And unless you give of yourself — and give away from yourself — you may never be able to help anybody again."

I said, "You are reminding me of the tree, aren't you?"

He said, "Yes."

I had told many times of how a tree drops its acorns or seed. Seldom do the seeds fall at the base of the tree. Instead they are given to the winds, which blow them away from the tree. They fall, take root, and become new trees. But no seed falling at the base of the tree reproduces itself. Likewise, Jesus teaches us not to lavish our seed upon ourselves but to give away from ourselves. That's how our seeds are multiplied back to meet our own needs. And each seed contains a harvest greater than itself.

From deep inside I felt a knowing that I must look away from my grief and see the hurting of others during those soon-coming four days. However difficult it would be to preach five days after that Saturday, and three days after the funeral, *my inner self could see and hear and smell and taste and touch one of the greatest miracles of my life.*

Well, we got through that first night before a packed auditorium. As we gave of our faith, we felt their faith and love come pouring back to us. Evelyn and other members of our family felt it. Richard sang as I've never heard him sing. He was reaching out to others. They felt it and their care for him in his hurt came pouring back to him.

It was with determination — and joy — that we were able to get through the next day, the next, and the final day. Our

The ORU students are seeds that will be scattered around the globe, bringing to people everywhere the Good News.

students, faculty, staff, and board members told us we had reached into their hearts and shown them Jesus in the *NOW*. They could see He was real in us, in our deepest grief. And we will never forget what we received from them as God worked through them to help us. We had sown seed away from ourselves. The faith which we had felt so small was really working wonders. *We had walked on the water.*

BREAKTHROUGH FROM HEAVEN IN '77

Now it's months later that I am writing this book. 1977 is drawing to a close. Walking on the water has calmed many terrible waves of fear. We no longer cry out in fear over Rebecca and Marshall and our dear grandchildren they left. Here's what Evelyn and I are *seeing:*

A Breakthrough from Heaven in '77 for my darling Rebecca and dear Marshall, in that their children have wonderful new parents!

A Breakthrough from Heaven in '77 in constructing the new ORU Medical School and paying the bills each month! (Our partners have never been so magnificent in their seed-sowing!)

A Breakthrough from Heaven in '77 for inner healing as Evelyn and I remember our word from the Lord when we prayed in the Spirit that fourth night and were able to withstand the pressures of sharing our faith nationwide while our grief was still trying to pull us under. (Thousands wrote that their lives were changed through that 30-minute telecast.)

A Breakthrough from Heaven in '77 as I write this book for you — believing through it God will help you to get through your struggles and walk on the water.

A Breakthrough from Heaven in '77 as the full plans of ORU's undergraduate and seven graduate schools take form, and as students literally cover the campus, with thousands of others wanting to attend.

A Breakthrough from Heaven in '77 as our ministry of preaching and healing reaches more people than ever before. (The testimonies of healing are pouring in to our office every day.) To see people healed is the greatest call upon my life.

And we're expecting even more breakthroughs in '78. God is working in powerful ways. Let me assure you that life is at your very fingertips. And it won't escape you when you let your spirit rise above your physical senses. God won't be late in '78. Your breakthroughs will come. Just keep on believing!

NOW ASK YOURSELF . . .

LIFE'S QUESTION: Why am ➤ **GOD'S WAY**
I so afraid?   SAY IT: FEAR IS THE RESULT OF LIVING BY WHAT MY SENSES TELL ME AND NOT BY FAITH. I WILL TRUST GOD WITH MY SPIRIT AND STOP BEING AFRAID.

LIFE'S QUESTION: How can ➤ **GOD'S WAY**
I get faith?   SAY IT: GOD HAS ALREADY GIVEN ME FAITH. I WILL BEGIN TO EXERCISE MY FAITH AND BELIEVE GOD.

LIFE'S QUESTION: How can ➤ **GOD'S WAY**
I fulfill the gift I feel inside myself?   SAY IT: LIKE THE OLD MAESTRO HELPING THE LITTLE BOY BECOME A MASTER PIANIST, JESUS WILL HELP ME — AS I KEEP MY EYES ON HIM.

LIFE'S QUESTION: How can ➤ **GOD'S WAY**
I in the midst of my grief face doing what I have to do?   SAY IT: I WILL GIVE SEED AWAY FROM MYSELF. I WILL GIVE TO OTHERS OUT OF MY OWN HURT AS A SEED OF MY FAITH.

PUTTING IT ALL TOGETHER FOR MYSELF

FEAR IS THE RESULT OF LIVING BY WHAT MY SENSES TELL ME AND NOT BY FAITH. I WILL TRUST GOD WITH MY SPIRIT AND STOP BEING AFRAID.

※※※※※※

GOD HAS ALREADY GIVEN ME FAITH. I WILL BEGIN TO EXERCISE MY FAITH AND BELIEVE GOD.

※※※※※※

JESUS WILL HELP ME AS I KEEP MY EYES ON HIM. I WILL SEE AND HEAR HIM SAY, "YOU'RE ON THE RIGHT TRACK. JUST KEEP IT UP."

※※※※※※

AS I GIVE SEED AWAY FROM MYSELF, GIVING OUT OF MY OWN HURT, I WILL BE ABLE TO RECEIVE MY BREAKTHROUGHS.

※※※※※※

GOD WILL NOT BE LATE IN '78.

※※※※※※

AS I USE MY FAITH I WILL WALK ON THE WATERS AGAIN AND AGAIN.

Chapter Ten

How you can know God is real
... real to you

*"And when the disciples saw him walking on the
sea, they were troubled, saying, It is a spirit ..."*
(Matthew 14:26).

One of the biggest questions I ever had, one that I asked
my parents most often, was: "Is God real?"

When they would reply, "Yes, son, God is real," I would
ask, "But how can *I know?"*

WHAT ABOUT GOD AND ME?

The worst moment I had with that question was when
I was a teen-ager and I realized I might not make it. I might
die. I might live a little longer by being admitted to the
tuberculosis sanatorium in the mountains of eastern Oklahoma. But the doctors told my parents, "Oral is now in
the hands of God."

In the hands of God? All my life I had been taught
about God. Papa was a preacher. He saw to it that we
children went to church, that we entered into family prayer,
that we knew a lot about the Bible. I even won a Bible-
reading contest once in our church. It impressed people

that the preacher's son had that much interest in the Bible.

Lying there in bed, I continued taking my medicine. It was in liquid form and bitter to the taste. Suddenly I came to a climax of frustration and lost hope. My diet of milk and eggs beaten together was not enough. The fever, the hacking cough, the hemorrhages were too much.

Sweeping bottles of medicine to the floor and crying out in my frustration, I remember saying to Mamma and Papa, "God! God! What about me? What about God? Is He real? Can He help me?"

THE UNKNOWN GOD

I tell you, I was hurting outside and inside. Like the disciples who thought Jesus was a ghost, I couldn't make Him out to be real, either.

St. Paul while preaching in Athens, Greece, spoke of "the Unknown God" (Acts 17:23).

My fears made God an unknown God to me. And I think the disciples' fears caused them to fail to recognize Jesus.

I was looking at my condition with my physical senses, not with my spiritual sight. I wasn't seeing God as my spirit could have been able to see Him.

The disciples' physical sight distorted Jesus, making them think He was ghostly, not real. Well, it did the same to me.

All of us go through things like that. We face something so hard we can't really see Jesus. And it scares us. I got a letter not long ago from someone facing a terrible problem. She said one day she couldn't do anything but shake her fist toward the sky and say, "God, if You're up there like they say You are, You'd better do something because I'm scared to death!" And probably every fourth letter I receive says something like that. Is God real? If He *is* real, why isn't He doing something?

You may wonder why they write. If they're so full of doubt, why write at all? Well, it helps a person to tell the truth about his feelings toward God. It gets him into a position where he may be open to hear something about God he can feel is real.

In almost every letter I write back I try to relate some personal encounter I have had with God that has made Him more real to me. People appreciate that because it helps them understand more about Him. And it helps them know God can be that real in their lives too.

AN AIRLINE HOSTESS ASKED ME, "HOW CAN I KNOW GOD IS REAL?"

Sometimes when people talk to me, the issue of "how to know God is real" is often raised.

Recently I had two such experiences.

The first one I want to tell you about happened when I was traveling. An airline hostess sat down by me and said abruptly, "Mr. Roberts, I was raised in church as a child. But I want to ask you, How can I know God is real to me?"

Instantly I thought of the twelve disciples out there in the storm wanting to believe in God. But all they saw was something ghostly and frightening. Even though it was Jesus, and He was saying, "It is I, Jesus," somehow they couldn't believe it. They couldn't believe He was real.

Then, of course, I thought of myself.

I said to the hostess, "Ma'am, the best way I know to tell you how to believe God is real is to tell you how I came to believe He is real."

She said, "How was that?"

I answered, "I had a need, a desperate need. Until then, I never felt the need of trying to believe God is real."

She started crying then. I asked, "Are you in trouble? Do you feel that need now yourself?"

She wiped her eyes again. "You see, I have a teen-age son. He has just told me he has turned gay."

Through blurred sight she looked at me, "And there's nothing I can do about it!" she said.

"Well, I think I can give you a thought to help you on that."

She looked expectantly. "Just remember that your child just passed through you into the world. He's now his own person. You gave him birth but actually he's not yours. He just passed through."

She said, "I never thought of that. Do you really believe it?"

"I have to," I replied. "I love my children so much. But there came a time Evelyn and I had to realize that they had just passed through us. Try as we will we cannot successfully lay any more claim to them. We can love them and hope they will return our love. But the real fact is they have passed through us."

She thought that over. "That helps me. But it is so hard to see my son turn out this way . . . "

"I understand. You've done the best you could. You've put the seed in. Remember the farmer who plants his seed. He waits for the harvest. Even when he has a crop failure he plants more seed and keeps expecting the harvest."

She nodded, thinking on what I had said. I continued, "I've been through things with my children. Not this particular thing, but others that hurt Evelyn and me. Believe me, whatever goes wrong in a parent-child relationship hurts."

She said, "You? I never thought of something bad happening to you."

I said, "Struggles have been the story of my life." Then I told her, "There is one hopeful thing about your son. He can change!"

"Can he, oh, can he?" she asked.

"Yes. Over the years I've seen it happen to many people. Conversion to Christ brings a miracle of new desires, a regeneration of the way God made us. In the case of homosexuality, God can wipe it out by a person's will to renew the way God made him or her — male AND female. He didn't make us male and male, nor female and female. He made us male and female. I told her to read Genesis 1:27.

She said, "You've personally known of people changing back to the normal way?"

"Yes, I have. Usually it happens quite quickly. And permanently. I do not believe homosexuality is inborn but is a giving in to weakness, and then cultivating that weakness until it becomes ingrained into the nature. The new birth gives you a new nature. Second Corinthians 5:17 says, 'If any man be in Christ, he is a new creature: Old things are passed away, behold all things are become new.'

She thanked me, then added, "If I could only believe in God myself, if I could only know He is real."

I HAD TO LEARN TO BELIEVE IN GOD

I said to her, "As I said earlier, there was a time when, even though I was young, I had to learn to believe in God. The important thing is learning *how.*"

She said, "Oh, you mean it's not just a business with you, being a minister and all? I thought it was just your business to believe." That hurt when I saw she thought my faith in God was a business or profession with me. I decided to level with her.

I said, "I was studying and dreaming of being a lawyer."

"Don't you feel you are chosen to do what you're doing?"

"*Now,* I do. Maybe I did then but I was fighting it. I didn't want to be a minister. I wasn't thinking about believing in God until I became desperately ill with tuberculosis. I didn't really get serious until the papers were being filled out to put me in the state institution for tuberculosis and I was told I was going to die."

"You weren't ready to die?"

"I didn't think about being *ready.* I wanted to *live.*"

This aerial photo of Oral Roberts University shows th
hand corner is the new graduate student housing pr

dical School building almost completed. In the upper left
re will eventually be 1,500 apartments in the complex.

"What happened?"

"The same thing that will probably happen in your life. Somebody crossed my path who contagiously believed in God and knew He is real. I could see it in her eyes. I could feel it coming from her heart. It was my sister Jewel."

She said, "She had enthusiasm?"

"Whatever she had, she believed. She told me God was going to heal me. That excited something in me to believe and eventually I did. It led me to believe in God, to be converted. It led me to recovery and to this ministry I am in today."

"Do you think that it could happen to me, that I could believe God is real?"

"Oh, it *will* happen. Somebody will cross your path. Today it's me. Tomorrow it will be someone else. Whoever it is will have a contagious belief in God. Believe me, it's catching."

She smiled and said quietly, "I want it to happen to me."

I told her how my brother Elmer was the next to cross my path, telling me of a man who prayed for the sick. "That's when it seemed so natural to believe God was real. My need had brought me to the point of questioning. My brother and sister had offered me hope and I grabbed for it.

"Soon I was being carried to the man who prayed for sick people. His prayer got through to my believing and a strong, healing warmth went clear through me. I could breathe. I stopped hemorrhaging and started getting well. It took about a year, but I got well.

"Then I became aware of the calling of God on my life to the ministry, of being chosen. God has been real to me ever since. He is more real to me now than ever before."

The twelve disciples upon the raging sea had had a childhood of being taught to believe in God. Later, as grown men, they had lived with Jesus. They had seen and heard and talked with Him. They had witnessed His miracles. Yet there in the troubled waters they were like the airline hostess. They had a problem they couldn't handle. Today it's hard for us to understand why they found it hard to believe Jesus was real, that He was coming to them even when He had to walk on the water.

How could the disciples not believe He was real? They had a great opportunity to believe. But when He came to them they thought He was a ghost.

HE'S REAL, MAN! HE'S REAL!

Another experience I want to share with you is an encounter I had with a famous star of motion pictures and television that caused me to understand a little better how a person can have trouble believing God is real. Really, we even have trouble believing another person is real.

Sammy Davis, Jr., a man millions believe is one of the most talented performers alive, was in his dressing room right down the hall from ours at NBC. At that time we were doing all our television shows at the NBC studio. (Of course, when Mabee Center was completed at ORU we taped most of our programs there. But now we are taping them in "Baby Mabee" — the nickname our students gave the new Television Production Center added to the original Mabee Center because it is a smaller version of Mabee Center.)

Word came to the studio where we were taping that Sammy wanted to meet me. When I finished that portion of the taping, I went down the hall to his dressing room, which was literally jammed with people. I walked in and as I looked around, a small dynamic black man got up, came over and stood in front of me. He looked me up and down and didn't say a word. I put my hand out to shake his but he didn't take it. So I just stood here.

He walked all around me, stopped in front of me again. Gingerly he put forth a hand and touched me.

I said, "Is there something wrong?"

He seemed to realize I was somewhat taken aback by his actions. "Oral Roberts," he said, excuse me for not shaking your hand and for looking you over so closely."

"What is it?" I said.

"What it it? Oh, it's not you. It's me. You see, I've been watching you on television. I wanted you to be real, man, but I was afraid you were not. I've had this desire to know God, to know if He's real. He seems so real to you. But I was afraid when I met you that you wouldn't be real. I wanted so much for you to be real."

There in the background of the tinsel of show business, I began to understand why a famous star wanted to find someone real and to touch that person. What he really wanted was to touch beyond the human. He wanted to touch the ultimate reality — GOD.

I smiled, "Well, am I real?"

He breathed a sigh and said, "Yeah, man. You're real all right."

Then he yelled, "Everybody listen. This is the Oral Roberts we've all been seeing on television. He's real, man, he's real."

Then, his eyes filling with tears, he said, "Thanks for coming. I gotta go in now and do my thing. But, man, I'll never forget this moment. You are real. I can feel it."

I said, "Thank you, Sammy. But the most real Person I know is Jesus Christ of Nazareth. Whatever is real about me comes from Him. He is in me."

Sammy Davis, Jr., looked at me and said, "Yeah, I know."

GET ON THE ROCK

I think the day I began to learn that God is real — and is real to me — was the beginning of my ability to live, really live.

Years ago a little boy heard me preach. I was talking about Jesus being a spiritual rock. And it must have made a great impression on that youngster. When he got home to his parents he blurted out, "God came into me tonight."

The mother said, "Oh, son, you're too little to know God came into your heart."

But he replied, "I got saved. Jesus saved me."

So his faither said, "Son, how do you know Jesus saved you?"

And he answered, "I knew when I got on that rock Oral Roberts talked about."

The parents told me, "Such a change came over our son we had to believe that in spite of his being only a child, God had become real to him. It beats anything we've ever seen."

When you act through your faith and let your spirit rise above your senses, you can get on that Rock too. Jesus will be so real to you that your faith will be greater than any doubt you have. And you'll walk on the water — you'll get through your struggles. You'll make it. God will help you do it.

NOW ASK YOURSELF...

LIFE'S QUESTION: I wonder ➔ **GOD'S WAY**
if God is even real?   SAY IT: GOD IS REAL BUT I CAN ONLY SEE HIM WHEN I GO BEYOND MY PHYSICAL SIGHT AND SEE WITH MY SPIRIT.

LIFE'S QUESTION: What ➔ **GOD'S WAY**
makes God sometimes seem   SAY IT: MY FEARS MAKE GOD
like an unknown God to me?   AN UNKNOWN GOD TO ME.

LIFE'S QUESTION: Does be- ➔ **GOD'S WAY**
lieving in God make other   SAY IT: SINCE JESUS CHRIST
things more real to me?   OF NAZARETH IS THE MOST REAL PERSON THERE IS, HE MAKES ME A REAL PERSON TOO. WHATEVER IS REAL ABOUT ME COMES FROM HAVING HIM IN ME...AND WITH ME.

LIFE'S QUESTION: If I be-➤ **GOD'S WAY**
lieve that God ... that Jesus   SAY IT: THE DAY I BEGIN TO
Christ ... is real, will my life   LEARN THAT GOD IS REAL
be different?   IS THE DAY I'LL HAVE THE
                                 ABILITY TO REALLY LIVE. I
                                 WILL HOLD ON TO THE
                                 ROCK OF MY SALVATION.
                                 JESUS IS REAL!

PUTTING IT ALL TOGETHER FOR MYSELF

GOD IS REAL BUT I CAN ONLY SEE HIM WHEN I
GO BEYOND PHYSICAL SIGHT AND SEE WITH MY
SPIRIT.

✳ ✳ ✳ ✳ ✳ ✳

MY FEARS MAKE GOD AN UNKNOWN GOD TO ME.

✳ ✳ ✳ ✳ ✳ ✳

SINCE JESUS CHRIST OF NAZARETH IS THE MOST
REAL PERSON THERE IS, HE MAKES ME A REAL
PERSON TOO. WHATEVER IS REAL ABOUT ME
COMES FROM HAVING HIM IN ME ... AND WITH
ME.

✳ ✳ ✳ ✳ ✳ ✳

THE DAY I BEGIN TO LEARN THAT GOD IS REAL
IS THE DAY I'LL HAVE THE ABILITY TO REALLY
LIVE. I WILL HOLD ON TO THE ROCK OF MY
SALVATION. JESUS IS REAL!

How to let God take your hand when you begin to sink

"And Peter beginning to sink cried out . . ."
(Matthew 14:30).

When Peter stepped out of the boat and into the storm, he started his walk really well. But something happened and he began to sink.

THAT SINKING FEELING

I know that feeling, don't you? Many times in my life, after I've started an act of my faith, something has gone wrong. I've felt that sinking feeling in the pit of my stomach. It's a panicky feeling. All reason or ability to think rationally seems to leave. I cry out, "Oh, no! Not that! Oh, no! Not again!" But there seems to be nothing I can do. Nothing! It's a hopeless feeling.

I remember early in this ministry I was returning home after a crusade. I was by myself. And as I drove, I thought about the great miracles God had performed, the lives He had touched. I was nearing Little Rock, Arkansas when a sudden downpour of rain struck. In a matter of seconds the rain was so heavy I couldn't see through the windshield.

Instead of stopping, I tried to go on. My car hit a slick spot and I felt it veering sharply to the left, going over an embankment and hitting something.

Just at that moment the rain let up enough for me to see that my car had struck a fence line. The fence posts went down one at a time. My car cleared out the posts, gradually slowing as it leveled each one. Finally the car stopped.

I was sort of stunned so I just sat there a moment. A farmer whose house was nearby came running and yelling toward me. I got out of the car.

"Are you hurt, Mister?"

"I don't think so."

We both looked the car over and saw the damage to the front end. I asked who owned the fence row and was told it belonged to the former governor of Arkansas. I said, "How can I reach him?"

The farmer reached in his pocket and gave me a card with the phone number on it. But he advised, "Aw, go on. He'll never know it. And I'll have it fixed up in no time."

I said, "Thanks, but I'll know it. I've got to call him and pay the damages."

Suddenly the man reached out his hand and put it on my shoulder. He said, "Just who are you, son?"

"Oral Roberts."

"What do you do?"

"I preach and pray for people."

He said, "I live right there in that farmhouse and I've got a sick wife. Would you come pray for her?"

"But you don't even know me," I said.

I was just starting this ministry at that time and was not known at all.

"I may not know you by name, son, but look at that fence row your car plowed up. By all rights you ought to be dead or bad hurt. I know Someone bigger than you has His hand on you. And I still want you to come and pray for my wife, if you will."

I said, "All right." And after I had prayed I went to the nearest town and phoned the governor. When I told him what I had done and that I wanted to know the charges, he too asked me who I was. I told him.

And he said, "Seems like one of my workers mentioned something about a young fellow over in Oklahoma praying for folks. I guess if you'd just say a prayer for me over the phone, I'd say things were even."

So I prayed for him and drove on toward home, feeling in my heart that God surely had His hand on my life. I thanked Him for it and knew deep down inside me that He would be getting me out of a lot more tight spots as I worked for Him, ministering to the people.

I didn't know what to call it then. But *I had taken some of my first steps walking on the water.* What I started learning then, I've learned even more forcefully with each storm I've come through — every time I start to sink, God will be there to take my hand. God will be there!

SEED-FAITH CAN MAKE THE DIFFERENCE IN SINKING OR ARRIVING

Every day of your life you face the very real possibility of sinking, of going under in your struggles. You also face the possibility of getting on top of your troubles and arriving at your destination. Every day you face both of those possibilities. From my personal experience I can say there are no exceptions. There is struggle. But there is also something pulling you up. It's God — an invisible power calling to you to come to Him.

THE INNER TUGGING

That inner tugging you often feel is Jesus telling you to walk on the water and to get through your struggles.

There's a story I'd like to tell you that will illustrate this point. A little boy was flying his kite when a man walked up and asked him what he was doing.

"Flying a kite," replied the youngster.

"Flying a kite?"

"Yep."

"Well, I can't see any kite."

"Yeah. But it's up there."

"It's out of sight."

"Yep."

"Well, how do you know it's up there?"

"Mister, I can feel it tugging on the line."

I made kites and flew them too when I was a boy. And like this youngster, I've flown them out of sight. What a thrill it was to stand there holding that string of cord, with the kite riding the winds on the other end. The only way I knew it was there was to feel it tugging on the line.

JESUS COULD FEEL IT TOO

When Jesus came toward the disciples on the Sea of Galilee that night, He could feel an inner tugging. He felt the excitement of walking on the water in His humanness. He felt the excitement of using His faith. He knew there was no reason to be afraid because of the tugging of the line.

Jesus wanted the disciples to feel it too. When He went to them He told them to be of good cheer, not to be afraid. But they were afraid. They were so afraid they couldn't feel the tugging. They couldn't feel Jesus' magic moment tugging on their line. What He was doing was "out of sight." It scared them. They couldn't believe it because their physical eyes couldn't see the reality of what was happening. They weren't using their spiritual sight. So they didn't feel the tugging on the line.

Suddenly Peter cried out, "Lord, if it be thou, tell me to come to you on the water." He had a desire to feel the tugging on the line of miracles. He wanted a magic moment. Although the kite was out of sight, the bold voice of Jesus saying, "Come" meant Peter COULD do it. He felt the tugging inside. And that's where the tugging of God really is.

I can see in my mind what happened then. The eleven others on the boat looked at Peter and realized what he meant to do.

"Peter, what are you doing?"

"Walking on the water."

"Walking on the water?"

"Yep."

"But you can't do that."

"Well, I'm doing it."

"Peter! You're out of sight!"

"Yep."

"How did you know you could do it?"

"Fellas, I felt the power of my faith. I felt it tugging on the line."

Peter did what no one else had ever done except Jesus himself. He had done the impossible. And you can do it too when you learn what it means to feel the faith of God tugging on the line of your spirit. One of the greatest things you can do is accept the fact that it can happen to you.

And there's something else that's equally important. You have an opportunity every day to plant a seed of your faith. *That will make the difference between your going over or going under.*

IT'S YOUR DECISION ... AND YOU CAN MAKE IT

Someone said, "God has a vote, the devil has a vote, and your vote decides the election."

In my own experience I know God has a will for what happens to your life, the devil has a will for what happens, and you have a will for what happens.

No matter how strong God's will or the devil's will is,

your will decides it. Even Jesus, in facing the Cross, faced the three wills. *First,* the devil's will was that Jesus disobey God's purpose for His life and by His own will put God aside. *Second,* God's will was that Jesus face the Cross and let the Father plant His life as the "Seed of David," which God would raise up in the harvest of the Resurrection, thus providing the power for our salvation and everlasting life. *Third,* Jesus' will was to decide whether to do the devil's will or God's will. Jesus used His will to cast His vote with God's. And that decided the way things went. Jesus said, "Not my will but thine be done." *He was really saying, "I vote with You, Father."*

GOD WANTS YOU TO GO THROUGH YOUR STRUGGLES

Just as God's will was that Jesus face the Cross and come through it, He wants you to come through your problems and struggles. And I know something about your struggle. You struggle because you're trying to go somewhere. You have dreams and hopes and goals, don't you? I know they are very important to you.

Whenever you're trying to get somewhere with your life the most important thing in the world is for you to get there. The most important thing is for you to arrive — or at least to make progress in getting there.

God WANTS you to arrive. Jesus commanded His disciples to get in the boat and "go to the other side." They were to start, to go, to arrive, to reach the other side safely. This was part of Jesus' plan for the success of their lives. If they had gone under during the journey through the storm, they wouldn't have reached the other side. Jesus would have gotten no glory from their failure and defeat. Their failure would have been His failure too.

God is a God of success, not failure.

God is a God of going over, not under.

God is a God of going through the storm,
  not being destroyed by it.

God is a God of walking on the water, not the
  water rolling over Him in destruction.

God is a God of getting to the other side,
  and of getting you there.

THE SEED YOU PLANT MAKES SUCCESS POSSIBLE

Too many people think:

"If God wants me to get there,
  He'll see to it that I do.

"If God wants to prosper me,
  He'll see that I do.

"If God wants to heal me, He will.

"If God wants things to work out
  for me, they will."

That leaves your *choice* and your *will* out. That leaves out your seed-planting. It leaves the devil voting NO and God voting YES. But it leaves you without a vote.

Well, in every one of my struggles I've had to vote, I've had to exercise my will to choose to do something and do it with God. I've had to plant a seed. I've had to make my faith an act of believing specifically, my love an act of giving — which is voting to go against the devil and taking God's way. It has become A WAY OF LIFE WITH ME — THE SEED-FAITH WAY.

Peter planted a seed. He chose to make his faith an act. He didn't just hang onto the boat, leaving it all up to the Lord by saying, "Jesus told me to go over to the other side and He'll get me through." NO! He willed to do something — TO GO TO JESUS.

Please notice that Peter did not make a blind leap of

faith. Faith is not blind. Faith is seeing with the inner self, with the spirit. Faith is a knowing inside that God is God. Faith makes you know that you know that you know.

Remember, when Peter first saw what looked like a ghost he was not seeing with his spirit. He was seeing through his physical eyes. And he couldn't see Jesus clearly enough to know Who He was. Because he wasn't seeing with his inner self that it was Jesus, the real Jesus, he was doubting. And his doubt almost kept him from walking on the water.

Peter got his faith going. How did he do it? He began seeing with his spirit. Then he planted a seed. What was the seed he planted? The seed Peter planted that dangerous hour was to give of himself in behalf of the eleven other frightened disciples. Sure, he planted the seed for himself which he should have done. But there were other struggling people on his heart too. They needed to come in their *humanness* and *will* and *faith* and walk on the water — but they couldn't get their courage up. Peter could. Peter did! It was a good seed he planted . . . and he planted it *first*.

PETER GAVE ALL HE HAD OUT OF HIS NEED

Peter put his life on the line. Usually when we talk about giving, we talk about a seed of money, a seed of time, a seed of talent, a seed of love, a seed of encouragement. But Peter risked everything with the seed of his total being. He became very vulnerable. Seed-Faith always makes you vulnerable. For then you have to trust.

The others didn't do what Peter did. They used their will to vote with their fear instead of with their faith. They were not willing to test Jesus. They were not willing to plant a seed for themselves or for Peter.

But Peter, out of his need and theirs, made a leap of faith. And it became a seed of faith planted toward Jesus Who was the Source of his support to get through the struggle of that storm — to get through the struggle to the other side.

In asking God to help you successfully get through your struggles, *it comes down to your very life.* Are you willing to give, and give first? Are you willing to plant a seed for a harvest you can't yet see? Are you willing to step forth in faith, trust in God your Source, and then expect a miracle? If you're not, then you're like the rest of the disciples, just stumbling around in the boat, scared and full of doubt and going under. Planting your seed is the magic moment that starts you to walking on the water to go to Jesus. It starts you really believing that you will arrive! Believing that you will arrive is very important to you.

GOD PLANTED A SEED

Think about your struggles for a moment. They are very real to you, aren't they? They hurt. Now think a moment about God and His struggles.

Yes, God has struggles. Does that shock you? What are His struggles?

Well, God made man and gave him the power of communication. He gave him the opportunity to walk and talk with Him, the Creator. He also gave him the power of dominion, telling him to take dominion over all things (Genesis 1:28).

Now how was that a struggle for God? Here's how. When man lost his first estate (the Garden of Eden) by doubting God and believing Satan, he lost his power of *direct communication with God.* He could no longer walk and talk with God *easily and naturally.* That was such a struggle for God that He finally sent His own Son to die for us to redeem us from the clutches of Satan and to restore to us the power of communication so that now by using the prayer language of the Spirit we can again communicate with God AS IN THE BEGINNING. And we can get His answer back to our intellect. We can reach the place where this comes easily and naturally.

God also gave man in the beginning the *power of dominion* telling him to take dominion over all things. By doubting God man also lost his power of dominion to a great degree. Fear took the place of dominion — man was no longer the *master* God had made him to be.

This was brought sharply to my mind when last summer Evelyn and I spent a few days in Wyoming. We were fishing with a friend — a friend who is a very devout servant of Jesus and communicates with Him daily in the Spirit.

This friend told us of an experience she had when she and her son had gone out on a boat in the ocean on a fishing trip. They were not having any luck. Finally she said to her son, "Gary, the Bible says 'to take dominion over the fish of the sea.' I believe if we do what it says, we'll catch

Evelyn couldn't understand how I managed to catch so many fish until I explained that I was taking dominion over them, just as we are told to do in Genesis.

some fish." So they began to talk to God about taking dominion. Immediately they began to catch fish — big ones — sailfish, dolphins, etc. When the boat went in, the people from other boats were amazed to see so many fish come in from that one boat.

Well, Evelyn and I were fishing for trout, but not having had much experience we weren't having any luck. So I began thinking of what our friend told us. Soon I began catching trout. Evelyn said, "Oral, what are you doing to catch those fish?"

I said, "Evelyn, I'm taking dominion over these fish." Well, she tried it and when a fish got on her line she was so shocked she almost fell out of the boat.

Later that day when I sat down to read my Bible and work on this book, I realized we had stumbled on to something very important. We can take dominion, not only over fish but over the struggles of our lives. Instead of letting them get us down, we can ride on top. We can walk on the water with Jesus.

NOW ASK YOURSELF...

LIFE'S QUESTION: Do I really have a choice of which way I go when I'm going through a problem?

➤ **GOD'S WAY**
SAY IT: EVERY DAY I FACE THE POSSIBILITY OF SINKING OR GETTING TO THE OTHER SIDE. BY TRUSTING GOD AND PLANTING SEEDS OF FAITH I CAN DO SOMETHING ABOUT MY STRUGGLES.

LIFE'S QUESTION: What if I become afraid?

➤ **GOD'S WAY**
SAY IT: I WILL NOT ALLOW MY FEAR TO TAKE OVER MY SPIRIT. I WILL PAY ATTENTION INSTEAD TO GOD TUGGING ON THE LINE OF MY FAITH.

LIFE'S QUESTION: Can I → GOD'S WAY
exercise my will in my life?   SAY IT: I WILL REALIZE GOD
HAS A WILL FOR MY LIFE,
THE DEVIL HAS A WILL FOR
MY LIFE, AND I HAVE A WILL.
I WILL VOTE WITH GOD. AND
THAT WILL MAKE THE DIF-
FERENCE. THAT WILL CAUSE
GOD AND ME TO WIN.

LIFE'S QUESTION: I have → GOD'S WAY
dreams and hopes and goals   SAY IT: GOD WANTS ME TO
for my life. Is that important   GO THROUGH MY STRUG-
to God?   GLES. I WILL REMEMBER
IT'S AS IMPORTANT TO GOD
AS IT IS TO ME THAT I MAKE
IT THROUGH TO ALL MY
DREAMS, MY HOPES, AND MY
GOALS.

LIFE'S QUESTION: Is there → GOD'S WAY
something I can do to help   SAY IT: I WILL MAKE MY
God help me?   FAITH AN ACT AND DO
SOMETHING TO EXPRESS IT
TOWARD GOD. I WILL PLANT
A SEED OF FAITH TO HIM.
I WILL GIVE AND GIVE FIRST.
AS GOD GAVE JESUS OUT OF
HIS NEED, I WILL GIVE TO
HIM OUT OF MINE.

LIFE'S QUESTION: Can I → GOD'S WAY
give for a specific need to be   SAY IT: ANY TIME I FACE A
met?   PROBLEM, I HAVE A NEED TO
PLANT A SEED. I CAN GIVE
FOR A DESIRED RESULT. AND
THE MORE I GIVE, THE MORE
I RECEIVE.

LIFE'S QUESTION: Can I → GOD'S WAY
really take DOMINION   SAY IT: GOD SAYS HE HAS
OVER MY STRUGGLES?   GIVEN ME DOMINION BUT I
MUST "TAKE DOMINION" —
AND I WILL!

PUTTING IT ALL TOGETHER FOR MYSELF

EVERY DAY I FACE THE POSSIBILITY OF SINKING OR GETTING TO THE OTHER SIDE. BY TRUSTING GOD AND PLANTING SEEDS OF FAITH I CAN DO SOMETHING ABOUT MY STRUGGLES.

******

I WILL NOT ALLOW MY FEAR TO TAKE OVER MY SPIRIT. I WILL PAY ATTENTION INSTEAD TO GOD TUGGING ON THE LINE OF MY FAITH.

******

I WILL REALIZE GOD HAS A WILL FOR MY LIFE, THE DEVIL HAS A WILL FOR MY LIFE, AND I HAVE A WILL. I WILL VOTE WITH GOD. AND THAT WILL MAKE THE DIFFERENCE. THAT WILL CAUSE GOD AND ME TO WIN.

******

GOD WANTS ME TO GO THROUGH MY STRUGGLES. I WILL REMEMBER IT'S AS IMPORTANT TO GOD AS IT IS TO ME THAT I MAKE IT THROUGH TO ALL MY DREAMS, MY HOPES, AND MY GOALS.

******

I WILL MAKE MY FAITH AN ACT AND DO SOMETHING TO EXPRESS IT TOWARD GOD. I WILL PLANT A SEED OF FAITH TO HIM. I WILL GIVE AND GIVE FIRST. AS GOD GAVE JESUS OUT OF HIS NEED, I WILL GIVE TO HIM OUT OF MINE.

******

ANY TIME I FACE A PROBLEM, I HAVE A NEED TO PLANT A SEED. I CAN GIVE FOR A DESIRED RESULT. AND THE MORE I GIVE, THE MORE I RECEIVE.

******

GOD SAYS HE HAS GIVEN ME DOMINION BUT I MUST "TAKE DOMINION" – AND I WILL!

Chapter Twelve

How to find what's missing in your life
. . . then get it and hold on to it

". . . . Lord, if it be thou, *bid me come unto thee on the water"* (Matthew 14:28).

When the storm struck that night and poured out its fury, Peter discovered there was something missing in his life. The ingredient missing was the *reality* of Jesus. Jesus was right there before Peter. He was there. He was there where Peter was struggling. But He seemed so unreal.

DO YOU REALLY KNOW JESUS?

Peter had found Jesus real before, but never in a life/death situation. He had never faced anything like the struggle he was in now.

I think one of God's greatest concerns about you and me is that we learn to know the reality of Jesus in the storm so we can know Him also when all is peace and quiet.

Recently Evelyn and I received a letter from Tay Thomas, wife of Lowell Thomas, Jr., Lieutenant Governor of Alaska. Lowell Thomas, Sr., is a good friend and partner of ours and it was because of him I think that Tay wrote us.

She wrote that she and her family had barely escaped

with their lives during the great earthquake that struck Alaska in 1964. This was when she first realized the impermanence of what she had built her life on. She said she didn't know the reality of a good God, a stable force, Someone she could really depend on in good times and bad. "When the earth broke up under my feet I had nothing to hold on to but my fear. And it left me in the same shambles as the earthquake had left our home."

She said her husband, Lowell, Jr., once told her that if the house begins trembling and shaking under the force of a tremor, "It's safer outside. Get outside!" They did and it saved their lives. An instant later the house crashed down with the quake.

Tay recalled, "From that moment on, I began to search for a faith that would take away my fear and give me an inner serenity, a serenity that would be stronger at the end of a problem than at the beginning . . . .

"What I wanted was to leave my old habits and ways and take on the ability to depend completely on God and His caring for me and my family. I wanted to be held in God's keeping power — not my own . . . ."

She wrote later that she had found this inner strength when the Holy Spirit filled her heart, giving her a new language of prayer and praise to God, opening up the deepest parts of her being to the glorious Savior and receiving His everlasting, ever-abiding Self in her. Going from the point of not knowing Who or where God was to being able to find Him in every detail of her life gave her an energy and permanence that was making her a whole person.

THE STORM THAT NEARLY SUCKED ME UNDER

Like Tay, we all go through storms and struggles. And if we can find Jesus there, the storms will strengthen our lives. Let me tell you about a storm I went through that at first I thought would destroy me.

In 1947 as I began this ministry, I was quickly enveloped in a storm that nearly kept me from taking my first step onto the water.

I felt God wanted me to go beyond the small view most people around me had of Him. I knew He could heal. I began to see that He wanted people to have health, to prosper, to be whole spiritually, physically, financially. I saw He wanted people to have the ability to love when they were not loved back.

I began to preach this message. The people I preached to were good people. They gave me a decent hearing and went on about their lives, unchanged, without really having heard what I was saying. The truth of it had not found a place in them.

Taking matters into my own hands, I announced I would pray for any sick person who had enough faith to ask me. There were some pretty sad failures at first. I was scared to step out in faith away from the common view that going to church and being a part of its formal services was all that was necessary. I wanted to stay in the boat (the way the church had always done things) even though it was not strong enough to weather the storms that swept over me. I knew God was out there with something more — but where? How could *I* make direct contact with Him? How could I grasp *His* view of life, His faith, His serenity?

THE STRUGGLE GOT FIERCE

You would think that a young preacher wanting Christ to be that near and real to him, wanting to be able to bring healing to people, would excite and thrill everybody. But not so! It upset the "status quo" of the church services. It was so hard to find anyone who believed that Jesus is actually in the now, that what He was 2,000 years ago He is now. That He is really closer now because He is no longer confined in a body that is limited to time and space. That

He is in the now in His invisible, unlimited self, His presence closer to us than the very breath of our body.

In 1947 that was a scary mind-boggling thought. And I had it. I had it. But with problems!

My problem, I see now, was like Peter's as he was trying to make up his mind to walk on the water toward Christ. He simply couldn't see or understand. The truth had not dawned on him yet. He wanted Jesus to be more visible, more recognizable. And so did I.

In my prayers I kept saying, "Lord, 2,000 years ago the twelve disciples actually saw You. They physically touched You. They heard Your human voice. But I've never had this experience. Those 2,000 years make too much distance between us.

"I can't go back in time 2,000 years . . .

I live in the now . . .

Please do me the favor of appearing to me in the
    physical way You did to them.

Then I could see You for myself.

I could see You heal people.

I could see You do miracles.

Seeing You, I could then do all these things myself."

I CONTRIBUTE TO THE FURY OF THE STORM

That's the way I talked to God. At first I got no answer. Day by day I kept asking. I brooded over it. Since I was pastoring a small congregation and at the same time continuing my education at the university, I had even greater difficulties.

I had to minister to the church in the old accepted manner — opening the service with prayer, having a trained choir sing, making boring announcements, preaching and giving the benediction.

I had to carry a normal college load of credit hours and pass them.

I had to support my family on the meager amount my church paid me. The salary was so small I often thought of the preacher who complained to the church board about his low pay. They said, "Pastor, poor preach, poor pay." It's funny now, but it wasn't then.

Then a blow was struck against me by a few prominent men in the church. They told me I was off the beam in starting a healing ministry. They questioned my motives — something I would encounter again and again a hundred times more severe in the next twenty years.

Quackery was also brought up. It was said I had a desire to get rich off the poor sick people. They accused me of planning to get into a racket.

I went to pieces. Like Peter, I was starting to sink. "Evelyn," I said, "I can't go on with this. Everything I'm dreaming and planning is being questioned. I am under heavy suspicion even before I start. It's too much. I can't make it."

Putting her arms around me she proved what a treasure a good wife really is. She said, "Oral, you've been saying Jesus healed the sick. He cared for people, including the poor and certainly the sick. He cared for everyone, and that included those who thought He was fooling the people. They even hated Him and eventually killed Him."

As I listened she continued, "Honey, I know you. You haven't a dishonest thought in your being. You are just beginning to understand the real Jesus and what He went through to help the people. Our relationship with God is coming alive. Don't let a few who don't understand, and who don't want to change, defeat you. The devil doesn't want people to see miracles, to be healed by the Lord. And the devil certainly doesn't want someone around who is young and vigorous and able to undertake this mission."

Then she added, "Whatever you do, I'm with you, even if it means leaving here and going to the ends of the earth. But YOU'VE got to decide."

That was a voice from the Lord across the troubled waters speaking directly to me in the midst of the storm and the sinking boat I was in. Still, the storm raged on.

Almost overnight there was a coldness toward me by most of the congregation. I couldn't understand it. They loved me. I loved them. They had strongly indicated their desire for me to stay at least seven years as their pastor. Now we could no longer relate to each other. I allowed myself to be hurt by this. Then suddenly I contributed to the fury of the storm. I threatened to quit. I even slipped downtown and secured the promise of a secular job if things didn't work out and I had to leave the ministry.

THEN I SAW WHAT I WAS MISSING

Through all this, my physical senses were trying to take the place of my spirit, making what I heard these men say drown out what God was saying inside me. The thought came to me that sometimes people accuse another person of something they know they would do themselves under similar conditions.

Then came my magic moment. From deep inside I heard Jesus' voice again. It was as clear to me as it was to Peter when Jesus, balanced on the storm-tossed waves, said, "Be of good cheer. It is I; be not afraid."

He said to me, "Do you have the Holy Spirit?"

"Yes, Lord, I do."

"Do you know what you have?"

"Some, but I'm sure not enough."

It was then that He said, "Having the Holy Spirit is the same as having Me with you physically — only better. Through the Holy Spirit I am not only WITH you, as I was with My disciples 2,000 years ago, but I am IN you."

It was breathtaking to get this information. I said, "But, Lord, I never realized having the Holy Spirit was the same as having You with me, by my side."

He said, "I am by your side. But I am much more than being *with* you. Through the Holy Spirit I am IN you. Therefore you have My power to take healing to the people."

Well! All the lights of the world seemed to come on inside my spirit and mind. My physical senses came alive. Vibrations went through me. I could do it because I had the Holy Spirit! Through Him — Christ was IN me — in ME, Oral Roberts.

I SAW JESUS IS IN THE NOW

That's when I saw that I could do it. What I had to do was start preaching that Jesus is in the NOW. I had to allow the compassion I felt for the sick start flowing out of me to the people. I was to touch them and pray for God to heal them.

I felt shaky inside because these were new truths about Jesus to me. Yet I felt solid as a rock as I began to know Jesus was IN ME . . . IN ME TO TAKE HIS HEALING POWER TO MY GENERATION. Within the next few days I went through that storm by having my first healing service. God had given me the assurance He would heal the people through my faith — and He did!

I WAS WALKING ON THE WATER TO GO TO JESUS. I had learned that where Jesus is, there is also His healing power. Since He was in me, His healing power would flow out of Him through me.

FILLED WITH THE HOLY SPIRIT

I am "charismatic" in my experience with God. That is, the Holy Spirit fills my life with the unlimited, invisible presence of the Living Christ. As St. Paul says, "Christ living in me" (Galatians 2:20). Jesus, while on earth in the flesh, was *with* His followers. He told them that He had fulfilled

His mission in coming to earth as a man and must return to His Father. He would pray the Father to send "another Comforter," which is the Holy Spirit. He said the Father would give us the Holy Spirit. He said, "I will come to you." So the Father had first sent Jesus in the flesh to be *with* man. He sent Him back in the invisible, unlimited form of the Holy Spirit to be *in* us — both *with* and *in* us. It is through the invisible, unlimited Christ (the form in which God sends the OTHER COMFORTER) that the Holy Spirit fills my spirit and gives me the power to speak to God with my spirit in THE PRAYER LANGUAGE OF THE (HOLY) SPIRIT.

Still as a man, I get scared at times. But I get full of faith too. The prayer language helps me to have more faith than fear. I find in my humanness my faith can work for me the same way faith worked and made the stormy water become a liquid pavement beneath Jesus' feet.

From that first moment of finding what was missing, I knew I could walk on the water. To be filled with His Spirit and use the prayer language of the Spirit intelligently is the most exciting thing I've ever discovered in getting through to Jesus and allowing Him to get through to me. By using the prayer language, I can talk with Him easily and naturally, and He can talk easily and naturally with me.

This is a valid experience. I intend to hold on to it . . . to use it daily.

I'm going to share one of the greatest testimonies I've ever heard about the work of the Holy Spirit. It's from one of the partners of this ministry. I'll just use his own words to tell it.

I had been drinking off and on for twenty-five years, only lately, much worse. Presently I was sweating out the effects of my latest drunk . . . probably should have been in the hospital. But even worse, my heart ached because our eight-year-old daughter had just gone through a tonsillectomy and I was too strung out even to be with her. While my wife watched and waited with her at the hospital, I sat alone, fighting to control a body and mind near d.t.'s. I went to bed, hoping to find peace in sleep, but there seemed to be strange creatures crawling on the bedroom ceiling. It was hopeless.

I got up and went back into the living room. There was a book on the table, TWELVE GREATEST MIRACLES OF MY MINISTRY, by Oral Roberts. Something made me pick it up and begin reading. I became so engrossed in every word that I didn't put it down until I had finished the entire book.

Well, that was last night. Today it appeared it was all for nothing. My wife was leaving.

Maybe not, I thought. Oral Roberts spoke about miracles. I picked up the book, went into the bedroom, and dialed the Prayer Tower number. A very nice lady answered the phone and listened as I told her of my problems. Then, with my hand on the book, she said a prayer, the most beautiful prayer I've ever heard.

After we hung up, something made me reach out for a miracle. I knelt beside my bed and prayed, asking God to rid my body of this terrible disease. Suddenly the power of the Holy Spirit came upon me. The words I prayed in English instantly ceased and were transformed into a new prayer language of the Spirit. Then I felt something coming up from my stomach. It continued through my chest and throat and came out of my mouth. I actually spit the foul substance out. Then a calm feeling came over me. From the inside out, I felt clean!

My wife was sitting on the patio and when I came out she asked, "What's wrong? What was all the noise about?" I smiled but only told her that everything was all right now, that the demon of alcohol was no longer inside me.

Sunday morning I got up bright and early and went to church — a new man! Though the gulf between me and the Lord was now bridged, the distance between me and my wife was still uncrossable.

That night while we sat at the dinner table I asked her, "Do you believe in miracles?" "Yes," she said. Then I told her all that had happened to me the previous day. Gradually her heart softened and it wasn't long before we were really talking together, communicating for the first time in a long time.

Then she showed me a letter she had written to you, Brother Roberts, and your reply. And with that the three of us — my wife, my daughter, and I — got down on our knees, took each other's hands, and prayed like we've never prayed before. We praised God for the miracle He had given us and asked His blessing on our renewed marriage.

We went to tell our pastor what had happened. I can assure you there were three happy people in his study that day!

Today our family is closer than we've been in a very long time. I have absolutely no desire to drink, and as God holds my hand each day I can truly say that He is in the NOW of our lives and is able to meet any and every need we will ever have.

EMPTY WON'T WORK

Whenever you reach out to God, He is there. He will help you through any struggles — any storm. That's why He walked on the water. You need only to look to Him . . . to be filled with His Spirit . . .

You see, in your humanness you cannot live in a vacuum. Your life must be filled with something greater. Jesus confirmed this truth. One day He told the scribes and pharisees about a man who got an unclean spirit out of himself but he didn't get anything positive back in. He left his inner self swept out but empty.

There is no place quite as attractive to the devil as an empty life. The unclean spirit was delighted when he came back to this man and discovered his former residence clean but empty. He looked around and found seven devils more evil than himself and together they entered the man again. And the last state of that man was worse than before (Matthew 12:43-45). The man had been cleaned up but had not gone on to be filled with the Living Christ through the power of the Holy Spirit. Satan entered the vacuum and it was disaster for the man.

Find out what's missing in your life. *Empty won't work.* The storm that day was filling the boat with water, it was swamping it. Peter said, "Lord, I've got to get out of this boat that's filling up with water and sinking. I need to walk with You *on the water.* If I stay in this boat, I'll drown. Tell me to come to You!"

Peter knew something had to change in his life that moment. It was now or never. In his spirit he finally saw it was the real Jesus and could hear Jesus calling, "Come." The moment he recognized Jesus, he left the boat and went walking on the water to Jesus. Then Peter and Jesus walked back on the water to the boat, entered it, and another miracle — a magic moment — happened. The boat which had been sloshing around in the water was emptied of water and filled with the presence of God. The boat got to the other side. They arrived! They got through!

What is Jesus saying to you? Get your mind off the storm, get in your spirit and see Jesus, hear Him tell you, "Come . . . walk on the water to Me." Go to Jesus. You'll reach Him, even if you stumble and doubt some. His big strong hand will catch you and stand you up in the midst of your struggle. Together you'll come through — and *you will arrive.* I guarantee you, you can make it to the other side — through your struggle.

This is the Jesus I have come to know. I risk everything I am and ever hope to do and be in His hands. He's here for me, He's here for you — IN THE NOW!

NOW ASK YOURSELF...

LIFE'S QUESTION: How can I know Jesus in the storms and struggles the way I know Him when all is peace and quiet?

GOD'S WAY
SAY IT: I CAN BE FILLED WITH THE SPIRIT AND USE THE PRAYER LANGUAGE OF THE SPIRIT TO GET THROUGH TO JESUS AND ALLOW HIM TO GET THROUGH TO ME . . . ANY TIME!

LIFE'S QUESTION: What should I do when I am scared to step out of the boat and trust God even though I am failing to find answers where I am?

GOD'S WAY
SAY IT: I WILL LEAVE MY OLD HABITS AND WAYS AND DEPEND COMPLETELY ON GOD AND HIS CARING FOR ME AND MY LOVED ONES.

LIFE'S QUESTION: Is God still there when I feel like my life is coming apart in the fury of the storm, everyone is against me, and nothing is working out right?

GOD'S WAY
SAY IT: WHEN THE STORM IS THE ROUGHEST, FROM DEEP INSIDE ME I CAN HEAR JESUS' VOICE ACROSS THE STORM-TOSSED WAVES SAYING, "IT IS I. BE NOT AFRAID! COME, WALK ON THE WATER TO ME."

LIFE'S QUESTION: I want Jesus to be more visible and more recognizable in my hurts and problems . . . but how?

GOD'S WAY
SAY IT: I WILL REMEMBER THAT HAVING THE HOLY SPIRIT IS THE SAME AS HAVING JESUS WITH ME PHYSICALLY — ONLY BETTER — BECAUSE IN HIS INVISIBLE UNLIMITED FORM HE IS *IN* ME.

LIFE'S QUESTION: I can't go back in time 2,000 years. How can I make direct contact with Jesus now?

GOD'S WAY
SAY IT: THROUGH THE HOLY SPIRIT, JESUS IS ACTUALLY IN THE NOW. AND WHAT HE WAS 2,000 YEARS AGO, HE IS NOW — TO ME!

LIFE'S QUESTION: Even → GOD'S WAY
though I am filled with the   SAY IT: I WILL REMEMBER I
Holy Spirit, at times I go to   HAVE MORE FAITH THAN I
pieces with fear and start to   HAVE FEAR. AND I WILL RE-
sink like Peter. What one   LEASE MY FAITH KNOWING I
thing must I remember?   CAN WALK ON THE WATER
                                OF ANY STORM COMING
                                AGAINST ME.

PUTTING IT ALL TOGETHER FOR MYSELF

I CAN BE FILLED WITH THE SPIRIT AND USE
THE PRAYER LANGUAGE OF THE SPIRIT TO GET
THROUGH TO JESUS AND ALLOW HIM TO GET
THROUGH TO ME . . . ANY TIME!

******

I WILL LEAVE MY OLD HABITS AND WAYS AND
DEPEND COMPLETELY ON GOD AND HIS CARING
FOR ME AND MY LOVED ONES.

******

WHEN THE STORM IS THE ROUGHEST, FROM DEEP
INSIDE ME I CAN HEAR JESUS' VOICE ACROSS THE
STORM-TOSSED WAVES SAYING, "IT IS I. BE NOT
AFRAID. COME, WALK ON THE WATER TO ME."

******

I WILL REMEMBER THAT HAVING THE HOLY
SPIRIT IS THE SAME AS HAVING JESUS WITH ME
PHYSICALLY — ONLY BETTER! BECAUSE IN HIS
INVISIBLE, UNLIMITED FORM HE IS *IN* ME.

******

THROUGH THE HOLY SPIRIT JESUS IS ACTUALLY
IN THE NOW. AND WHAT HE WAS 2,000 YEARS
AGO HE IS NOW — TO ME!

******

I WILL REMEMBER I HAVE MORE FAITH THAN I
HAVE FEAR. AND I WILL RELEASE MY FAITH
KNOWING I CAN WALK ON THE WATER OF ANY
STORM COMING AGAINST ME!

Chapter Thirteen

The fear you can't afford to have is —not letting Jesus do for you what He can do

". . . It is I; be not afraid . . ." (Matthew 14:27).

Fear is one of the most natural emotions of man. The disciples felt fear that night. And there was only one person who could help them overcome their fear — Jesus. He could do it in only one way, and that was to say:

"Come, walk with Me ON the water."

The disciples had more than fear of the storm that night. They feared Jesus wasn't real, that He was a ghost.

They also had a fear to leave the boat in the midst of the storm, although it was sinking. They feared turning loose of the familiar. These fears, combined, nearly did them in.

I understand that kind of fear, one fear piling upon another. I'm sure you do too. In addition to those fears, they had a fear to test Jesus, to ask for proof. I think their fears demonstrate to you and me our own fears. Thank God, one of their group, Peter, tackled his fears and as he acted upon what little faith he had, overcame them!

"IT IS I..."

When I think of the fear these disciples of Jesus had that night in the storm, I am reminded of the little boy who took part in a church play. He was given the line, "It is I; be not afraid." It was his only part in the play. They coached him over and over until he learned it.

On opening night when the time came for his part, the little boy walked out on the stage and started to say his line. Suddenly the bright lights and the crowd made the situation unfamiliar and frightening to him. So he just stood there.

From behind the curtain came the prompter's voice, "It is I; be not afraid."

The little boy just stood there.

Again the voice, "It is I; be not afraid."

The little boy shifted from foot to foot but still didn't say his line.

Finally, the voice rose a little higher, "It is I; be not afraid."

The little boy finally blurted out, "Folks, it's only me. And I'm scared to death."

When Peter heard Jesus say, "Be of good cheer, it is I; be not afraid," he knew those were his lines. He knew that was his cue to settle down and follow through the way Jesus had prepared him. Scared to death, he took Jesus' strong urging and stepped out onto the water.

I heard from a young woman the other day who wrote about her own step onto the water. She was divorced and had three small children. She had severe financial problems. She had been giving, but not with much gladness of heart. As she had been taught, she said she had never expected to receive anything back from her giving to God. She began to learn the principles of Seed-Faith. She was afraid at first. She said she had to plant a very small seed so she could build up her courage. One day she finally came to the place where she was no longer afraid. She planted something of real value in her life. It was out of her deep, deep need. Then knowing she had planted her seed out of her need and beginning to understand that she could expect God to multiply her seed sown, she began to watch and see when God would give the harvest. She had stepped out of the boat. She had gone toward Jesus. She had obeyed His prompting. As she watched and expected, her miracle came. In a matter of days, she got a good job offer, took it, and was able to go off welfare. She said:

> "My case workers wanted to do a success story on *me* but no one gets this kind of credit but God. Because I finally learned *He* was my *TOTAL* Source of supply. I could plant my seed, expect Him to supply my needs, and He did."

This woman had acted out of faith. She too heard Jesus say, "Be of good cheer, it is I; be not afraid."

How well I understood her experience of seeding to God for a miracle. It is the continuous story of our ministry. It's what keeps me going in times of great stress and need, just knowing God will multiply the seed I sow.

"... BE NOT AFRAID"

But when we don't hear Jesus in our spirit, or when we don't pay attention to the inner voice, our fear remains with us. And fear does strange things. When I was a stuttering boy, I was asked my name the first day I went to school. I opened my mouth but nothing came out. I was paralyzed with fear. I couldn't say, "My name is Granville Oral Roberts and they call me Oral." I couldn't say anything.

The kids laughed. *Then* the teacher laughed. I can't remember anything that ever hurt me more, or did more to give me an inferiority complex that nearly wrecked my chances of amounting to anything.

That same thing happened once when I was a young

preacher. Evelyn was with me. We were in a group and everyone was asked to introduce himself. At my turn, fear hit me and again I couldn't speak. I couldn't say my own name. Evelyn spotted my predicament and said, "He is my husband. His name is Oral Roberts."

It was terrible sweating that one out.

The disciples were sweating something out too. When we look on that scene today and think of Jesus coming down from the mountain, leaping on the tossing waves, balancing Himself on the waters that were threatening His disciples, we say:

Oh, how great. Wouldn't it be thrilling
to be in on something like that?

Well, they didn't feel that way at all. They were in that storm because they were His disciples. They had done what He'd told them to do. They couldn't understand the struggle they were going through, or why all this was happening to them.

We think of the disciples as bright-eyed, Spirit-filled, fearless men. But like the little boy, they were saying, "It's only us, and we're scared to death."

LET JESUS DO WHAT HE CAN DO

Like the little boy, they too had a Prompter standing in the shadows. He was determined to get through to them. And Jesus did get through to *one* person. But the eleven others had run into the one fear no one can afford to have. They had allowed themselves to get so afraid that Jesus' voice seemed unreal to them — and they allowed themselves to become even more afraid.

Just think a minute about these men.

They couldn't afford to be so afraid they
couldn't listen to Jesus' voice.
But they *didn't* listen.

They couldn't afford to fear so much that Jesus'
voice could not get through to them.
But they *didn't* let it get through to
their inner selves.

They couldn't afford fear so great it would
prevent Jesus from doing for them what
only He could do — get them out of that
sinking boat and on the water safe with Him.
But they did *prevent* it.

Only Peter walked on the water. Only Peter let Jesus do
what He could do for him.

WHAT CAN JESUS DO FOR YOU?

We all face storms. Jesus can't do anything if you are
afraid to let Him. Can you see that? You've got to let Him
do what He can do, or He can't do it.

I know people who will go to others when they face
problems, but they won't go to Jesus.

They will go to a doctor when they need healing, but
never think of God's delivery system of prayer.

They will ask for prayer, but not accept God's delivery
system of healing through medicine.

They will get worried to death over their finances, never
remembering that God cares about supplying their financial
needs, that He can reveal ways and means to them about
the money they need that no human mind can do. God can
make a way for your finances where man can never make
a way.

I would be lost without having overcome the fear of
letting God in on helping me financially. Or helping me
with my health. Or helping me get answers I can't get from
any human beings I know.

I know the fear of turning to Jesus in the storm of leaving the old usual way of getting through. As I said earlier,

I am scared even as I write this book. I confess this fear. But I battle it with my faith. Every day I say to myself, "Oral Roberts, do what you can do, then don't be afraid to let God do what He can do!" It helps so much as I do this. I urge you to do it. It's God's way.

MY MAJOR ASSIGNMENT

God has given me my major assignment in life. To fulfill His complete calling to take His healing power to my generation, He has commanded me to build the CITY OF FAITH here on the ORU campus — a great new Health Care Center. There will be a building complex of more than 1,600,000 square feet. These towering buildings will rise from a common base. The structure will signify a new kind of health care for body, mind, and spirit — whole man healing — and will house:

> A clinic and diagnostic center.
>
> A center for research into a cure for
>   cancer and other dread diseases.
>
> A medical center for acute cases.
>
> A center for continuing education for the ORU
>   medical, dental and nursing students and
>   graduates.
>
> A center for the re-certification of
>   current physicians, surgeons, dentists,
>   nurses, and other medical professionals.

An atmosphere of prayer will permeate the CITY OF FAITH in every person, in every department, in every relationship with the sick.

A thorough training program will be established to raise up healing teams consisting of young doctors, dentists, nurses, and preachers. They will go to nations where missionaries are no longer welcome, as well as to countries still open to the Gospel. The ORU healing teams will carry on this healing ministry long after I have finished my work on earth.

I'M GETTING INTO THE BOAT

But right now I face the staggering task of assembling skilled men and women who are also dedicated to the healing Christ. I face the staggering cost of building the CITY OF FAITH and building it AS GOD SAYS — BUILD IT AND OPEN IT DEBT-FREE. I am getting into the boat to go to the other side. On the other side I can, by obeying God, join the healing hands of prayer and medicine, bringing together these two most powerful delivery systems. The CITY OF FAITH is the dream God gave me as a part of the abundant life Jesus promised us (John 10:10). It's part of the call of God upon my life to take His healing power to my generation.

It's thrilling.

It's scary.

I've got to do it.

I've got to obey God.

He alone is my Source. My own seeds of faith have started it. Other seeds are being planted by partners, and some by people I don't even know. I've got to expect a miracle, the greatest I've ever known. In short, I must not be afraid to let Jesus do through me what I can't do myself.

Right now I'm in the storm. I'm seeing the problem but I'm working on the answer. In my spirit I'm seeing Jesus, I'm recognizing Him as He is, I'm hearing Him say, "Come! Walk to me on the water!"

Yes, I feel the waters swirling around me. My heart pounds. My stomach gets queasy. Some nights I toss and turn. I hurt inside. Because what God has called me to do has never been done before in history.

GOD WILL BUILD IT THROUGH ME

But there's one thing I must understand in building a Health Care Center that's never before been built. I must understand that *God* will build it through me. I understand there are things *I must do myself* and there are things *God alone can do* — and I must trust Him to do them.

There's another thing I'm learning. To get God's help, *I have to feel my need of it. I have to want it more than anything else in the world.*

I've already had some magic moments in getting the CITY OF FAITH under way.

I've walked on the water to Jesus and found He has begun to supply me with:

> Able associates in the medical and spiritual
> fields who are in a unity of purpose with
> my calling.

> The architectural and engineering plans that will
> create the most people-oriented Health
> Care Center the world has ever known.

> Partners who feel the spark of it in their hearts,
> as I do in mine, and who know they and
> their loved ones will receive the greatest
> help they've ever had.

> An anointing in my spirit to see this is a great
> task in this healing ministry — bigger than
> He has ever asked me to do before. And
> it will operate until the Second Coming
> of our Lord.

NOW ASK YOURSELF...

LIFE'S QUESTION: How can I overcome the fear of letting Jesus prove Himself to me? → **GOD'S WAY** SAY IT: I WILL REALIZE THERE ARE THINGS ONLY JESUS CAN DO. I WILL TURN LOOSE OF THE FAMILIAR AND LET JESUS DO WHAT HE CAN DO.

LIFE'S QUESTION: What happens when my fear keeps increasing? → **GOD'S WAY** SAY IT: I WILL NOT LET MYSELF BE SO AFRAID THAT I CANNOT HEAR JESUS SAYING, "BE OF GOOD CHEER, IT IS I. BE NOT AFRAID." AT HIS WORD I WILL FOLLOW THE WAY HE HAS PREPARED FOR ME.

LIFE'S QUESTION: How can I learn not to be afraid to go to God with my problems instead of to other people? → **GOD'S WAY** SAY IT: JESUS HAS THE ANSWERS NO HUMAN CAN PROVIDE. AS I LEARN THAT, I WON'T BE AFRAID TO GO TO HIM WITH MY STRUGGLES. I KNOW HE WILL HELP ME WALK ON THE WATER.

LIFE'S QUESTION: If God gives me something to do, how can I do it? → **GOD'S WAY** SAY IT: WHEN I AM CALLED TO DO SOMETHING FOR GOD, I WILL NOT BE AFRAID TO LET JESUS DO THROUGH ME WHAT I CAN'T DO MYSELF. I WILL DO WHAT I CAN DO, THEN I WON'T BE AFRAID TO LET GOD DO WHAT HE CAN DO.

LIFE'S QUESTION: How can I receive God's help? → **GOD'S WAY** SAY IT: I WILL UNDERSTAND THAT AFTER I HAVE DONE WHAT I CAN DO, AND HAVE ASKED GOD TO DO WHAT HE CAN DO – THEN I MUST EXPECT TO RECEIVE; TO SEE MIRACLES HAPPEN.

PUTTING IT ALL TOGETHER FOR MYSELF

I WILL REALIZE THERE ARE THINGS ONLY JESUS CAN DO. I WILL TURN LOOSE OF THE FAMILIAR AND LET JESUS DO WHAT HE CAN DO.

* * * * * *

I WILL NOT LET MYSELF BE SO AFRAID THAT I CANNOT HEAR JESUS SAYING, "BE OF GOOD CHEER, IT IS I. BE NOT AFRAID." AT HIS WORD I WILL FOLLOW THE WAY HE HAS PREPARED FOR ME.

* * * * * *

JESUS HAS THE ANSWERS NO HUMAN CAN PROVIDE. AS I LEARN THAT, I WON'T BE AFRAID TO GO TO HIM WITH MY STRUGGLES. I KNOW HE WILL HELP ME WALK ON THE WATER.

* * * * * *

WHEN I AM CALLED ON TO DO SOMETHING FOR GOD, I WILL NOT BE AFRAID TO LET JESUS DO THROUGH ME WHAT I CAN'T DO MYSELF. I WILL DO WHAT I CAN DO THEN I WON'T BE AFRAID TO LET GOD DO WHAT HE CAN DO.

* * * * * *

I WILL UNDERSTAND THAT AFTER I HAVE DONE WHAT I CAN DO AND HAVE ASKED GOD TO DO WHAT HE CAN DO, THEN I MUST EXPECT TO RECEIVE – TO SEE MIRACLES HAPPEN.

Chapter Fourteen

How you can know God is bigger than anything that comes against you

"But straightway Jesus spake unto them ..."
(Matthew 14:27).

A pastor who had just seen me on television wrote and told me about the first sermon he had preached as a young man right out of seminary.

After the sermon was over and several had shaken his hand, an elderly minister approached and said, "Young man, that was a nice sermon."

The young preacher said, "I sensed in my spirit that the older minister had something else he wanted to say to me. I asked if he had any advice for me."

GOD IS GREATER

The elderly minister said, "Well, I do have one suggestion. If you can accept it and learn it, you'll be a better preacher and you'll be able to help many people you won't be able to reach otherwise."

"Certainly. Just tell me anything," the young preacher said.

"Son, you said a lot of good things. But you made sin

and fear and problems so big, and God so small, that if I had not known better I would have left here believing those things were bigger than our Savior."

Then he added, "Son, when you preach about sin, always remember the Bible says 'where sin abounds, grace does much more abound.' When you preach about fear, always remember the Bible says 'God hath not given us the spirit of fear, but of power and love and a sound mind.' When you preach about problems, always remember the Bible says, 'Greater is he who is in you, than he who is in the world.' *Tell that to the people.* And remind them Jesus told His followers to 'go over to the other side,' that He has a way for us to go through instead of being defeated."

The young man said he shook the elderly minister's hand, saying, "I'm going to accept this. I'm going to try to do it because I feel it's the best advice I've ever had."

The letter continued. "As I heard you on television, and you were telling us how good God is, how strong and powerful God is, how very close He is to each of us, even at the point of our need, I remembered the advice of the old preacher. What a profound influence his advice has had on my ministry. From that day I have put God in His proper place. I have told everyone He is bigger than anything that comes against us. As you do, Brother Roberts, I now preach that God is bigger than any problem I have."

I wrote this pastor back and told him I was encouraged by any minister who has the ear of a lot of people, for a minister's words and spirit are used by God to lift them up into a new understanding that God can do anything. The preaching of the Word of God causes faith in a person to be released. It is only through our faith that we are going to make it.

JESUS WANTS YOU TO TAKE HIS HAND

A woman in an automobile accident, trapped underneath

her car, was screaming, "Somebody help me." A crane was requested to lift the car off her. Meanwhile a crowd had gathered. And one man crawled as close as he could get to the woman and said, "Take my hand."

She took his hand and in a few moments she calmed down. She didn't go into shock.

When the crane arrived and the woman was released, she said, "I never thought an outstretched hand could mean so much."

Jesus stretched His hand out to Peter in the midst of his struggle to survive. When He put out His hand and took Peter's, He showed us something. Jesus does more than come to us at the point of our need. He stretches His hand out for us to hold onto. In fact, whether we know it or not, His hand is always pulling us up. I'm sure I've been pulled up by Jesus without knowing at the time that He'd done it. Gradually I've learned the nature of God as expressed in Jesus. It's simple yet profound.

God is bigger.

God is here.

God will take your hand.

God will walk with you and quiet the storm.

God will speak to you in every need you have.

Yes, God will speak to you.

HOW MY DARLING WIFE EVELYN DISCOVERED GOD WOULD SPEAK TO HER

The day I started writing this book, May 18, 1977, Evelyn slipped out of the house for her usual two-mile walk. We usually go together, for we enjoy walking together. And it helps us keep ourselves physically fit.

Well, pretty soon she came back from her walk. She casually said, "Oral, would you let me tell you how God talked to me during my walk?"

I said, "Sure, I'd love to hear it."

You see, Evelyn and I are opposites except for two things. We are the same in our deep love for each other. We are the same in our deep love for God. In other things we are quite opposite.

She's quiet, steady, the same every time you see her. I'm moody and often irritable, especially if I can't get things done. I have to hear God's voice. I do nothing of an important nature in my ministry until God speaks to me. Through much suffering I've learned to obey His voice. Without hearing God's voice, quite often I grow tense. And I know I'm often hard to live with. I have mountaintop and valley experiences. I plumb both the heights and depths. Evelyn says I have thunder one moment and quietness the next. She says the only thing about me that never changes is that I will obey God. No matter how low I get, how hard the situation facing me, how tough it is on me or anybody else, she says, *"Oral will obey God."*

She adds, "When Oral understands what God wants him to do, he's going to do it — with or without people's approval. But until he understands what God wants him to do, he goes through periods of uncertainty, fear, frustration, irritation. And you better stay out of his way."

She says my associates at ORU will call her and ask, "How's the president doing today? Is he in one of those moods? Is he wrestling with a problem or is he coming out on top?" They don't want to bring one of their problems to me without knowing that God and I have been communicating with each other and I have reached a state of knowing within myself.

The morning I started this book I had been walking the floor. I had not slept well the night before. I was even snapping a bit at Evelyn. But I was really crying out in my heart to reach out to God and hear His voice again. There had been so many struggles and more in sight. I needed one of the greatest miracles of my life and it looked like it wasn't coming. I was hurting and it was showing. I desperately needed to walk on the water.

Evelyn was taking all this in, cooking for me, encouraging me, and sometimes staying as far from me as she could — "to let you and God work this out," she'd say.

That morning in the midst of this struggle, she got to wondering why God didn't speak to her like He does to me. On her walk, she told me, she had really gotten into praying, talking straight out to God. As she started telling me what God said to her, I said, "Wait, honey. Write it down. I'll read it. And perhaps others will have the chance to, also!"

Here are Evelyn's own words:

"Lord, You know this struggle we're going through. If You want our decision to be yes, then show us definitely. If *no* then block the way. Remove the thought from our mind and let Oral be satisfied with a no.

"Now, Lord, I want to ask You something. It's been on my mind a long time. Why can't I hear Your audible voice? You have never given me an earth-shaking experience. Oh, I won't deny that You have spoken to me many times since I was a little girl through reading the Scriptures, through a sermon I heard or a song. Or by someone sharing an experience of faith with me. Or by a knowing I have sometimes felt inside. But, Lord, although I'm grateful for all these, I'd like to hear Your voice as Oral does. And another thing, Lord, when I'm praying in the Spirit in my private devotions, I'd like to have You speak back to my mind in an interpretation that is clear and unmistakable. St. Paul teaches that we can do this and I want to very much."

(Just before this walk I had finished reading an article in *Daily Blessing* in which Richard had written the story of a minister who had a parishioner who called to talk and talk but would never listen for the minister to answer. Well, I got the message loud and clear. I was to stop now and listen for God's answer.)

So as I walked I prayed in the Spirit at length. I couldn't

understand the prayer language coming over my tongue. It sounded Oriental to me. But I waited to see what the Lord would give me and the interpretation came back in my own language, one line at a time.

No, you will not hear my voice as others do. You will know, however, that it is I speaking. Oral is the one I've called to do great things for the healing of the people and you are his helper. I speak to him in an audible voice but I will not speak to you audibly. I will speak to you out of the everydayness of your life and that is the way I designed your life. It is my way for you.

Creative people like Oral are sometimes explosive and get upset easily. You are to calm him by your love and by being with him. You have not been given big tasks as I've given him (to which I said, "Thank You, Lord"). *However, you have your work to do. As you give yourself to him whom I've called, you are giving your best to Me, and I will give My best to you.*

Whether Oral returns the giving is not up to you. It's up to Me. So look to Me, not to him.

Evelyn, again I say I speak to you out of the everydayness of your life in ways you will understand. This is my will for you.

"Well, Lord," I replied, "You know light shone upon Paul and he heard a voice from heaven. You've never given me an experience like that."

But you are not Paul and your calling is not the same as his. I speak to you the way you are called.

"All right, Lord. Then I'll be satisfied with the way You make Yourself known to me. I'll keep on doing what I'm doing, knowing it is Your way for me. When I help Oral answer his mail, or write a book, or when I listen to him when he's upset or exploding, or when we pray together, or when I just sit quietly by his side knowing he wants me there, I'll be giving my best to You and I'll expect miracles in return."

By the time I returned from my walk, God had begun to answer us in our struggle. The phone was ringing. The decision was made and it was *yes*.

I felt very much that God had answered. I had heard. That phone call was as much a confirmation of God's will for us as any answer we've ever gotten from Him. We had gotten through another hard decision and struggle.

My mind is now at peace about the way God chooses to talk to me in the *everydayness* of my life instead of an audible voice at different intervals or in thunderous tones as He did to Paul. I feel now as I pray daily in the prayer language of the Spirit that I will receive the quiet interpretation in words I can understand or in His words in the Bible which I read so often. I feel with Him all things are possible. And I believe God.

PETER TOO HAD A STORY TO TELL

When Peter got back to the boat, he had gotten an answer too. He shouted to his fellow disciples, "Look, here's the Master. It WAS Him we saw. I walked on the water to go to Him. I actually walked on the water. And when I got my eyes off Him, when I looked back at the storm, when I started to go under, I cried for Him to save me. He put His hand out and caught me just in time. Together we walked on the water back to the boat. And you see? The storm is over! We've arrived! We've gotten to the other side, like He said when we started. I've tested Him and He's REAL, He cares about us. He sees us and knows where we are all the time." What a testimony! Peter always saw Jesus in a different light after that. He felt a deeper understanding, a closer walk, a greater faith. He knew Jesus in a different and better way. Jesus had done so much for him. And He had worked through him to help the others. Peter had planted good seed.

THIS, JESUS DID FOR ME

There's no substitute for personal experience, for knowing Jesus and what He can do in your struggles.

An early American missionary asked one of his Indian

converts what he thought of Jesus. The Indian expressed his feelings in a most unusual way.

Stooping to the ground, he formed a circle with some dry leaves. He dropped a worm in the middle and then set fire to the leaves. The flames quickly encircled the helpless worm, causing it to squirm and wriggle as it searched in vain for some way to escape its fiery ordeal. Finally it sank motionless, exhausted by its futile efforts to save itself.

At that moment the Indian stretched forth his hand, gently lifted the helpless creature from certain death, laid it on the cool ground, and simply remarked, "This, Jesus did for me."

JESUS IS STILL REAL ENOUGH

That reminds me of another story that means a lot to me. Father Francis MacNutt, a Spirit-filled Jesuit priest, spoke once at ORU. In his heartwarming message he told of going on a mission to a North Dakota Indian reservation. He and a group of priests and nuns were having a dialogue with a group of Indians who had accepted Christ.

Finally an Indian man asked, "You say your Jesus did miracles for the people?"

"Yes."

"He healed the sick?"

"Yes, many times."

"You're His follower?"

"Yes."

"Do you do any miracles? Do you heal any sick person?"

Father MacNutt said they all were suddenly very quiet. When no one answered, the Indian said, "You say Jesus heals. You say He does miracles. But you don't heal. You don't do miracles. How do you explain that?"

With tears streaming down his cheeks, Father MacNutt told us that was the beginning of the change of his thinking about Jesus being real enough to intervene as miraculously in our lives today as He did 2,000 years ago.

What the Indian wanted was to know if the followers of Jesus Christ can still walk on the water. The answer is yes. We can when we use even our "little faith."

NOW ASK YOURSELF...

LIFE'S QUESTION: What should I do when my problems look so big my fear almost overcomes me? → **GOD'S WAY** SAY IT: I WILL REMEMBER THAT NO SIN OR FEAR OR PROBLEM IS BIGGER THAN MY SAVIOR. GOD IS GREATER THAN THE DEVIL AND BIGGER THAN ANYTHING THAT COMES AGAINST ME.

LIFE'S QUESTION: What can I do when everything around me is wrong and I'm going under? → **GOD'S WAY** SAY IT: I WILL REMEMBER JESUS' HAND IS STRETCHING OUT TO ME. HIS HAND IS ALWAYS THERE TO PULL ME UP.

LIFE'S QUESTION: What does it mean when God seems to talk to other people in such a big way and not to me? → **GOD'S WAY** SAY IT: GOD HAS GIVEN ME A WORK TO DO. HE WILL SPEAK TO ME OUT OF THE EVERYDAYNESS OF MY LIFE, OUT OF THE WAY HE DESIGNED MY LIFE. THAT IS HIS WAY FOR ME.

LIFE'S QUESTION: Sometimes I'm going along just fine but I get my eyes off Jesus and begin to go down. Will He still be there? → **GOD'S WAY** SAY IT: ANY TIME I CRY FOR JESUS HE WILL REACH DOWN TO ME. HE WILL CATCH ME JUST IN TIME.

LIFE'S QUESTION: Will I remember what God has done the next time I find myself going through problems and struggles? → **GOD'S WAY** SAY IT: THERE IS NO SUBSTITUTE FOR PERSONAL EXPERIENCE WITH GOD. I WILL FEEL A DEEPER UNDERSTANDING, A CLOSER WALK, A GREATER FAITH IN JESUS AFTER I'VE COME THROUGH MY FIRST STORM.

LIFE'S QUESTION: Can I ➤ GOD'S WAY
count on Jesus? Is He as able   SAY IT: I WILL BELIEVE WITH
to intervene in *my* life the   ALL MY HEART JESUS CAN
way He did 2,000 years ago?   STILL WALK ON THE WATER.
                                    AND HE CAN HELP ME WALK
                                    ON THE TOP OF MY STRUG-
                                    GLES. JESUS IS AS REAL TO-
                                    DAY AS HE EVER WAS.

PUTTING IT ALL TOGETHER FOR MYSELF

I WILL REMEMBER THAT NO SIN OR FEAR OR
PROBLEM IS BIGGER THAN MY SAVIOR. GOD IS
GREATER THAN THE DEVIL AND BIGGER THAN
ANYTHING THAT COMES AGAINST ME.

******

I WILL REMEMBER JESUS' HAND IS STRETCHING
OUT TO ME. HIS HAND IS ALWAYS THERE TO
PULL ME UP.   ******

GOD HAS GIVEN ME A WORK TO DO. HE WILL
SPEAK TO ME OUT OF THE EVERYDAYNESS OF MY
LIFE, OUT OF THE WAY HE DESIGNED MY LIFE.
THAT IS HIS WAY FOR ME.

******

ANY TIME I CRY FOR JESUS HE WILL REACH
DOWN TO ME. HE WILL CATCH ME JUST IN TIME.

******

THERE IS NO SUBSTITUTE FOR PERSONAL EXPERI-
ENCE WITH GOD. I WILL FEEL A DEEPER UNDER-
STANDING, A CLOSER WALK, A GREATER FAITH
IN JESUS AFTER I'VE COME THROUGH MY FIRST
STORM.   ******

I WILL BELIEVE WITH ALL MY HEART THAT JESUS
CAN STILL WALK ON THE WATER AND HE CAN
HELP ME WALK ON TOP OF MY STRUGGLES. JESUS
IS AS REAL TODAY AS HE EVER WAS.

Chapter Fifteen

What to do when Jesus tells you how to get the greatest miracle of your life!

"And Peter . . . said, Lord, if it be thou, bid me come unto thee on the water. And he said, COME . . ." (Matthew 14:28, 29).

Does Jesus have a way to tell you how to get the greatest miracle of your life?

Can you do what He tells you?

Is it as possible now as it was when He told Peter?

Can you really get your miracle?

YES, YOU CAN HAVE YOUR MIRACLE

You have a right to ASK FOR YOUR MIRACLE. GOD IS A GOD OF MIRACLES. And HE WANTS YOU TO HAVE your miracle. I know it! I experience it constantly.

Let me remind you that Peter cried, "Lord, if it is really You, tell me to come to You walking on the water. Tell me how to have the greatest miracle of my life. Tell me in this struggle how to save my life."

Jesus answered with one simple, powerful word: "COME!"

Now, instead of instantly obeying Jesus' command, Peter

could have said, "Lord, if I were you, I could walk on the water."

And Jesus could have answered, "Well, you are not Me."

EVIDENCE FOR YOUR FAITH

But that is not what Peter said or what Jesus answered. It's important for you to know this. Peter was really asking for evidence for his faith to act on. And Jesus gave him that EVIDENCE. He gave it to him. He said, in essence, "Yes, Peter, it is I, and you can prove Me by stepping out of the boat and coming to Me on the water. Although you have never walked on the water before, if you will obey and come as I have, you can walk to Me on the water."

When Peter received that evidence he made a decision to obey. He had a choice to make and he made it. With his "little faith" he made a *leap of faith.* He jumped out of the boat. When his feet touched the stormy waves, a miracle happened. The harvest came for the seed he was planting. The water became a liquid floor beneath his feet just as it had for Jesus: PETER WALKED ON THE WATER!

As I wrote that last paragraph I couldn't stop for a breath. I didn't want to stop until Peter's feet hit the water and he had his miracle. It excites me to think about that. Because actually I'm living it now. I'm saying, "Lord, that's me. That's me walking on the water of my struggles. I'm making *my* leap of faith."

I remember watching Richard when he was a little boy tottering on the edge of the pool. Rebecca, his older sister, was standing in the water coaxing him to jump! "Come on, Richard, jump, jump. I'll catch you. I won't let you go under. Come on!" I can feel the look on his face right now in the pit of my stomach. He'd shift from one foot to the other. Every muscle in his body would tighten. His face would display a combination of fear first. Then a look of daring excitement would light up his eyes and he'd make

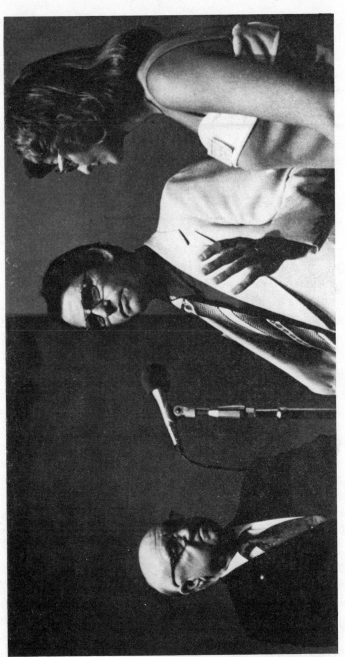

This man received inner assurance about a new job after learning about Seed-Faith. Now he's really getting ahead! He and his wife tell their story at an ORU Seminar.

his leap. I'd catch myself tensing with him as he was leaping out. And Rebecca never let his head go under. One time I caught myself yelling out, "He did it! He did it!" Everybody was looking — but it was OK! The expression on Richard's face was the look of an eagle. He swam half way across the pool, then his big sister had him in her arms. He'd made the big leap and he hadn't gone under. He had confidence to try it again, and this time he swam all the way, again and again.

LEARNING TO ACT ON THE EVIDENCE

I've seen this same thing happen to many others, too. It's simply a matter of getting *evidence for your faith,* then acting on that evidence and expecting God to give you your miracle.

A young couple who came to a seminar at ORU shared what happened to them when they received the evidence for their faith and acted on it. They had a little baby and were having trouble meeting their expenses. They planted seed here and there and said they got by on their Seed-Faith. The husband had unexpectedly been offered a job that was not exactly in his field of experience, but it offered a tremendous opportunity. He honestly didn't know whether to take the job or not. It was just a few days later that the couple came to the seminar. And something that happened there gave that man the evidence he had needed to know that he could handle the job and that it really had come to him as a result of his faith in God. It was the night when our Dr. Jimmy Buskirk, Dean of the ORU Theological Seminary, who preaches with me on many occasions, was giving his testimony of the healing of his eyes from blindness. Dr. Buskirk had told how a lady in his church approached him with a word from the Lord which he acted on and through which he got his miracle of healing. Our friend took Brother Jimmy's words as evidence upon which to allow his faith to work. It was evidence he needed for his faith to be released. He said, "I felt faith rising inside me, a kind of knowing, and I made my decision to take this job. My wife and I took a Seed-Faith project, giving out of our need for this desired result. As we left we had an inner assurance."

In a letter from him later, he told us he had fitted right into this new opportunity. They had found a new home, a church for their family, and a new outlook on life. The last letter I got from him said, "Brother Roberts, things are going so well with me and I know I must remember Who my Source is and keep trusting Him."

I agreed with him and wrote and told him so.

THE LEAP OF FAITH

Before Peter was willing to make his leap of faith, to actually jump out of a boat that was already sinking in the waves, he had to have evidence for his faith. He asked for evidence and got it.

An important thing to remember is faith is not blind. Faith *is not* a leap into the dark. Faith is not an unknowing state of mind. Faith is reaching an unshakable conviction, the deepest "gut feeling" you can ever have. This is stated clearly in Hebrews 11:1 —

"Now faith is the substance of things hoped for,
  the evidence of things not seen."

Faith is . . . the evidence. Evidence. Everything in life is based on evidence.

Evidence is all important. A court of law demands evidence to be presented before a verdict can be reached. You require evidence even that a chair will support your weight or you won't sit on it. You demand evidence the food you eat is not poisoned or you will not eat it. You do everything based upon evidence. Without evidence you draw back. You say, "No. I'm not going to do it!" And that's the way it should be.

Just before writing this chapter and as I was living Peter's experience with him, I was praying with Evelyn and a small group. We all had needs. Of course everybody thinks his need is the biggest. I was feeling that way about my need to obey God and have the courage to start building the CITY OF FAITH. I led the group in prayer in the Spirit. Since there were only about ten of us, and we were not in a public meeting — and we all used the prayer language — I felt it was proper for me to lead them in tongues and interpretation. As I prayed "in the Spirit," the interpretation quickly came from the Lord. In my own langugae I spoke it. The interpretation was:

> "The riches of Christ will eradicate the poverty of
> your spirit, and any material need you are suffering.
> Christ's riches in heaven will fill your mind and supply
> your financial needs. You will receive His riches with-
> out measurement by any human standards."

As the interpretation was given a hush fell over the group. Then God gave me a word of knowledge: "The evidence has been given and we rest our case before God. And it will stand up in God's court."

We were richly blessed in our hearts but more than that. God had given evidence that our minds could grasp. He gave us a knowing for our faith to act upon. Each of us left there believing the riches of Christ are real, they are for us, and we will receive them.

I am absolutely sure God will give an honest and believing heart solid evidence for his faith to act upon.

Let's remember the evidence Jesus gave Peter for his walking upon the water.

1. He gave Peter the evidence that He Himself was
   walking on the water and that He was doing it
   as a man.

2. He gave Peter the evidence by saying, "Come."

Giving assurance that if He in His humanness
could use His faith, Peter could use his also.

That is the evidence Jesus gave then. And it is the
evidence He gives you in the *now* of your troubled waters.

THE BIBLE IS THE GREATEST EVIDENCE FOR YOUR FAITH

The greatest basis for the evidence of faith is the Bible,
God's Holy Word. I believe the Bible, all of it. The Bible
tells us of the evidence of things not seen but nevertheless
very real. Now you really don't need faith *for the things you
can see.* You need faith for the *"things not seen."*

St. Paul states it like this:

> *"Eye hath not seen, nor ear heard . . . the things
> which God hath prepared for them that love
> him"* (1 Corinthians 2:9).

Paul makes it clear there are things God has prepared for
us that our physical eyes and ears cannot see or hear. He
adds:

> *"But God hath revealed them (these things eye
> can't see or ear hear) by his Spirit . . . because
> they are spiritually discerned"* (seen and heard
> only by your inner self, your spirit) (1 Corin-
> thians 2:10, 14).

JESUS IS THE NORM

I keep remembering that when Peter stepped onto the
water, he couldn't actually *see* that the raging waves would
become a pavement for him. He couldn't *hear* the calm, the
quiet that would follow when the storm ceased under his
feet. *Only his spirit* could see and hear that. But the things
that couldn't be seen physically COULD be seen spiritually.
The evidence was Jesus' own word, "COME."

A BUSINESS FRIEND

I have a very good friend who was able to start a business of his own about five years ago. He's done very well and today his business reaches worldwide. He began that business when he had the courage to get out of fear and into faith. He stepped out when he heard in his inner self Jesus say, "COME." Since I knew he had this faith, I was surprised when he said, "Oral, I'm scared to death about business in 1977. Inflation is getting bad. The political situation in countries I do business in is very touchy. I've about decided to pull back. Yet I know that may be the wrong move. I'm scared."

I said, "Listen, I remember when you started your business with just yourself, then with three people you hired. I remember the seed you planted for your miracle. You had faith and you expected God to guide and bless you, isn't that right?"

He said, "You're right. But I've grown to ninety employees and I've got to be careful."

I said, "OK. But be careful to stay in Seed-Faith. You've been walking on the water. Jesus isn't going to change no matter what the economy does or the political situation turns out to be. Your faith will work exactly as it has been working if you will work it."

He said, "Are you telling me it's all between me and God?"

I said, "You better believe it. Just remember it was all between Peter and Jesus out there on the stormy sea. They made it and so can you."

He smiled. "Oral, you've made my day. I'm going right now and call my head people together, tell them what you said, and start laying plans for the best year we've ever had."

Now I believe Jesus walking on the water is *not the exception*, it is the NORM. That's really what I was sharing with my friend. It is the norm for you to move forward, not backward. It is the norm for you to face your present situation and your future with faith, not fear. It is the norm to go through your struggles, not under with them.

It takes spiritual insight to grasp this truth of God for your life. This is why Jesus said to a man named Nicodemus:

"Except a man be born again he cannot enter into
the Kingdom of God."

He added, *"You must be born of the Spirit"* (John 3:5).

It is your *spiritual* rebirth and by seeing with your spirit that you see things not seen, you hear things not heard, you dream dreams not dreamed, you do things not done. The person inside you — the real you — gets up, stands up, and says, "Yes, Lord, I will come to You on the water. I will expect my miracle."

LORD, IF IT IS REALLY YOU . . .

We are not told how long it took for Peter and Jesus to join their spirits closely enough for Peter to know he could leave the boat. We probably have only the gist of their conversation. Still there was something in Jesus' voice to Peter that he couldn't let go of. And neither can you. Hear Jesus' word again: "Come!"

Peter wanted to come. But words were not enough. They never are.

Peter shouted, "Lord, if it is really You, command me to come to You on the water."

What did Peter mean? He was really saying:

"Jesus, I know You. I've walked and talked with You. You've shown me Your humanness. I know You're a man, a human being just like I am. You've taught me You have not used anything against the problems of life except the same thing available to me — faith in God. So if it's really You walking on these waters of danger and death, if it's really You, Jesus, then I can walk on them too through my own faith. They will become a liquid pavement under my feet. This storm will cease around me as it has ceased around You. The waves will no longer be dashing over me. They will be under me and I will be on top. If it's really You walking on the water in Your humanness, I can walk on it in my humanness!"

And Jesus said, "COME."

Let me tell you, that's powerful. I feel it now.

USE YOUR FAITH FOR MIRACLES

Don't forget that Peter was just an ordinary person at that time. He had not become the great apostle Peter, the man of mighty miracles which were later recorded in the book of Acts in our New Testament. He was an ordinary, impulsive, scared human being who had chosen to follow Jesus but had not yet come to fully know Jesus as He really is. He was struggling to know Jesus. He *wanted* to know. And that's what counts, when you want to know Jesus.

Don't forget that Jesus lived in His humanness in the exact way you and I have to live in our humaness. He used only His faith in God for miracles, the same way you and I can use our faith for miracles. Don't miss this great truth. It will do wonders for you.

One of my Missouri partners learned how to use his faith for miracles. He had to wait awhile for the evidence for his faith. But when he got it, miracles came his way so fast he could hardly count them. He learned of Seed-Faith at a Lay Seminar here at ORU, where he had reluctantly brought his mother. He said the things he heard at ORU were all new to him. While he wanted to ignore the feeling that was growing in him, he was still curious as to whether God was really as real as I had said He was. He talked to his wife about these things. And he began to study his Bible. Then a few days later he suddenly realized he no longer doubted. He knew if he planted a seed he would reap the harvest. He gave a sum of money as a seed. The very next day his miracles started coming. They've kept coming. They haven't stopped. And he hasn't stopped using his faith to receive them because he finally found the evidence!

I wanted to share that with you because it's important to realize the *time it takes* to receive the evidence for your faith is not as important as the fact *that you do receive it.* Getting yourself up to the moment when you can see with your spirit, when you can enter into that unshakable knowing, may take hours, days, even months or years, but it's worth it.

It took Peter only a moment — the flash of a second — to make his leap of faith *once he had the evidence to act on.* Releasing your faith then is quick. Then it is easy. You find that walking on the water is the most natural thing in the world once you have the evidence for your faith to do it. But however long it takes to get the evidence, get it. Just don't be misled into thinking that faith is presumption, or that faith is mere wishing. Faith is not jumping off the deep end. It's a knowing that comes in your heart, a knowing that won't leave. You can have evidence from God that will produce that knowing in your spirit. Long ago I made a decision that I will act only when I have that inner knowing. It's the only way I know to get miracles.

DARE TO TEST YOUR RELATIONSHIP WITH GOD

I remember one time when I shared an experience I had had in the very beginning of this ministry with a fellow minister. I had put God to the test for evidence that He had really called me to take His healing power to my generation. I described the steps I had taken and the conditions I had made. I told how those things had all been met. After hearing me, the minister said, "That would have scared me to death. I never could have lived it down if God had not answered me as He did you."

"In other words," I answered, "you are willing to trust

your life into the hands of God when you have not tested
Him and found the evidence that He will answer. Tell me,
without evidence, as is mentioned in Hebrews 11:1, how can
you exercise faith in God and know He will answer?"

He just shook his head. I watched that minister prosper
for awhile. But eventually he got involved in deals that
tested his credibility. I couldn't help but remember the time
he had admitted his fear of testing his relationship with God.

What I'm telling you about getting evidence for your
faith seems tough. But when the going gets rough — and it
will — you had better know in your heart you can *trust* God
to see you through.

FAITH IS SOMETHING YOU CANNOT DOUBT

I remind you that your faith becomes faith only after you
have done something with your inner self. It comes after
you've held on and secured solid evidence for knowing there
is a path in the trackless sea. It comes after you know that
you know that you know.

To put it another way:

> *Faith is not something you try to make
> yourself believe.*

> *Faith is something you cannot doubt.*

What that means is the Holy Spirit supernaturally
empties your spirit of doubt and fills you with an inner
knowing. Through this inner knowing, and in spite of
doubts that try to creep in, you actually cannot doubt in
the thing you are about to undertake.

Jesus said, *"Have faith in God"* (Mark 11:22). Jesus
means exactly what He says, "Have faith in God." He
wouldn't have told you and me to have faith in God if we
couldn't. So we can.

Having faith in God is being empty of doubt and full of

knowing. Knowing that you know that you know. That is the faith Jesus had even in His humanness. That is the faith Peter found he could have there on the tossing boat — a knowing inside.

When Peter made his decision to leap, to walk on the water, he *KNEW* he could walk on the water. He could not doubt it because the knowing filled his spirit and permeated his whole being. It was a whole-man experience of faith being released.

My friend, this is no wishful thinking. This is an indisputable fact. And it will be proven in your heart every time you feel a knowing inside and act on it, and discover you can do what you know you can do.

ONE WORD FROM JESUS CAN BE EVIDENCE ENOUGH

When Jesus said "COME" to the scared human being leaning over the edge of the tossing boat, He was giving His Word. And you can walk on His eternal Word.

The Word Jesus said, meant:

Yes, I am your Lord.

I am this same Jesus you have known.
Yes, I am walking on these troubled waters
by the faith of God in My heart, the
same faith of God that is in yours. This
is not an exception, it is the norm.

As you are human, I am human.

As you are in a storm of danger and death,
so am I.

The winds and waves are striking at Me the
same as they are at you.

The same kind of problem you are facing,
I am facing. And by My faith I am
walking on these problems.

So COME! COME! COME! WALK ON THE WATER
TO ME!

Jesus' Word is the evidence for your faith. His Word
will never fail. "Heaven and earth shall pass away, but my
words shall not pass away," Jesus said (Matthew 24:35).

I stand on the Word of God.

God speaks through it to me.

To me in my struggles, my storms.

To me in my hopes, my dreams, my calling to take His
    healing power to my generation, which includes you
    and your loved ones.

To me, Oral Roberts, a human being just like yourself.
    No difference at all. Depending on God just as you
    do.

Standing on the Word of God I faced a new life, the
beginning of my whole self coming into being. No longer
a stuttering, fearful person but one who knows in my heart
Jesus' Word tells me to *come* and *I can do it!*

That's exactly how I feel about you — and what I believe
for you.

NOW ASK YOURSELF...

LIFE'S QUESTION: What do ➤ **GOD'S WAY**
I do when I'm facing a SAY IT: I WILL REMEMBER
problem and can't find the JESUS HAS A WAY FOR ME TO
answer? GET MY MIRACLE AND IT IS
POSSIBLE FOR HIM TO TELL
ME WHAT IT IS.

LIFE'S QUESTION: How do ➤ **GOD'S WAY**
I take the first step toward SAY IT: I WILL ACT ON JESUS'
finding the answer to my COMMAND TO COME. I WILL
problems? WALK ON TOP OF MY STORM
— TO HIM.

LIFE'S QUESTION: How can → GOD'S WAY
I be sure I am taking the   SAY IT: GOD'S WORD IS THE
right step?   GREATEST EVIDENCE FOR
                             MY FAITH. IT PROVIDES A
                             KNOWING IN MY HEART
                             THAT I KNOW THAT I KNOW
                             THAT I KNOW . . .

LIFE'S QUESTION: What → GOD'S WAY
should I do when I have re-   SAY IT: I WILL ACT ON THAT
ceived the evidence of my   EVIDENCE AND MAKE MY
faith?   LEAP OF FAITH. I WILL
                             WALK THROUGH MY PROB-
                             LEM TOWARD JESUS.

LIFE'S QUESTION: Are mir- → GOD'S WAY
acles the exception rather   SAY IT: I WILL LEARN THAT
than the rule?   THE MIRACLES BROUGHT
                             ABOUT BY MY ACTION ARE
                             NOT THE EXCEPTION BUT
                             THE NORM. AND I WILL EX-
                             PECT THOSE MIRACLES IN
                             EVERY NEED I FACE.

LIFE'S QUESTION: How do → GOD'S WAY
I overcome the feeling that I SAY IT: I WILL HOLD ONTO
can't accomplish things as   THE FACT THAT JESUS AC-
Jesus did because I am just COMPLISHED HIS MIRACLES
a human being?   BY USING THE SAME THING
                             THAT IS AVAILABLE TO ME
                             — HIS FAITH IN GOD!

LIFE'S QUESTION: What is → GOD'S WAY
true faith?   SAY IT: WHEN I GET INTO
                             TRUE FAITH, THE FAITH OF
                             GOD, I CANNOT DOUBT. I
                             COME TO A PLACE WHERE I
                             KNOW AND THEN THROUGH
                             FAITH I CAN DO WHAT I
                             THOUGHT I COULD NOT DO.

PUTTING IT ALL TOGETHER FOR MYSELF

I WILL REMEMBER JESUS HAS A WAY FOR ME TO GET A MIRACLE AND IT IS POSSIBLE FOR HIM TO TELL ME WHAT IT IS.

* * * * * *

I WILL ACT ON JESUS' COMMAND TO COME. I WILL WALK ON TOP OF MY STORM — TO HIM.

* * * * * *

GOD'S WORD IS THE GREATEST EVIDENCE FOR MY FAITH. IT PROVIDES A KNOWING IN MY HEART THAT I KNOW THAT I KNOW THAT I KNOW...

* * * * * *

I WILL ACT ON THAT EVIDENCE AND MAKE MY LEAP OF FAITH. I WILL WALK THROUGH MY PROBLEM TOWARD JESUS.

* * * * * *

I WILL LEARN THAT THE MIRACLES BROUGHT ABOUT BY MY ACTION ARE NOT THE EXCEPTION BUT THE NORM. AND I WILL EXPECT THOSE MIRACLES IN EVERY NEED I FACE.

* * * * * *

I WILL HOLD ONTO THE FACT THAT JESUS AC-COMPLISHED HIS MIRACLES BY USING THE SAME THING THAT IS AVAILABLE TO ME — HIS FAITH IN GOD.

* * * * * *

WHEN I GET INTO TRUE FAITH, THE FAITH OF GOD, I CANNOT DOUBT. I COME TO A PLACE WHERE I KNOW AND THEN THROUGH FAITH I CAN DO WHAT I THOUGHT I COULD NOT DO.

Chapter Sixteen

How to pray short prayers and get the job done

"And Peter, beginning to sink, cried, saying, Lord, save me" (Matthew 14:30).

"LORD, SAVE ME!"

That's one of the shortest and best prayers I've ever heard. Somebody said, "If Peter had prayed any longer, he would have drowned."

There are several things I want to share about this.

FIRST. Peter did walk on the water. He got out of that tossing boat and walked on the water to Jesus. He DID it! And this can never be taken away from Peter, a human being like you and me. He walked on the water!

SECOND. In only seconds something went wrong. Out there on the water Peter did a very human thing. He got his eyes off Jesus — his Source — and began using his physical senses. He *listened* to the roaring of the storm. He *watched* the waves raging on either side of him. Suddenly what he *heard* and *saw* was too much. It was overpowering. His physical senses had failed him again. With a sinking feeling, Peter started to go down.

THIRD. But just before he went under he cried for Jesus!

Now you can criticize Peter for getting his eyes off his Source. You can criticize him for going back to his physical senses and failing when he was getting the job done by using his spirit first.

You can criticize Peter all right. But there's one thing you've got to say he did right. When he was in trouble, he cried for Jesus!

He cried just three words. "Lord, save me."

That reminds me of a story about two little girls who were playing outside. The older girl said, "Go in and tell Mommy to make us some jelly sandwiches."

The youngest girl went in and hurried right back without them.

"Well, where are the sandwiches?"

"Mommy said she was too busy."

"Well, you go back again."

Again she returned empty handed.

Then the older girl said, "You stay right here. I'll get 'em."

Pretty soon she returned, loaded down with delicious jelly sandwiches.

The baby sister said, "Mommy wouldn't fix 'em for me. How did you get her to do it for you?"

"I bawled for 'em," she replied.

Well, there's a time for crying, even bawling to God, as Peter did. I've done it many times, and will probably do it many more.

EVEN SHORT PRAYERS DO THE JOB

FOURTH. When Peter cried to Jesus, he spoke only three words. *There's something to be said for short prayers.*

A partner of this ministry wrote me and told me about

On one of our TV programs Evelyn reads aloud a letter from one of our dear partners who faced such terrible storms that she almost went under. But a short prayer from her heart opened up a whole new world for her.

the greatest struggle she had ever faced and how a prayer of only a few words had changed her life.

> Before I read your books, *Miracle of Seed-Faith* and *A Daily Guide to Miracles,* I lived in spiritual darkness. Almost everything I did was sinful. Almost every word that came from my mouth was putting the Lord down. I smoked two to three packs of cigarettes a day. I hated the world, the people around me, and myself. I got to the point where I couldn't even stand myself anymore because of the way I was living. If I wanted something, I took it. I was five years old when I started shoplifting. I am now twenty-four years old and have been arrested many times for shoplifting. I even went to a shrink but nothing seemed to help me. The temptation was too great. Every time I walked into a store I would come out with things I didn't even have a use for. Half the time I would throw the stuff away. I would just laugh to myself, saying, "I got away with it! No one saw me!"
>
> I never felt guilty about anything I did. I even involved myself in witchcraft, black magic and demon worship. I made a pact with the devil and denounced God. I got myself hooked on drugs. It was costing me a fortune and I found myself stealing to support my habit. One night I came to the end of my rope. I fell on my knees and cried, "God, what has happened to me?" I started crying. I had no right to call on God. But He answered. I have studied the Bible along with your books. I know now how much God loves me and wants to be involved in my life. I now have a good job, a nice place to live, enough food and money to pay my bills. But best of all, I have found Jesus. And I have learned to expect miracles in my life from Him.

It all happened because she had meant that short simple prayer of just six words: "God, what has happened to me?"

SHORT PRAYERS FROM THE HEART SAY A LOT

In the same way, when Peter cried, "Lord, save me," his heart was in it. And in these three words he was saying a lot.

His heart was talking. His spirit knew that regardless of the towering waves and the terrible noise of the storm, Jesus could save him.

Your spirit is so powerful. It is so much more powerful than any of your five physical senses. I keep telling you that because every time I tell you I am telling myself.

When I lay so ill with tuberculosis, my physical senses could see or feel no hope. Mamma would come to the side of my bed and say, "Oral, pray."

"Why, Mamma?"

"Jesus can raise you up."

"Mamma, I don't know how to pray."

Her answer was a classic. And it's helped me so many times. She said, "Oral, you don't have to know how to pray. Just talk to Jesus out of your heart. He'll do the rest."

I finally did exactly that. And I found she knew what she was talking about. The short prayer that came from my heart got things going in the right direction for Jesus to give me my miracle. That short prayer started me toward my magic moment. I said one word: "Jesus!" But my whole being was in the word, "Jesus!"

A little later I added two words: "Save me!" Then: "Heal me!"

I can feel it now right in the pit of my stomach, and it feels good.

JESUS' HANDS WILL LIFT YOU UP

Peter's short prayer captured a magic moment for him.

Usually we only say a short prayer if we're in trouble. And you know, if Peter only had enough time to pray a little three-word prayer, he was going down pretty fast.

But faster still two powerful hands reached down and pulled Peter back up. They were the hands of the Man who was walking on the water, the Man who had told Peter to prove Him by coming.

Those same hands had scooped out the bed for the oceans. They had flung the stars into place. They had sculptured the mountains. They had painted the sunrise.

But at that moment — Peter's moment of need — those hands were concerned about one sinking human being who was trying to walk on the water. Those hands made the difference!

Peter felt the lifting power of Jesus' hands. And by this time he knew who Jesus was. Jesus had given proof that not even a storm could suck him under when he said even a three-word prayer.

Even if he had only said "Jesus," I believe those hands would have pulled him up. Really, I believe, if he only had the thought strong enough in his heart, Jesus would have felt it, and pulled him up.

LIFE BEGINS WITH A PARTNERSHIP WITH JESUS

I received a letter from a young girl who had gone almost all the way under. She had somehow gotten involved in homosexual relationships and had accepted that as her way of life. Just when it seemed no hope was left, this girl reached up for Jesus. She told me in her letter that so many didn't believe she could change into a normal person again. But she said as she started to read the Bible she was deeply impressed and strengthened in her inner self by a thought that kept leaping up in her, "There is nothing impossible with God." Finally, she cried out, "God, You can do anything." She said, "The only way I can describe what happened is that in the deepest part of my being something changed. I knew it. Even when people thought I was putting them on, I knew I was changed. Today I am living a normal and happy married life with two lovely children. The homosexual tendency had gotten such a hold on me, there seemed no way out. But when the Bible showed me

God can do anything, I knew that meant He could change me — and He did!"

She added, "My life began when I started a partnership with Jesus."

Don't you know there must have been a moment when it dawned on Peter that JESUS WALKING ON THE WATER meant that God can do anything?

Peter's life really began when he entered into a partnership with Jesus. It was in that partnership that they walked on the water together. And they walked back to the boat together. It was their partnership that caused the calm, and the boat to arrive on the other side.

This is very meaningful to me. It takes me all the way back to my first prayer, short as it was, and to that magic moment when Jesus healed my stuttering tongue, when He healed my tuberculosis, when He told me He was giving me the Call of God to bring His healing to the people. I want to keep my partnership with Jesus going. *There are so many more magic moments ahead.*

NOW ASK YOURSELF...

LIFE'S QUESTION: Should I ➤ GOD'S WAY
feel defeated when all of a sudden my miracle seems to stop?

SAY IT: I WILL REMEMBER THAT WHATEVER HAS BEEN ACCOMPLISHED BY MY FAITH CAN NEVER BE TAKEN FROM ME. WHAT HAS HAPPENED ALREADY CANNOT BE REVERSED.

LIFE'S QUESTION: What do ➤ GOD'S WAY
I do when I start to sink?

SAY IT: WHEN I'M IN TROUBLE I'LL CRY FOR JESUS. THERE'S A TIME FOR CRYING — EVEN TO GOD.

LIFE'S QUESTION: If things → **GOD'S WAY**
crowd in on me so fast I don't   SAY IT: PRAYER CAN BE ONE
have time to really pray, what   WORD OR A THOUSAND. NO
should I do?   MATTER HOW SHORT MY
                                    PRAYER IS, JESUS WILL HEAR
                                    AND IT WILL BE ENOUGH.

LIFE'S QUESTION: How can → **GOD'S WAY**
I pray? I don't know how to   SAY IT: WHEN I DON'T KNOW
talk to God.   WHAT TO SAY I WILL JUST
                                    TALK OUT OF MY HEART.
                                    JESUS WILL RESPOND TO MY
                                    HEART'S TALKING.

LIFE'S QUESTION: When it → **GOD'S WAY**
seems like I'm about to go   SAY IT: I WILL REST IN THE
under, what can I do?   KNOWLEDGE THAT I WILL
                                    NOT GO UNDER. JESUS'
                                    HANDS ARE ALWAYS THERE
                                    TO PULL ME UP.

LIFE'S QUESTION: Can I be → **GOD'S WAY**
sure Jesus is with me?   SAY IT: JUST AS JESUS AND
                                    PETER WALKED TOGETHER
                                    BACK TO THE SAFETY OF THE
                                    BOAT, I CAN KNOW JESUS IS
                                    WALKING WITH ME. TO-
                                    GETHER WE HAVE A PART-
                                    NERSHIP THAT WILL LEAD
                                    TO MANY MIRACLES . . . TO
                                    MANY MAGIC MOMENTS.

PUTTING IT ALL TOGETHER FOR MYSELF

I WILL REMEMBER THAT WHATEVER HAS BEEN
ACCOMPLISHED BY MY FAITH CAN NEVER BE
TAKEN FROM ME. WHAT HAS HAPPENED ALREADY
CANNOT BE REVERSED.

WHEN I'M IN TROUBLE I'LL CRY FOR JESUS. THERE'S A TIME FOR CRYING — EVEN TO GOD.

* * * * * *

PRAYER CAN BE ONE WORD OR A THOUSAND. NO MATTER HOW SHORT MY PRAYER IS, JESUS WILL HEAR AND IT WILL BE ENOUGH.

* * * * * *

WHEN I DON'T KNOW WHAT TO SAY I WILL JUST TALK OUT OF MY HEART. JESUS WILL RESPOND TO MY HEART'S TALKING.

* * * * * *

I WILL REST IN THE KNOWLEDGE THAT I WILL NOT GO UNDER. JESUS' HANDS ARE ALWAYS THERE TO PULL ME UP.

* * * * * *

JUST AS JESUS AND PETER WALKED TOGETHER BACK TO THE SAFETY OF THE BOAT, I CAN KNOW JESUS IS WALKING WITH ME. TOGETHER WE HAVE A PARTNERSHIP THAT WILL LEAD TO MANY MIRACLES . . . TO MANY MAGIC MOMENTS.

Chapter Seventeen

How to expect a miracle in your struggles

"Wherefore didst thou doubt?" (Matthew 14:31).

You may have many questions about the possibility of God's miracles coming to your life. Perhaps, like me, it is hard for you to grasp. My trouble was that my doubt would get in the way of what God really wanted to do. Here are questions I asked (and sometimes still do):

Can I afford to believe God is near me?

Is He really at the point of my need?

Can I depend on it that Jesus is sending a miracle toward me in the struggle I am in NOW?

YOU CAN'T AFFORD NOT TO BELIEVE

At times my struggles hit me so hard I find myself asking, can I afford not to risk believing? Can I really afford not to believe? Is there anyone or anything I can turn to, with any hope at all, except God? Do I have any other choice?

Here's what I learned and am still learning that really has helped me get through my struggles or to be in a position to get through them — things that have helped me deal successfully with the doubts the devil throws at me.

When their little girl received healing from a serious burn, this family learned that God is always at the point of their need.

JESUS WILL BE THERE ON TIME

I learned that before you can stop doubting, you have to come to the realization that there is a *direct and very personal connection between you and God in your present condition.* I say present condition because Jesus came to the disciples in their immediate condition, in their immediate need. He didn't wait until it was all over and they had gone under. He was there on time. And Jesus will always be on time. I am not embarrassed to tell you that I often have to say: God will always be on time to help me in my need. I say it out loud to myself. I say it under my breath. And I say it again: GOD WILL ALWAYS BE ON TIME.

I received a letter from the parents of a little girl several months ago. They told me about an accident their daughter had had that would have meant her death if the Lord had not come to her at her exact moment of need. The child had accidentally pulled some boiling coffee over on herself and suffered third degree burns. The second day after that her temperature started rising. As her mother was dialing the doctor, the little girl started having convulsions. And when she got off the phone, it looked as though there was no life left in her daughter. Her husband was there by this time. And knowing nothing else to do, the couple dropped to their knees beside the child and began to pray in the Spirit. When they opened their eyes their child was breathing again, and by the time the ambulance arrived, she was just fine. Jesus had gotten there first with a direct miracle. And He had been on time. After that there was no room in that family for doubt. They had learned that Jesus was at the point of their need — ALWAYS AT THE POINT OF THEIR NEED. Every time I get a letter like this I find my own faith strengthened to believe God will always be on time in *my* need.

THERE IS NO REASON TO FEAR GOD

It was scary out there on the troubled waters. As your struggle envelops you, it is impossible to see with your eyes the help you must have to get through. For your eyes see the struggle —

> Disappointment
> Discouragement
> Loneliness
> Rejection
> Guilt
> Frustration
> Failure
> Helplessness
> Fear of the unknown
> Fear you will go under

You see that human resources are *not* enough. That your problem or hurt is bigger than any answer you can see. You can see no change in sight. You can see no hope for miracles. I know this feeling of helplessness. And you know when you keep encountering storms, there's the danger of growing used to them. You begin to have a feeling of helplessness.

So in your feelings of helplessness, you do exactly what the disciples did in their storm — you get frightened. They got so frightened that the appearance of Jesus on top of the water walking toward them didn't seem real. Doubt filled their minds, driving out their faith and increasing their fear until "they cried out for fear."

The fear of the twelve disciples did not reach its height until Christ appeared walking on their troubled waters. Isn't that strange? Jesus was coming to them at the point of their need. He was on time. But they were accustomed to what their physical eyes could see, not to what their spirit could see. They were more accustomed to the storm than to having Jesus come to them — in their need, and on time. Well, Jesus came. He was there. They had no reason to doubt, or fear, but they did.

Let me tell you about a couple who came to ORU for a seminar. The woman had been ill for a long while. They had done all they knew to do in the way of medical help for her. And they didn't know where to turn. She had been ill for so long she had become accustomed to the pain and he to the drawn look on her face. They said, "Yes, we thought we knew God was near but it was so hard to condition ourselves to look to Him for help." As a matter of fact, they weren't looking for a miracle!

They said later, "We weren't sure we should expect God to do anything. At the end of the four-day Seminar when the time came for the healing service on Sunday morning, you invited all of us with needs to come through the line to be touched and receive healing prayers. This was new to us, in spite of the fact we had been watching you on television."

Then the wife said, "When my husband brought me down with all the others I felt more and more that I had a little faith. I was remembering you had told us we had no reason to fear God because He is a good God. You had told us to keep our hopes up, that God was closer to us than the breath in our nostrils. You even said we had to want to get well."

Reading her letter, I nodded to myself. I was thrilled and a little amazed how well she had heard what God was saying through me.

She finished her letter by saying, "The Lord showed me I couldn't continue to be afraid and still expect to get well. I was actually trembling with expectation when you gently touched my forehead. Although I didn't hear your exact words as you prayed, your touch carried something in it I had never felt before. Then I remembered your saying: 'Let my hand be an extension of God's hand.' Well, that's when I saw — really grasped it — that God's hand was touching me. Me. My doubt was gone. My husband and I were weeping. My miracle had started and we knew it."

This couple has written me several times since. Sometimes just to praise the Lord. Sometimes to tell me of other struggles. They keep learning. I keep learning how near God is, how He wants us to take our doubts to Him, to remember HIS HANDS CAN TOUCH US, and we can have a miracle!

ALWAYS EXPECT A MIRACLE

One of the most important things to learn is that before you can stop doubting, you have to stop being afraid of miracles. In spite of the fact that the disciples had been with Jesus and had seen Him perform miracles for other people, they were afraid when He came with a miracle for THEM. They were not expecting a miracle for themselves. And when it came it frightened them. They almost missed receiving the very miracle Jesus was bringing them in the midst of their struggles.

Is this the way it is with you? Are you afraid of a miracle happening to you? How grateful I am that I have learned not to be afraid, but to expect miracles. *I believe the very secret of life is in expecting miracles.*

That was also the case of a man from California who came to Tulsa for a visit with his relatives. While at their home, his wife came down with a sudden case of uremic poisoning, which was followed rapidly by a heart attack. The doctors gave her very little hope to live. At first the man went into panic. He was away from home. His wife was dying. But suddenly a suggestion helped him to keep his hopes up. His relatives suggested he telephone our Abundant Life Prayer Group in the Prayer Tower. He had never done anything like that before. He'd always had sort of a fear to think of God in terms of asking for a miracle.

But now, he not only asked for one, he made some very specific requests. Naturally, his wife's healing was his main concern. But he also wanted her to be able to drive with him back to California. And he wanted her to be able to return to Tulsa with him again the next year. It looked impossible. But the call to the Prayer Tower, and the prayer offered with him on the phone by the prayer partner, helped him to start believing God for a miracle for his wife. It was touch and go but he kept saying, "I called the Prayer Tower. They prayed with me for a miracle. They made me feel God really cares. God is at the point of my wife's need of healing."

He got his wife to think of God in this way. In spite of everything, however, it *looked* like she would die. Then one morning after a terrible night things changed. His wife had a different look on her face.

Sixteen days later he took her home to California with him in their station wagon. Her healing is progressing rapidly and they currently have plans to return to Oklahoma for another vacation. It turned out like that because they reached the place in their spirit where they were no longer afraid to ask for a miracle. They were no longer afraid to be specific with God. They learned they could walk on water. God could get them through this terrible need.

BEING SPECIFIC WITH GOD IS A GOLDEN KEY TO MIRACLES

I remember the very first time I experienced God's healing power working through me. As a young preacher it was part of my ministry to pray with people. But I only knew how to offer general prayers. In the pulpit I would pray for the congregation's health, their spiritual welfare, their betterment in life. I wasn't familiar with any other way of praying for people. I didn't really know how to pray in a specific way for a specific need to be met. I didn't know I should be specific. As I look back I don't think people expected specific personal prayers. Even today, I find some are a little afraid for me to get specific, to call out their specific problem to God, to ask God to give a miracle for *it*.

But the day came when a terrible need was thrust upon me. I received a phone call from the wife of a deacon in the little church I pastored. "Clyde is hurt," she said. "Come quick."

I asked another man from the church to go with me and we went rushing to the garage that this man owned. He had dropped a heavy motor on his foot and crushed it. His wife had called the doctor but we got there ahead of him because he was tied up with another difficult case. We found our friend rolling on the floor in excruciating pain, holding his foot.

The motor had cut through the shoe leather and blood was seeping out. I stood there a moment, looking and listening as Clyde Lawson groaned with the pain. He twisted and turned and actually yelled, he hurt so badly.

Without conscious thought I felt something sweep through me. I wanted to reach out and touch the foot. Instantly I leaned down, brushed my hand over it, and said a short prayer, something like, "Jesus, heal Clyde of his crushed foot."

Raising back up I turned to the man who had accompanied me. But just then Clyde got up from the floor. He started moving his foot around and around. He sat back down and took the blood-stained shoe off. He stood up and started stomping his foot on the floor.

I didn't understand. Why was he stomping his foot when seconds before he had been writhing on the floor in pain?

I BEGAN TO UNDERSTAND

"Oral Roberts," he said, calling me by my full name.

Still confused, I said, "Yes!"

"Oral Roberts, what did you do to me?"

"Nothing!" I said, "Nothing!"

A shadow of fear, and then awe came over his face.

"Yes, you did," he said.

"No, I didn't. I didn't do anything!"

"Well, what did you do when you touched my foot?"

"Well, I just had a feeling that I wanted to touch your foot and ask God to heal you of the pain." I still didn't know quite what he was driving at.

He said, "Look at my foot. There's no cut. The blood is dried up. It doesn't hurt. It's well."

Holding the shoe, cut through from the top, he said, "See? Here's the shoe. And there's the motor I dropped on my foot. I tell you, my foot is healed!"

Actually, all three of us were overwhelmed. I left quickly. My friend, Bill Lee, who had come with me, was nearly in a state of shock.

"Oral Roberts (he too called me by my full name. I was to learn later that most people would do that. I don't know why but they do), can you do that all the time?"

I was so surprised by his question all I could blurt out was, "Good Lord, no!"

Quietly he said, "If you could, you could bring a renewal to the Church. You could really bring Christ to people in their needs."

Then I began to understand. I had seen Jesus walking on the water in the storm of pain a friend was going through. And I had been a part of that walk of healing for his injury. I had done it partly because I got *specific* in my prayer for him. But it went further than that. It was the beginning, although I didn't know it then, of all I am doing now in the healing ministry.

DEAR LORD ... WHAT IF???

As I pondered this miracle I thought, "Dear Lord, what if I COULD be an instrument of Yours to bring Your healing to people? What if . . .?"

I remembered in a vague sort of way what God had said when He healed me, "Son, you are to take My healing power to your generation."

I continued to ponder this in my heart. But months passed before I came into a knowing in the deepest part of my being that I could be God's instrument of healing. It was through that knowing within that I began to stop being frightened of the supernatural.

That happened in 1946. A year later I began this healing ministry.

I KNEW I COULD DO IT AGAIN AND AGAIN

Only last year, thirty years later, I received a beautiful letter from Clyde Lawson recounting again the details of his miracle and renewing his friendship. Although it had been thirty years before, it still had a tremendous positive effect upon me. I know Clyde's healing was an act of God at that particular time to prove to me if I could walk on the water once for someone's healing I could do it again, and again, and again.

Without that proof, I would never have begun the following year to enter the full-time healing ministry that has consumed my whole being ever since. I would never have made my leap of faith. There would be no Oral Roberts University, no joining of the healing hands of God through prayer and medicine that God is helping me accomplish today. The test that day with Clyde left no more room for doubt. I could take the next few months to sort things out in my believing and thinking. I was beginning to see I could face my doubt, face my lack of praying for people in a specific way for their needs. I was beginning to see there were a lot of Clyde Lawsons in the world who were hurt with all kinds of problems and struggles and had to have somebody who would follow his inner feeling to touch and pray for them.

The moment of understanding may have come to you too. It may not have. But I've got a feeling it will come. You will learn you can stop doubting and start believing. You will learn you can get specific with God.

NOW ASK YOURSELF...

LIFE'S QUESTION: When → **GOD'S WAY**
I'm facing a need, can I af- SAY IT: I CAN'T AFFORD NOT
ford to believe God is at the TO BELIEVE. THERE IS NOTH-
point of my need? ING AND NO ONE I CAN TURN
TO WITH ANY HOPE BUT
GOD. PEOPLE AND THINGS
ARE INSTRUMENTS TO HELP
ME BUT GOD IS MY ANSWER.

LIFE'S QUESTION: What if → **GOD'S WAY**
my need is urgent and I have SAY IT: I WILL REMEMBER
to have an answer RIGHT JESUS DEALS WITH ME IN MY
NOW? PRESENT CONDITION, MY IM-
MEDIATE NEED. HE DIDN'T
LET THE DISCIPLES GO
UNDER. HE WAS THERE ON
TIME. AND HE ALWAYS WILL
BE ON TIME FOR ME.

LIFE'S QUESTION: What → **GOD'S WAY**
should I do when I'm so used SAY IT: I WILL LEARN TO
to being surrounded by prob- LOOK THROUGH THE STORM
lems that I'm scared when FOR JESUS. I WILL EXPECT
Jesus comes to me with a HIS MIRACLES INSTEAD OF
miracle? FEARING THEM. I WILL WEL-
COME HIS PRESENCE IN-
STEAD OF SHRINKING FROM
IT.

LIFE'S QUESTION: Should I ➤ GOD'S WAY
pray specifically about my needs rather than in a general way?

SAY IT: I CAN BRING CHRIST MORE POWERFULLY TO MY NEED WHEN I AM SPECIFIC IN MY REQUEST. I WILL TELL HIM EXACTLY WHAT MY NEED IS.

LIFE'S QUESTION: What ➤ GOD'S WAY
will happen when I come into a fuller understanding and a closer relationship with God?

SAY IT: I WILL REALIZE I CAN BE GOD'S INSTRUMENT OF HEALING AND BLESSING. I CAN LEARN TO STOP FEARING THE SUPERNATURAL AND GOD CAN WORK MIRACLES THROUGH ME AGAIN AND AGAIN AND AGAIN.

PUTTING IT ALL TOGETHER FOR MYSELF

I CAN'T AFFORD NOT TO BELIEVE. THERE IS NOTHING AND NO ONE I CAN TURN TO WITH ANY HOPE BUT GOD. PEOPLE AND THINGS ARE INSTRUMENTS TO HELP ME BUT GOD IS MY ANSWER.

* * * * * *

I WILL REMEMBER JESUS DEALS WITH ME IN MY PRESENT CONDITION, MY IMMEDIATE NEED. HE DIDN'T LET THE DISCIPLES GO UNDER. HE WAS THERE ON TIME. AND HE ALWAYS WILL BE ON TIME FOR ME.

* * * * * *

I WILL LEARN TO LOOK THROUGH THE STORM FOR JESUS. I WILL EXPECT HIS MIRACLES INSTEAD OF FEARING THEM. I WILL WELCOME HIS PRESENCE INSTEAD OF SHRINKING FROM IT.

I CAN BRING CHRIST MORE POWERFULLY TO MY
NEED WHEN I AM SPECIFIC WITH MY REQUEST.
I WILL TELL HIM EXACTLY WHAT MY NEED IS.

❋ ❋ ❋ ❋ ❋ ❋

I WILL REALIZE I CAN BE GOD'S INSTRUMENT OF
HEALING AND BLESSING. I CAN LEARN TO STOP
FEARING THE SUPERNATURAL, AND GOD CAN
WORK MIRACLES THROUGH ME AGAIN AND AGAIN
AND AGAIN.

Chapter Eighteen

How to find the purpose in your struggles and make it work for you

"And when they were come into the ship, the wind ceased" (Matthew 14:32).

One of the most valuable lessons Peter learned from his experience that night of walking on the water was that as long as he kept his eyes on Jesus, as long as he kept his inner belief working, the storm was subject to him the same as it was to Jesus. Even in his humanness he found that his faith, though it was only little faith, was stronger than the destructive forces around him.

As soon as he looked to the Greatest Reality of all — our Lord Jesus Christ, he immediately came into the protective power of that Great Reality. It became a magic moment in which he actually walked on the water.

PURPOSE OF OUR STORMS

Though Peter started to sink and had to call on Jesus to help him, he was able to walk back to the boat arm-in-arm with his Lord. And at that point the Scriptures tell us *"the wind ceased."* The storm was over!

You see? As soon as Peter's miracle was accomplished,

the storm had spent itself. There is *purpose* in our struggles!

It doesn't come easy for me to say, there is a purpose in our struggles. I've always had a difficult time understanding it. There are times now that it baffles me. I know from Peter's experience, and through hundreds of my own, THERE IS PURPOSE IN OUR STRUGGLES.

But what was the purpose of this storm for Peter and the other disciples? Why did they have to go through this struggle?

Well, first of all, the disciples discovered that wherever Jesus sent them, there would probably be a storm. And second, they discovered that within that storm was the possibility of a miracle. (Will you read that again please?)

I've put this to the test many times. Wherever I go, whatever I do, in trying to do God's will, I invariably find struggle, conflict, fear, danger. A storm of some kind seems always to be in my path. I hear myself saying:

"This looks bad."

"I cannot do it."

"I'll never make it."

I admit I get tired of the struggle. I wish I didn't have to go through it so often. But it always happens.

And you know I rarely ever discover the purpose of a storm while I am in it. When I suffer, the reason for it seems to escape me. My pain has a way of clouding my brain, of blinding my vision, of blunting my understanding that all things work together for my good (Romans 8:28). Over and over I ask WHY. And even that question increases my suffering.

Only after I get control of my inner self, only after I stand up on the inside, only after I respond with my spirit can I think of expecting a miracle that will take me through the struggle. Sometimes it's only after the miracle has brought me through that I can see there was a purpose for it. Only then can I see I have made progress through that struggle and am doing something about it with my faith. Only then am I better able to face the next struggle. And I know another will come my way as surely as the storm struck the disciples that night. I am no bettter than they were, I am no worse off than they were. A storm is a storm, a struggle is a struggle, and Jesus is Jesus, and He is still walking on the water to us — to you and me.

OUR PURPOSE IS TO LEARN MORE
OF JESUS' HUMANNESS

I think Peter had to go through this storm for the purpose of learning more about the humanness of Jesus. He certainly didn't know very much about it at this time in his life.

Jesus was a man in every sense of the word. He was just like us. He felt what we feel. He saw what we see. He went through struggles the same way we do. And in facing His conflicts and storms He used the same things available to us — *the Word of God, prayer,* and *faith.*

Even in his conflicts with the devil when He was tempted on the mount, Jesus used no more than the Word of God, prayer, and faith. And He won over the devil. He came through that fearful storm of temptation. He got through His struggle. He made it! (Read Matthew 4:1-11.)

Now you may be tempted to think Jesus could walk on the water because He was the Son of God. But He did it as a man! We're not told how He used the Scriptures in this situation. We are told though that He had been in *prayer.* And we also know He used *faith* which was available to all His disciples.

Peter was a man too, a rather ordinary man at this time. We know Peter today as a very powerful man of God in the Early Church. But during this storm Peter's greatness had not yet developed. What's important here is that even as an ordinary man he was able to grasp the fact Jesus wanted him to get out of the storm. Jesus wanted him to get through the struggle of his life. Jesus wanted him to walk on the water and experience the miracle of deliverance.

Right at this point, many people don't know that God is a good God. They fail to understand the humanness with which He clothed His only begotten Son when He had Him born of a woman, to walk among us as a man. It's hard for them to see, as it was for me, that Jesus is really part of their lives on this earth — that He came to enter into their sufferings and to bring them abundant life.

It's been a struggle for me to get this fact across to people. It's been my message, my mission, my calling of God. Like Peter, I have been in the valley of the shadow of death. Like Peter, I came to know that Jesus wanted me to come through it, to come to Him walking on the water.

No matter how little or ordinary you feel, Jesus wants you to come through your struggles. Believe that half the battle is won when you know He wants you to come through.

PETER LEARNED SOMETHING NEW ABOUT FAITH

Peter saw too that Jesus wanted to show him something about faith. He wanted Peter to learn that faith is faith, even if it's a little faith — just like gold is gold, even if it's a little gold. Jesus wanted Peter to know little faith is enough to get you started walking on the water. It's enough to start you through your struggles.

I think after the wind had ceased, Peter could see the purpose of the storm more clearly. He realized this wouldn't be the last storm or bad experience he would face. But he had seen Jesus in His humanness use His faith to walk on the water. He had heard Jesus urge him in his own humanness to use his faith and walk on the water too.

Peter had learned HE . . . COULD . . . FACE . . . EVERY STORM . . . WITH . . . AN . . . INNER . . . KNOWING. You and I can do it too and we're going to do it.

Listen with your heart to this letter from the parents of

an Oral Roberts University student. You'll be able to see that they have learned something about the inner knowing. This letter really touched my spirit as I read it. You'll appreciate it too.

Dear President Roberts:

I want to share with you the feelings my precious wife and I have experienced this past twelve months.

Our daughter Sue was about to graduate from high school. We were looking for a college with a school of music for her to attend. She received an invitation from ORU to attend the spring youth seminar. We were all delighted for her to have this opportunity.

Then the big question. Could she audition and be enrolled as a voice major at ORU?

We contacted the Chairman of Fine Arts. He arranged an audition for our Sue. Then the worrying hit me. How, God, could I afford this? Six hundred miles from home, little money, and never had our daughter been away from us. Was it to be a possibility?

After the youth seminar was over, I wish I had been able to tape our daughter's praises for the University. I knew she wanted very much to enroll in the fall. But again that big question. How, God, can I afford this for her?

About two weeks later we were officially notified by ORU of her acceptance. We prayed. God told me, "You can do it!" Our business was not doing good, we needed to rebuild or buy a new press. But, I told my family — "I can do it! Sue, send the room deposit, quick. Send all they ask for. WE WILL MAKE IT!" Then I said, "Sue, God, not me alone, will pay your tuition." Together we started to work, God as my Guide and my Source.

My wife and I work long hours. We miss our Sue. But how the rewards keep coming! With God as our Guide and Source, our business has grown, profits are growing, the future is bright. My wife and I feel this past year has been our best year in thirty-five years of marriage. We know planting our seed and sending our Sue to ORU has reaped many dividends.

And now as this school year is drawing to a close we are already looking forward to our daughter's returning as a sophomore next year. We are so thankful — we have been blessed! The freshman year bills are paid in full. The first deposit of $100 on next year's room has been made. What a wonderful feeling. We have received our miracle.

This couple has learned one of the most important lessons of all. And that is by keeping our eyes on Jesus, by believing through Him that we can make it, God will act! God will be our Guide and Source. God will keep us going. God will keep giving us that wonderful feeling inside. We will continue to receive miracles.

HOW TO KEEP YOUR EYES ON JESUS

I believe the greatest purpose of your struggles is to learn through your spirit to see the face of Jesus, to see Him with your inner sight, which is the best way of all to see. I believe it is only through your struggles you can learn to see with your spirit . . . to *see* Jesus walking on the water and *hear* Him tell you to walk on the water to Him. Again I say, only through your struggles. Again I say, each struggle has a purpose.

JESUS IS IN A DIFFERENT FORM TODAY

Let me remind you that although Jesus is no longer in a human form, He is more alive, more real than ever. He was crucified, dead and buried. And God raised Him from the dead, giving Him a new form, a form that is unlimited and invisible. It is on that plane and in that form He comes to us today. It's the most thrilling thing in the world, for now we can get ALL THE HELP we need. Why? Because Jesus has come back in the invisible, unlimited form of the Holy Spirit to be IN us, as well as to be WITH us.

I know Jesus is here. In the NOW. In our struggles — with us and giving us inner power to rise up with faith and

One thing I always tell my ORU students is to keep their eyes on Jesus.

WALK ON THE WATER of every one of those struggles.
I know it. You know it too. I have to believe you do.

HOW WE CAN SEE GOD

Some say it's through a *sixth* sense that we see Jesus. I
call it something else, something better. It's our spirit, our
inner self. It is through our spirit we can see Jesus' face
illumined before us, we can feel His presence within us and
all over us. We can taste His goodness filling our being.

Here's a story that helped me see this. One night a little
boy was sleeping. He was suddenly awakened by the sound
of someone in his room. He saw a shadowy figure moving
about and it frightened him. He didn't know it, but his
father had gotten up to close the windows because it had
started to rain. The boy cried out, "Who is it?"

The father, not wanting to further frighten the boy, and
not wanting the boy to wake the other children, simply
took the flashlight that he had and shined it.

Now he didn't shine it on the boy. Because as we know,
to shine a light in the boy's face would have blinded the
little fellow. He would have become more frightened and
this would have made it all the worse.

So the father simply turned the flashlight on his own
face. And the little boy said, "Oh, it's you, Dad." He turned
over and went back to sleep.

That's exactly what Jesus did that dark night the disciples were in the storm on the Sea of Galilee. Roaring
thunder, flashing lightning, pouring rain, tossing waves,
shaking boat, terrified men. They too saw a shadowy figure.
The sight and sound frightened them. "Who is it?" they
cried.

Jesus told them, "It is I." But that was not enough. His
features were indistinct to their physical eyes. So they
couldn't really know it was Jesus unless the eyes of their
inner self began to see. It was Peter who made the best

use of his little faith. He wanted so much to know it was Jesus.

PETER'S FAITH ILLUMINED JESUS' FACE

Peter looked. And then he said, "Lord, if it's really You, tell me to come to You on the water." And Jesus did what the father had done in the room with his frightened boy. He told Peter to come and that activated the little faith Peter had. Peter's faith, like a flashlight, shined on Jesus' face. Peter said, "Oh, it's You, Jesus." And like the little boy who turned over and went back to sleep, Peter relaxed and unwound himself from his fear. He said, "You're not scared by the storm. You're walking on the water. Because You walk, I can walk on the water too." And he did!

There's a passage in 2 Corinthians 4:6 where St. Paul says, "For God has shined in our hearts the light of God in the face of Jesus Christ." What a magnificent thing. God, Whom we can't see with our physical eyes, has turned the flashlight of His miracle power full on the face of Jesus Christ. With our faith opening up our inner eyes, we can see that face. Fear leaves us. We turn loose of what is shaking our lives to pieces, we make our leap of faith, we walk on the water and go to Jesus. And soon the wind has ceased hissing at us, the boat has stopped rocking, and there comes the gentle whoosh of the waves and the soft slap of the oars dipping in water. We say, "Jesus, You hushed the sea to sleep. You are with us and we are not afraid anymore."

USING YOUR SPIRITUAL SIGHT

I want to share another letter with you right here. It's from a young woman who has really been through something. Her letter spoke to me in a great way.

Dear Oral Roberts:

I've been reading your book, *Miracle of Seed-Faith*. I feel the need to share something that's been happening in my life since September of 1976 that your book has helped me to understand.

I'm so overwhelmed by it all that it sort of scares me still, and at the same time I feel such a great need to share it with others. Yet I wonder if they would believe me!

My point of need came for me in the form of my eighteen-year-old brother who died suddenly and unexpectedly in September of last year. During the two weeks he was in intensive care (before he died of a brain hemorrhage), I opened my heart to Christ as I prayed for my brother's recovery. I had received religious training as a child, but was not truly a Christian until this point in my life.

In learning to cope with the loss of my brother, I began reading the Word of God daily as well as praying. At first, I prayed only for God's forgiveness and guidance and most of all, for His help in accepting the loss of my brother. God brought me through this crisis and is continuing to give me the strength to learn to live without him every new day. But somewhere along the line, I remembered hearing that nothing was too small to take to the Lord in prayer. Bless Jesus for that wonderful revelation!

Now, I began praying for God's help with everyday problems. Since then, my husband and I have had to face crises financially, emotionally, and healthwise. Specifically, my husband was injured on the job, and it looked as though he would not be able ever to return to his former occupation. The two months he was unable to work brought on a financial crisis in which it really looked as though we would lose most of what we had acquired through four years of marriage. So I began looking for work. The employment picture was bleak, to say the least. I prayed for God's help with these problems and sure enough He has answered every prayer.

My husband's back is healed, and he is back to work at his old job. I was healed of sickness myself and given a good job. After two weeks of fruitless job seeking, suddenly two jobs were offered to me in one day and were just the type I had been praying for! Financial assistance has come to us from unexpected places! I could go on and on! There have been miracles too numerous to mention!

The point is, unknowingly I had planted a few small seeds with the Lord. Since then, the outpouring of God's blessings in my everyday life has been so great that it shames me to receive so much when I feel I have given so little in return.

I hope that you can use my testimony so that someone else can find the truth so clearly explained in your book on Seed-Faith. Maybe it will help someone to find out about expecting miracles without having to learn as I did through a crisis time. I can't help but think sometimes, "Oh, Holy Father, what a great miracle we might have been given in the form of healing my brother if only I had known then what I know now."

You see, this woman had learned to see with her spiritual eyes. And when we learn to do that, we're like the little blind girl who, after an operation, saw for the first time. Sitting with her father, she took his hand and looked up into his eyes. A radiant smile spread over her face as she said, "To think I have had such a father all this time and I could not see him."

Do you think Peter had ever seen Jesus *before* he walked on the water the way he saw Him *afterwards?* Oh, he had seen His physical features. But soon, through the Cross, those features would be marred. In the Resurrection they would be changed. Jesus would come back in His glorious, unlimited, invisible form, in the power and presence of the Holy Spirit. Peter had never before seen Jesus' face like this. He had never seen it the way it would be after Jesus had gone through life, the Cross, the Resurrection, the Ascension and the return in the power of the Holy Spirit. This was the purpose of Peter's storm. *He met the real Jesus.* He met Him in the small amount of faith he had in his heart. He met Him in the storm and he met Him in the calm as they walked on the water, together, back to the boat.

You and I can have the experience of seeing Jesus with our faith, of seeing His face with the light of the Father shining on it. His is a face so unmistakable to our inner vision that upon seeing it, we know we can walk on the water of any storm, we will find its purpose, and we will make it work for our good. As we know the purpose, we will believe even stronger that the miracle we have experienced will be repeatable — it will continue to happen the rest of our lives.

NOW ASK YOURSELF...

LIFE'S QUESTION: Do I have to have great faith to get through my struggles?

➤ **GOD'S WAY**
SAY IT: FAITH IS FAITH, EVEN IF IT IS "LITTLE FAITH," LIKE GOLD IS GOLD EVEN IF IT'S LITTLE GOLD. LITTLE FAITH IS ENOUGH TO GET ME STARTED WALKING ON THE WATER, COMING THROUGH MY STRUGGLES.

LIFE'S QUESTION: Why do I have to struggle so much? I get so tired!

➤ **GOD'S WAY**
SAY IT: IN MY STRUGGLES I LEARN TO SEE THE FACE OF JESUS. NOT WITH MY PHYSICAL EYES BUT WITH MY INNER SIGHT.

LIFE'S QUESTION: How can I ever make it through this storm raging in my life?

➤ **GOD'S WAY**
SAY IT: I WILL SEIZE EVERY STRUGGLE AS AN OPPORTUNITY TO ADVANCE, TO MAKE PROGRESS.

I WILL PRAY . . .
I WILL READ GOD'S WORD . . .
I WILL BELIEVE . . .
AND GOD AND I WILL PASS THROUGH THIS STORM TOGETHER!

LIFE'S QUESTION: Is it of value for me to know the purpose of my struggles? ➤ **GOD'S WAY**
SAY IT: KNOWING THE PURPOSE OF MY STORM CAN MAKE THE MIRACLE MORE REPEATABLE IN THE FUTURE WHEN OTHER STORMS COME MY WAY.

PUTTING IT ALL TOGETHER FOR MYSELF

FAITH IS FAITH, EVEN IF IT IS "LITTLE FAITH," LIKE GOLD IS GOLD EVEN IF IT'S LITTLE GOLD. LITTLE FAITH IS ENOUGH TO GET ME STARTED WALKING ON THE WATER, COMING THROUGH MY STRUGGLES.

* * * * * *

IN MY STRUGGLES I LEARN TO SEE THE FACE OF JESUS. NOT WITH MY PHYSICAL EYES BUT WITH MY INNER SIGHT.

* * * * * *

I WILL SEIZE EVERY STRUGGLE AS AN OPPORTUNITY TO ADVANCE, TO MAKE PROGRESS.

I WILL PRAY...
I WILL READ GOD'S WORD...
I WILL BELIEVE...
AND GOD AND I WILL PASS THROUGH THIS STORM TOGETHER!

* * * * * *

KNOWING THE PURPOSE OF MY STORM CAN MAKE THE MIRACLE MORE REPEATABLE IN THE FUTURE WHEN OTHER STORMS COME MY WAY.

Chapter Nineteen

The fantastic miracle of seed-faith
I saw at another lake

". . . walked on the water . . ." (Matthew 14:29).

Lake Junaluska, North Carolina, is one of the oldest Methodist camp meeting sites in America. Tens of thousands continue to pour in to the great tabernacle there each summer.

I've preached at Lake Junaluska three different years, the last time was this past summer while I was writing this book.

Three times I've tried to lead the people there deeper into Seed-Faith. And as I relate this story you are going to see something important, and life-changing for yourself.

LISTEN TO WHAT JESUS TOLD US TO DO

In 1972 on the first night I was to preach, my friend, Bill Henderson, the lay leader of the Western North Carolina Conference, received the offering. Bill did it in the usual way, like, "Now, let's all remember the needs the camp has. As Christians we owe the Lord. It's our obligation to support His work. And we've got to get this met and out of the way so we can go on with the meeting."

Well, Bill took a long time to say these things. He was trying to say they were struggling. They were in a storm. They needed desperately to walk on water, but he didn't know how. The longer he talked the more I saw the lack of desire to give among the packed audience. After awhile he called for the ushers and had a brother lead the people in prayer. The prayer said virtually the same things Bill had said earlier.

Bill introduced me and I preached and ministered the healing love of God to the people with all the faith I had.

Afterward Bill drove me to the hotel there on the grounds. He asked the Bishop of the Western North Carolina Conference, one of the nine or ten conferences served by Lake Junaluska, to eat a sandwich with us. A few other officials joined us and we had a good hour of fellowship.

Finally a question arose about the amount of the offerings during the camp. They wondered why they had not been larger. The offering that evening, they had learned, was only $900. That was about 40 cents each for the 2,500 lay delegates who had come from the churches in the South Jurisdictional District of the United Methodist Church.

Bill said, "Oral, maybe you have a word on it."

I didn't reply. Bill said, "Come on, friend Oral, with all your experience, surely you can help us."

I said, "You may not like my answer."

He said, "Say it. We can take it! Because we sure need help. The way we're going the expenses of the camp won't be met, much less the missions we support."

I said, "I hope the Bishop will pardon my saying so, and that you won't be offended, Bill, but that was the sorriest way to receive an offering I've ever seen."

Their mouths dropped open. The Bishop gravely said, "Dr. Roberts, how would you have done it? Perhaps you can help us."

I said, "All my life I've been reared in the church. All

my life I've seen offerings received like this. The church never gets enough to carry on the most important work on earth. The people don't get blessed. Frankly, I think it's because we are not listening to what Jesus told us to do in our giving."

Someone at the table said, "Isn't this the way Jesus wants us to do it? After all, don't we owe a debt to the Lord?"

JESUS DOESN'T WANT YOU TO OWE HIM ANYTHING

I said, "Didn't Jesus pay our debt by dying in our place on the Cross?"

"Yes," the Bishop replied, "He paid it all. It is through His death that we live."

I asked, "Then if He paid what we owe, all of it, how can we still pay?"

Someone said, "Explain what you mean."

Briefly I explained my belief in the teachings of the Bible that since Jesus had paid it all, we no longer owed, nor could we pay. He gave us a New Testament, a *new* covenant. A covenant based on giving AND receiving, a covenant going all the way back to the original principle God gave Noah after the flood where He gave the promise, "As long as earth remains . . . there will be seed-time and harvest" (Genesis 8:22).

Then I said, "Jesus teaches us our giving is not a debt we owe, but a seed we sow."

Bishop Hunt nodded. "That's true. But it's a new way of putting it, isn't it?"

I said, "If you had all the money in the world it couldn't pay what Jesus paid with His life. Since He has paid it, you no longer owe it. All you can do is plant a seed of your faith. That means you make your love an act of giving. You make your love an act of giving as the Father did when at the Cross He made His love for man an act of His giving. "God so loved the world that He gave . . ." (John 3:16). And what He gave was His best, His only begotten Son.

"Another thing, God in giving His only begotten Son, His very best, did something else. He gave out of His need for man to be restored to Him, and not perish. He also gave *first*. He gave off the *top*. And He expected a *desired result*. The result of His giving being that whoever would believe in Him would not perish, but have everlasting life. That's why as New Testament Christians our giving is a seed of our faith, causing us to love so much that we make our love an act of our giving. Our giving is the seed of faith planted to expect a miracle — to expect a miracle not from those we give to, but from God, our Source of total supply" (Philippians 4:19).

IF YOU HAVE A NEED, PUT IN A SEED

Well, we had quite a discussion. Next morning Bill asked me if I would take up the offering at the 11:00 service. I said, "No, but I am preaching a message on the Miracle of Seed-Faith. Now if you won't take up the offering before the sermon, which is the usual way you do it, and wait until after my sermon, I believe you and the people will better understand Jesus' teaching on giving AND receiving, on sowing AND reaping. Then you can test Seed-Faith for yourselves."

Bill said, "But we always take the offering before the sermon."

I said, "That's before *you* give. Why not give to the people first, giving them the gospel, then give them an opportunity to plant their seed out of their need?"

He said, "How will I do it?"

I said, "Bill, you folks must have had confidence in me or you wouldn't have invited me here to minister. Isn't that right?"

Bill smiled, "Oral, you were our first choice. We believe in you, brother; we love you."

"OK," I said, "then will you do exactly as I tell you? Remember, I love you too. I believe a great renewing in the Holy Spirit is going to come in the Church. That's why I am here."

He said, "Just tell me what to do."

I said, "Tell the people you are departing from your usual custom and receiving the offering after the sermon."

That morning Richard sang, prayer was offered, then I preached on "Seed-Faith, God's way of meeting our needs." I shared my feelings that you can only love by giving, you can only have God's abundant life by following Jesus' example of making your life — every act of it — a continuous act of giving. Then as you plant your seed you can expect a miracle, or a harvest, from God for He always multiplies the seed sown (2 Corinthians 9:10).

I stated, "It is the giving of your love that God multiplies, not your receiving. Seed placed in the storehouse is not multiplied. It does not reproduce. Only seed given to the ground and cultivated is multiplied. If you give nothing and nothing is multiplied, it is still nothing. Zero times zero is still zero. A rejected opportunity to give is a lost opportunity to receive."

In my sermon I also told them that, "God loves a cheerful giver. But the only way you can give cheerfully, as the Father did in giving Jesus, is to know you are going to receive the harvest from God's supply according to His riches by Christ Jesus in glory (Philippians 4:19). The farmer cheerfully plants his seed for the joy of the harvest he will receive when the crop comes in. God gave His Son and expected the greatest miracle to happen — for us to be saved and for His own self to be fulfilled by our restoration. So put in your seed as an act of your love and expect a miracle. Keep on expecting miracles. Make Seed-Faith your way of life, as Jesus teaches by the giving of himself and by the Resurrection, which is the harvest produced by the seed of His life planted on the Cross."

After the sermon I gave the invitation to receive Christ or to rededicate to Him. Many responded. Then I said, "I turn the service to Bill Henderson; he has a word to say."

I had whispered, "Bill, I suggest you say only nine words in taking up the offering — say, IF YOU HAVE A NEED PUT IN A SEED."

He had said, "Oh, they're used to being really urged to give. We may not get much of anything this way."

I had said, "Remember, in the sermon God may have given them new light by which to see and give."

Well, bless my friend and brother in the Lord, Bill Henderson. Bravely he walked up and announced he would ask the ushers to come forward and the offering would be received. Then he said those nine magic words. *If you have a need, put in a seed.* And he sat down.

I suppose it took five minutes to pass the offering cups among the people. We waited. Then the benediction was given.

They took me to the plane and I flew back to Tulsa. Later I got a phone call from Bill. He was excited. "Oral! I've got great news!"

"What is it, Bill?"

"You remember the offering last night was $900? Well, we counted this morning's offering and it is $3,600! The best thing of all is the people remained after the service worshiping God as I've never seen before. All our hearts are open and full."

His voice was vibrant on the phone. "Oral, this will go through the whole area. It will bring new hope to the churches, to the people, and certainly it has to me already. We have a whole new understanding. God wants us to give and He wants us to receive. And we are to expect miracles."

Later Bishop Hunt wrote me a generous note, expressing his love and appreciation. They had been helped through this struggle. They had walked on the water to Jesus.

THEY DO IT AGAIN

In 1974 I returned to Lake Junaluska. Richard and Patti were with me and ministered in song. I preached on the Holy Spirit. Also I added new thoughts on God's love as expressed through Seed-Faith. The Spirit of the Lord was already greatly at work among the people. They were expectant.

This time there was a very special need above that of the camp itself. The Bishop's fund for the needy was being included. Again Bill Henderson was the lay chairman. He said, with a twinkle in his eye, "Oral, what do you think we should do? Should we use Seed-Faith as we did before, or do it the old way?"

I said, "Bill, I'm here by invitation to preach and minister. I'm not in charge of the meeting. But I strongly suggest you remember those nine words — *If you have a need, put in a seed.*"

It was the same tabernacle, again filled to overflowing, most of them having attended two years before. Bill decided to stay with Jesus' teaching on Seed-Faith. As he received the offering, he said it again, "If you have a need, put in a seed." Everybody smiled and started planting their seed.

Again I flew home and again Bill telephoned. Excitedly Bill said, "The ushers just told me the offering was over $12,000. It's a miracle. It's more than enough to meet our needs here. And it's a great boost for the Bishop's fund."

I said, "What about the spirit of the people who planted their seed?"

He said, "Well, it's even better than two years ago. Everybody I talk to says they know God is going to meet their needs. They are expecting miracles."

Bill told me also that he had heard reports from the first Seed-Faith giving two years before where miracles had happened to many people he knew, and that was why they were even more eager this time to plant their seed. They had discovered for themselves God's own proof. THE MIRACLE OF SEED-FAITH.

THEY HAD TO BE REMINDED

The climax to the Lake Junaluska story came in July 1977, when I returned the third time to minister. This time the crowds overflowed the tabernacle. Two adjacent buildings were equipped with closed-circuit television. Also the areas on both sides of the tabernacle were open. It was estimated that over 4,000 people were there. To get in the main tabernacle each delegate had to show his credentials. Visitors and guests had to sit in the adjacent buildings or sit outside.

To my surprise, the offering the first night was received the old way. A new lay leader was in charge and did about the same thing Bill had done the opening night in 1972.

My associates told me the next morning the officials of the camp were again concerned that the needs were not going to be met. Since I had made my part in the Conference an act of Seed-Faith each time and had not accepted an honorarium, I said, "They know I'm here seeding for my own needs, don't they? They have no obligation for my travel or expenses."

"Yes, they understand that and are appreciative. But their other needs are large and the offerings have not been coming in. They want your guidance in the service this morning."

I preached. And as I was concluding I made reference to Seed-Faith, which had not been the main thrust of my message the evening before. I shared that one of my greatest joys had been discovering Jesus' teachings on Seed-Faith. My own Seed-Faith planting was working miracles in my life and in the lives of many others. I told of my two previous experiences at Lake Junaluska, reminding them of how those attending had been blessed through Seed-Faith giving AND receiving.

I said, "I have a great *joy* through Seed-Faith. But I have a great *sadness* too. The sadness is that Seed-Faith has made such a small dent in the church. Almost every time I attend a church service the offering is received in the old you-owe-God-way instead of in Jesus' way of planting a seed out of your need and giving it as an act of your love, giving God your best and then expecting His best."

I said, "Like last night. The brother who received the offering used the old long method of giving out of loyalty, or a debt we owe, and because the church has such great needs. I love this brother. I can't quarrel with being loyal or about the great needs of the church. But my heart hurts because last night we were not giving God our best the way He gave His best for us — His only begotten Son. And we were not expecting His best."

A CHURCH IN TULSA

I told them of a church in Tulsa, a Baptist church among our black people. The man pastoring the church had been in prison, where Christ entered his life and called him to preach. When he was released he began to study for the ministry. Some time later he was ordained and built a church in Tulsa. The crowds overflowed it and a new structure was built.

While preaching there on one of the two or three open Sundays I have a year, I learned they were planning another new, much larger structure for the growing church. The pastor told me the vision of his heart to love and serve the people. My soul was moved. After my sermon, during which I had referred to the three miracle keys of Seed-Faith, I asked everyone there to give God their biggest bill. I asked them not only to give it, but to give it out of a need in their life, expecting God to supply that need according to His riches. I asked them to give God their best and then ask for His, and to expect it.

The people came forward in lines (their custom in that particular church) — men, women, youth, children. They put in their biggest bill. It was the first time I had seen an entire congregation crying and rejoicing at the same time when giving an offering to the Lord. It was a powerful spiritual experience.

Later, ORU conferred an honorary doctorate on that pastor for the outstanding work he was doing. He told of something unusual that happened the Wednesday after the Sunday I had been with them. A widow in his church telephoned him. He said she was quite old and very influential in the church, a woman everybody loved and respected. "She asked me if I would come right over and I hurried, thinking something was wrong. When I arrived she opened her purse and handed me a worn $20 bill."

I said, "Sister, you can't do this. It's too much. You need it more than we do."

She said, "Pastor, now you listen. Last Sunday Oral Roberts said to give God our biggest bill. He said not to listen to his voice but God's. If God's words came through his, we would know God wanted us to do it so He could supply our biggest need. Well, I didn't obey the Lord. I thought this was just Oral Roberts himself talking. I put in my usual few nickles. But ever since then I've been hearing not Oral Roberts, but the Lord. 'Give Me your biggest bill. Then trust Me to meet your biggest need.' I've saved this $20 bill for a time of need. Now God has told me my time of need is here. My need is to give so that my Lord can do what He said through His servant. Now, pastor, don't you refuse this $20 and cheat me out of my miracle. Take it! You hear?"

The pastor, his eyes wet with tears, told me, "Brother Roberts, I took the $20 bill. I held it in my hands. It was sacred. It was like it was on fire. A sensation went through me. And suddenly the widow said something else.

" 'Pastor, for years I've been living in fear. My little offerings to the church, well, I haven't enjoyed giving them very much. I was afraid I had lost what I had given. It wouldn't come back. But I wanted to be loyal, to pay what I owed the Lord. Oral Roberts showed me Jesus had already paid. He showed me Jesus didn't need my money. Instead, I needed to give so He could give to me. Now that I've given you my biggest bill for the Lord's work, I have a different feeling. I'm at rest in my spirit. I know the Lord is going to take care of me. Never again will I have to worry. In the future I'll have more seed to plant.' "

Again the pastor said to me, "That woman is a new person. God has been supplying her needs so much that we at the church don't even have to take her anything anymore. She's got everyone in our church excited. You'll never know what you did for our church, for this woman, for all of us."

I said, "I didn't do it. Unless God had put His Spirit on what I did it wouldn't have worked."

Today that church, that pastor, and that widow are doing great things in Tulsa.

THEY GOT THE MESSAGE

I ended my message there at Lake Junaluska by saying, "Now I'm going to give my biggest bill this morning. And I'm expecting God to meet my biggest need. I'm giving it because I have a need to plant a seed. Will you do the same?"

The offering was received, the service ended and as before, they took me to the airport and I flew back to Tulsa. Later that night the phone rang and my associate, Collins Steele, answered it. The voice on the phone said, "Tell

Brother Roberts the offering has already reached $30,000. We desperately needed $10,000 to repair homes for our missionaries. We have $30,000 in hand and it's still coming in."

Even I was astonished. I asked for this to be verified again. And through another call it was. They said, "Something is happening here. The people are on fire. The Spirit is moving as never before."

I thought, "Dear God, will Seed-Faith giving as You have shown in the Bible, ever, ever make a dent on the church — on people — in a lasting way? Will they ever learn to jump out of the sinking boat and walk on the water to get their needs met?"

WHAT IF YOU DIDN'T PLANT YOUR SEED?

If the people at Lake Junaluska had not planted their seed in such a great way, their needs would not have been so powerfully met. What if Peter had not planted his seed in that perilous hour on the Sea of Galilee? Suppose he had not taken that first step on the water. There was the biggest miracle of his life waiting to pull him out of the storm and enable him to walk on the water. But it never could have happened if he had left the seed unplanted.

I told the people at Lake Junaluska, "God isn't poor. God isn't weak. God isn't defeated. He has millions and millions of dollars for His great work. He has plenty of everything, including money for each of us in our needs. He is just waiting for us to realize our need, as Peter realized his need. He is waiting for us to turn loose of the stormy boat, turn loose of our worn-out ways of doing things, and make our leap of faith. He wants us to plant our seed. And God will multiply our seed by enabling us to walk on the water!"

And it will work in your life too.

NOW ASK YOURSELF...

LIFE'S QUESTION: Why do ➤ **GOD'S WAY**
I not get blessed when I SAY IT: I WILL START LIS-
want to be blessed so much? TENING TO WHAT JESUS
TELLS ME TO DO. I WILL
TRY TO LEARN HIS WAY
THROUGH GOD'S WORD –
NOT MAN'S.

LIFE'S QUESTION: What ➤ **GOD'S WAY**
should my spirit be when I SAY IT: I WILL TRY ALWAYS
give? TO GIVE AS A SEED I SOW
AND NOT AS A DEBT I OWE
– IN ALL AREAS OF MY LIFE.
I WILL MAKE MY LOVE AN
ACT OF GIVING.

LIFE'S QUESTION: What ➤ **GOD'S WAY**
can I do when I'm facing a SAY IT: I WILL PLANT A
deep need? SEED OUT OF MY NEED. AND
THEN I WILL LOOK TO GOD
FOR MY HARVEST – FOR MY
MIRACLE.

LIFE'S QUESTION: How can ➤ **GOD'S WAY**
I keep my spirit in a state of SAY IT: I WILL REMEMBER
expectation? A REJECTED OPPORTUNITY
TO GIVE IS A LOST OPPOR-
TUNITY TO RECEIVE. I WILL
PLANT MY SEEDS OF FAITH
CHEERFULLY WHENEVER I
GET THE CHANCE, AND ES-
PECIALLY WHEN I HAVE A
NEED.

LIFE'S QUESTION: What ➤ **GOD'S WAY**
should I do when I'm facing SAY IT: I WILL GIVE GOD MY
something so big I can't see BEST, THEN TRUST HIM TO
my way out? GIVE ME HIS BEST. I WILL
NOT BE AFRAID TO DO IT.
I'LL BE AT REST IN MY SPIRIT
BECAUSE I WILL KNOW THE
LORD WILL TAKE CARE OF
ME.

PUTTING IT ALL TOGETHER FOR MYSELF

I WILL START LISTENING TO WHAT JESUS TELLS ME TO DO. I WILL TRY TO LEARN HIS WAY THROUGH GOD'S WORD — NOT MAN'S.

* * * * * *

I WILL TRY ALWAYS TO GIVE AS A SEED I SOW AND NOT AS A DEBT I OWE — IN ALL AREAS OF MY LIFE. I WILL MAKE MY LOVE AN ACT OF GIVING.

* * * * * *

I WILL PLANT A SEED OUT OF MY NEED. AND THEN I WILL LOOK TO GOD FOR MY HARVEST . . . FOR MY MIRACLE.

* * * * * *

I WILL REMEMBER A REJECTED OPPORTUNITY TO GIVE IS A LOST OPPORTUNITY TO RECEIVE. I WILL PLANT MY SEEDS OF FAITH CHEERFULLY WHENEVER I GET THE CHANCE, ESPECIALLY WHEN I HAVE A NEED.

* * * * * *

I WILL GIVE GOD MY BEST, THEN TRUST HIM TO GIVE ME HIS BEST. I WILL NOT BE AFRAID TO DO IT. I'LL BE AT REST IN MY SPIRIT BECAUSE I WILL KNOW THE LORD WILL TAKE CARE OF ME.

* * * * * *

The next few pages can bring the greatest . . .

BREAKTHROUGH FROM HEAVEN FOR YOU

The next few pages unfold the most exciting and adventuresome challenge of my life and ministry.

The words are exactly what God revealed to me — and

I wrote them down straight out of my spirit. They didn't go through my mind until later. I kept my spirit open and responsive to God as I wrote.

> In October of 1977 — exactly when the Lord impressed me — I sent "I will rain on your desert" to my partners. They received the letter and these pictures as you find them in this book.

You have probably just completed nineteen chapters on how you can get through your struggles. This most important final chapter could be your launching pad into a whole new way of life, of miracles, of one leap of faith after another, until walking on the stormy waters of your life becomes the norm for you.

Read on carefully, and prayerfully. It may be that God will put into your heart a seed to be planted. That seed could very well bring you just exactly the miracle — the magic moment — you need. It could bring you the greatest Breakthrough from Heaven for you.

Read on and see what God puts into your spirit.

Chapter Twenty

'I will rain upon your desert!'

. . . A revelation of the Lord that came to me in the desert concerning the vision to rise up and build a new Health Care Center on the ORU campus for the unifying of our Lord's different delivery systems of prayer and medicine, a vision He had given me thirty years ago, but whose time has come for the more complete healing of the people to whom God has sent me with His healing power. The new Health Care Center to be named the CITY OF FAITH.

I had begun 1977 with God's words ringing in my heart, *"There is to be a Breakthrough from Heaven in '77."* I saw breakthroughs for the people, especially for my partners. I saw breakthroughs for myself in this ministry. God has never said anything to me more important than that these Breakthroughs from Heaven would come. The devil took notice of the breakthroughs and fought them as I've never seen before.

Suddenly I was plunged into a terrible desert experience. In February 1977 a plane crashed over a Kansas wheatfield, killing our beloved oldest daughter, Rebecca, and her dear husband, Marshall, who left three small children. It devastated me and my family. We thought we were going to die with the grief and loss. To get through it Evelyn and I knew we had to plant a seed out of our hurt and need. Our seed was to go on nationwide television almost immediately after the tragedy and bare our hearts, letting all our hurting and grieving hang out before millions, many of whom had lost loved ones.

As we finished the telecast we were holding to Jesus Christ of Nazareth; the Source of our supply, the Root System of our faith, the Resurrection and the Life. We were holding on. Our seed had been planted.

Millions wept with us and we knew our seed planted out of our hurting would bear fruit. But suddenly I knew there was more involved than the death of our dear ones and the hurting in our hearts. Satan was striking at us.

The devil was trying to mock me. "You have said God is a good God. Where is His goodness now? You have told the people there is to be a Breakthrough from Heaven in '77. Now where is the breakthrough, for you, for the people?" The devil was trying to scare me so much I would quit and the people would lose the hope of healing they had gained through this ministry.

"GO TO THE DESERT"

Then God spoke telling me to go to the desert.

Down through the years the desert had been one of the places I had gone at times of special need for God to reveal Himself to me.

In the vast quietness of the desert, I had been able to reach out to God . . . to listen in my heart to what He wanted to say to me.

There in the desert God spoke to me. He said, "I WILL RAIN UPON YOUR DESERT!" In my heart I knew this was a powerful thing God had spoken to me — something very special. He would rain upon my desert.

As I entered the desert I saw the stark barren land, the shifting sands, the gullies and scars in the environment. I saw the trackless miles beneath the burning sun and felt the land crying for rain from heaven . . . crying . . . crying.

I remembered another time I was there, great cloud-bursts pouring down on the parched land. Almost instantly I saw a miracle. Everywhere it was like an explosion of life bursting forth. The long, dried-up vegetation leaped into newness of life. Soon all over the desert the rain had brought to pass the prophecy of the Bible: *"The desert shall blossom like the rose"* (Isaiah 35:1).

My eyes saw the rain as a Breakthrough from Heaven for the desert which had been denied it for so long.

It was like this again. For there in the desert God rained upon my desert. Again He showed me the vision He had given for my life and ministry thirty years before. Again He let me see and hear people as He sees and hears them, all hurting, all suffering grief and loneliness, all sick in some way, and some so sick they are desperate. A desert in their lives. All needing a Breakthrough from Heaven.

Again I felt the powerful compassion of God in my spirit, the Holy Spirit filling me anew with the faith for people to be healed of their sicknesses of soul, mind, and body, bringing them into a new readiness — where they would have a Breakthrough from Heaven.

I felt that special faith of God in me, a deep *knowing* inside. I felt God giving me a new dominion over the devil and his oppression of the people. The devil was not going to win.

All I had been going through in my own loss and grief meant God had taken me through the experience of the desert itself where again I was crying for the rain of God from heaven. I was holding on to "GOD IS A GOOD GOD." I was holding on to "BREAKTHROUGH FROM HEAVEN." I was holding on to THE VISION OF TAKING GOD'S HEALING POWER TO MY GENERATION. I was holding on to His call to me to merge the healing streams of His healing power: medicine which had helped me and the entire human race so much, and the healing stream of prayer which had been the final method God had used to raise me up from sickness and call me to the healing ministry.

DETERMINED TO OBEY

I was determined more than ever to obey the vision of taking God's healing power to my generation by uniting the healing streams of prayer and medicine. To build for God on the ORU campus, directly across the road from the Prayer Tower and the new medical school, a national and international Health Care Center. It would be a complete medical center, but new and different, as God had revealed it to me. All through the years I knew that when it was God's time to build it, it would be different from anything existing in the world. There in the desert God made it dramatically clear that NOW IS THE TIME.

He said to me:

"Son, you cannot put the vision I have given you into a place where My full healing power is not freely accepted. It must not be in a place defeated by a lack of faith in My miraculous power. You must build a new and different medical center for Me. The healing streams of prayer and medicine must merge through what I will have you build. Every physician, every nurse, every person praying, must be in harmony with My calling to you in the healing ministry. All medical and surgical skill, all research for a cure

for cancer and other diseases destroying man, must be carried on in an atmosphere of prayer and a total dependence upon Me as the Source of Healing and Life.

"You build it exactly as I have given you the vision . . . .

"People from throughout the world will come to the Health Care Center to receive the best of medical science and the best of healing prayers. Then they will know: I AM THE LORD THAT HEALETH THEE" (Exodus 15:26).

HE SHOWED ME THE BUILDINGS

Then rising before me were the details of the buildings. Immediately I was led to read the last two chapters in the Bible. Revelation 21, 22. There I saw the City of God, the new Jerusalem, with its River of Life and its broad avenues. I saw the Tree of Life, whose fruit is for the "healing of the nations."

I saw the City of God as a reflection of God Himself bringing healing and health to those who entered there. Suddenly God gave me *a new name* for the Health Care and Research Center I am to build in His name.

"You shall call it the CITY OF FAITH."

THE CITY OF FAITH

I thought my heart would burst with joy. The CITY OF FAITH. What a name! I knew only God could give a name like that to the Health Care and Research Center He wanted me to build. FAITH! The CITY OF FAITH! My whole life and ministry have been built on faith. Everything I do is an act of my faith, it's a seed of my faith. The prayers I pray are prayers of faith for the healing of people (James 5:16).

When I am under medical care, as I have been all my

life, as a patient I come to the physician with faith in God,
knowing that my faith brings hope, and that hope makes
the physician's skill and medicines reach their highest potential of help for me.

Yes, God works medical miracles, and He works miracles
through prayer. *A miracle is a miracle no matter what re-
source of God it comes through.* I know that faith in God
is the real force that makes prayer and medicine effective
in bringing forth the power of God to "raise up the sick,"
and give the miracle of healing and health — for me, for you,
for others.

*Many doctors and ministers have told me that when they
were in medical school or a theological seminary, they were
not taught to tell people to have faith or hope in God to help
them get well or that God could heal them by a miracle.*

As a result of this lack of right teaching, millions of
people are cynical, fearful, frustrated, and often hardened
in their hearts not believing that God cares whether they
are sick or well.

God said to me:

> *"All this must be changed and I have chosen you
> to bring it about. In the new CITY OF FAITH on
> the ORU campus, I want My healing resources used.
> Prayer but more than prayer. Medical science but
> more than medical science. I want an atmosphere
> charged with faith and hope, where My healing love
> fills the entire place.*
>
> *"It is the ministry of My Healing Power I have
> given you that will make this atmosphere of faith and
> hope possible in the new CITY OF FAITH Health
> Care Center. It will be contagious. People coming
> for medical care will feel this atmosphere and I will
> have a greater chance to bring about their cure. Never
> permit anything to stand in the way of holding faith*

*in Me, and hope to all who come. I want you to cause
My love to flow toward all.*

*"You will pray for the sick all your life. The CITY
OF FAITH I have commissioned you to build will
enlarge and extend your personal healing ministry
throughout the world. It will be a seed multiplied in
millions of lives who otherwise will never know the
healing power that I have provided for them."*

TOWERING BUILDINGS

God showed me the details of the buildings. They were
not to be the usual low scattered buildings that are not
always people-oriented. They are to be towering buildings,
closely connected together, built on a single base, a crown
jewel rising in the sky, reaching up in praise to God, the
Source of all healing (see color picture).

The largest and tallest building will house a great clinic
and diagnostic center. Hundreds of thousands will come to
the clinic and diagnostic center for care.

Connected to the clinic will be *the most modern Research
Center* to help find a cure for cancer and other death-dealing
diseases. God told me to "go all out," to use the full power
of my own prayers and spiritual discernment to help the
dedicated scientists working to find a cure for cancer and
for other diseases. God told me that a breakthrough for
cancer, and for other diseases, will come by a miracle. It
will be a miraculous insight given to the scientists working
in a miracle-inspired atmosphere. I feel in the depths of my
soul at least a major part of cancer breakthrough will come
through our research program in the CITY OF FAITH. I
have carried this dream and now I know it will happen.

A DIFFERENT KIND OF HOSPITAL

A *third building* also rising from the single base will be
a hospital. But a different kind of hospital. It is to be inter-

connected with the great clinic and diagnostic center where
OUR PHYSICIANS AND SURGEONS will be located in
a unified group practice. The physician won't have to come
from his office across town or even across the street. He is
there in the CITY OF FAITH.

I personally know from my own hospital experience how
much it would have meant to me to have my physician's
office physically near. Just the feeling he or she was near
would have been immensely helpful to my faith and hope.
Also, it would have enabled them to *feel my needs better*,
knowing they could reach me in seconds or in 2 or 3 minutes.
(I have always felt this is a missing link in the healing
process of a hospital.)

I had a strong impression the hospital should have 777
beds.

The Prayer Partners in the CITY OF FAITH will work
in — and from — specially designed chapels, working in unity
with the physicians, with the full freedom of this ministry.

These prayer partners will be specially trained by us at
ORU in cooperation with the Abundant Life Prayer Group.
They will be trained when to visit the patient, how to minister, and how to cooperate with God's delivery system of
medical care. They will be part of the team.

The entire health care system of the clinic and diagnostic center, the research center, the 777-bed hospital, and
every physician, nurse, staff member, and prayer partner
will be working in close proximity with the patient AT THE
SAME TIME — AND IN THE SAME PLACE. To me that's
a miracle in itself. It will be a family atmosphere where
the full resources of the CITY OF FAITH will be directed
toward the sick person in an atmosphere of the best skilled
medical care AND the best prayerful support. Everybody
and everything will be working together for the benefit of
the person who has come — to help him *get well and stay
well!*

Extra effort will be made to give the best medical care in the shortest length of time to CUT DOWN MEDICAL AND HOSPITAL COSTS TO THE PATIENT! The time has come for this and God will help us cause it to happen in the CITY OF FAITH.

ACCESS TO ALL FACILITIES IN THE SAME PLACE

When the patient arrives at the CITY OF FAITH he will have access to all facilities necessary, not having to be sent to different parts of town. In seconds or minutes he can be at any lab, or the physician's office or the emergency section, or the hospital. The CITY OF FAITH will be designed for full service for the whole person!

The highest goal will be to have a whole-man approach to each patient, to help the patient become a whole person — body, mind, and spirit. That's what this ministry is all about.

God showed me a stream of pure water was to flow directly out from the front of the CITY OF FAITH, representing the River of Life in heaven, with evergreen trees symbolizing the Tree of Life lining the banks of this stream alongside the broad avenues approaching the CITY OF FAITH on the campus of Oral Roberts University.

In the vision, I will never forget, God showed me *His Healing Hands*. He reminded me that His hands had touched the sick and healed them. He reminded me that He had used my hands as an extension of His hands (I remembered how over the years I never touched the sick in prayer without thinking of His hands rather than my own, knowing if I could visualize *His* hands rather than mine, I would more completely believe for the person's healing).

HEALING HANDS

God said, "It is very important to the sick coming to the CITY OF FAITH to visually see the symbol of My Healing

Hands. Your arms and hands, as an extension of My hands, are to be used as a model for the symbolic Healing Hands some 60 feet high. The Healing Hands are to be set in the fountain of water directly in front of the CITY OF FAITH from which the stream of pure water will originate."

I saw that the Healing Hands will connect the stream with the buildings. I was shown the reason for this. The Lord said to me:

> *"As the people drive up the first thing they will see is the towering CITY OF FAITH as it reaches up to ME. Then driving down the avenue beside the stream they will see the water and the trees, giving them a glimpse of the River of Life and the Tree of Life. As they drive closer they will suddenly see the Healing Hands. Their attention upon the Healing Hands will help draw them closer to ME, and will help them release their faith.*
>
> *"Human beings live and work by their hands. In the Healing Hands, the right hand will represent the healing stream of My power through prayer, the left hand will represent the healing stream of My power through medicine — the hands joined will represent the unifying of the healing streams of prayer AND medicine as they both reach up to touch the hands of Me the Great Physician, the Source of all healing and health."*

IN MY SPIRIT I'VE SEEN THE HEALING HANDS OF GOD

The symbolism of the Healing Hands standing tall where the stream meets the CITY OF FAITH, visible both day and night, grabbed at all I know about God's healing power. I've seen those healing Hands of God in my spirit many times. I feel them touching my hands as I pray for people. I understand how important hands are in God's healing process, both the laying on of hands AND the work of the hands of skilled and dedicated physicians.

I felt that the beautiful sight of those powerful hands would do exactly what God told me — help the person know Whose hands it is that have the power to heal them.

> *God revealed something else about the Healing Hands. He reminded me the Prayer Tower is the CENTER of the ORU campus, a daily reminder to all students that PRAYER CHANGES THINGS. Then He showed me that the Healing Hands will be the UNIFYING CENTER of the CITY OF FAITH and will say to all who come for medical treatment, "God works His healing wonders through many instruments but He is the Source."*

PEOPLE WILL WANT TO GET WELL

Then God told me the most wonderful thing, something I feel will cause a lot of people to get well sooner. He said:

> *"As they drive up to the CITY OF FAITH and see that it reflects the City of God, that it is a city of faith, their hearts will leap with hope. Just seeing the CITY OF FAITH and the Healing Hands, they will want to get well . . . to start getting well that instant!"*

And, dear partner, when a person desperately wants to get well, half the battle is won.

In the vision I saw it all built. I was walking through every part praying and touching and dedicating it to Him Who knows the way we are made, the anatomy of our body, every joint, every muscle, blood vessel, vital organ, our five senses, and the relationship of each to the other (1 Corinthians 12:14-18). I heard my voice as an extension of God's voice commanding the devil to take his hands off God's property. I felt, rather than saw, the angels of God filling the place with light and hope. I felt the resurrection power of God. I heard Him say:

"Because I live, you shall live also."

I knew the CITY OF FAITH Health Care Center would be a place of life, an instrument of the abundant life Jesus promised to bring each of us (John 10:10).

WHEN DO I START, LORD?

I asked, "When do I start construction, Lord?"

He said, *"I told you there would be a Breakthrough from Heaven in '77. Therefore, you are to start in the fall of '77. This is the accepted time. People are ready for it. They have not been ready before, neither have you — but they and you are ready now. You must offer more than prayer by itself. You must offer more than medicine by itself. You must bring these streams of My healing power together. From the beginning I have planned for them to be unified in the wholeness of My healing power. I chose you for this purpose. Your ministry has helped prepare the people. Their own experiences with medicine and with prayer, have helped them to come to the point they are ready for this new total emphasis of healing and health through BOTH medicine and prayer. They know they need this properly combined health care and they need it now."*

Reflecting upon what God had told me I knew in my spirit we are ready for this. Thirty years ago when I started, no. Ten years ago, no. Even five years ago, no. Now there's a whole new change brought about by the Holy Spirit's opening up the hearts of people everywhere to God's great desire for people "to prosper and to be in health . . . even as their souls prosper" (3 John 2). This was the verse God gave me when I began this ministry in 1947.

When God said, *"You are to start in the fall of '77,"* it both thrilled AND frightened me. I had known the day would come when He would tell me to do it for the healing of the people. Now that affirmation in my spirit was His command to start it in the year in which He told me there would be a beginning of a Breakthrough from Heaven in '77. Over and over God had told me '77 would be the beginning year for BREAKTHROUGHS.

HOW MUCH DO I BUILD???

I asked the Lord, "How much of the CITY OF FAITH, consisting of the clinic and diagnostic center, the Research Center, and the 777-bed medical center, shall I start constructing now?"

He said, *"Starting now you are to build all of it at the same time, the whole of it, leaving nothing out that I have told you."*

"Lord," I replied, "I'm just completing the Medical School at ORU. Do you mean I am to start immediately on the entire CITY OF FAITH Health Care Center?"

He said, "Yes, this is the beginning year of special Breakthroughs from Heaven. It is in this new clinic and medical center that your young physicians will get much of their actual experience, also those of your team praying for the sick. And it is here you will form them into *healing teams* to carry my healing power to the ends of the earth.

"In addition, the ORU Medical School will give new knowledge to the Health Care system in the clinic and medical center. Also, the clinic and medical center will have a positive effect upon the Medical School. They will work in *perfect cooperation."*

Then He added a new word: "The ORU Theological School, with its spiritual leaders under your direction, will constantly interact with the entire medical program. You will see to it that HEALING PRAYER will be at the heart of every leader. You are A MAN OF PRAYER, an evange-list of My healing power for the whole man. You live under My authority and the power of the Holy Spirit. This is what ties everything together and makes it Mine for you, and Mine for those who follow you to take My healing power to your generation, the generation of man."

As I listened and thought, it occurred to me again that God is a good God. But not only a good God, a Mighty God! A MIGHTY MIRACLE-WORKING GOD — AND HE GAVE ME THE MASTER PLAN.

WHERE WILL THE MONEY COME FROM?

About this time I began to realize what God has enabled us to build already — over twenty major buildings at ORU and all of them cost money. I started every one of them with just our faith in God, and what little seed we had to plant. It constantly had us on our knees, sometimes we felt we couldn't go another day.

I can't describe the hard times and rocky roads we ex-perienced to get these buildings up, to provide a place for our students to learn, to hear God's voice, and to prepare themselves to obey God and go with His healing power to the uttermost bounds of the earth. The sleepless nights of fear, the admonitions, "You can't do it," all have haunted us, especially me.

At the same time we have stood up inside, put in our seeds of faith, worked and prayed and expected miracles. And those miracles have come. This whole ministry is a living miracle. I know that better than anyone.

As we finish our latest large building, for our Schools of Medicine, Dentistry, Nursing, Theology, Law, Business and Education, God is telling me His time has come to build the biggest complex of all, some 1,600,000 square feet — and just our faith and obedience to start with. Thank God we have the land.

Of the total campus acreage of 500 acres we have been strangely led to preserve a single block of 80 acres right across the street from the Prayer Tower and the new Medical School. It is perfect for the CITY OF FAITH with plenty of parking space. The land is paid for, thank God. Eighty beautiful acres ready to build upon. Only God could have directed us to set these 80 acres apart. How great is His foresight and planning.

Many times I've looked at that piece of land and wondered. Now I know that I know that I know. But the money to build — how? where?

GOD HAS NEVER FAILED ME

God said, "Have I ever failed you when you trusted Me as your Source? When you put your seed in? When you expected miracles?"

Thinking of this entire ministry I could not think of one time God had failed me. Oh, I remembered praying for the sick when there seemed to be no way for their healing. I remembered digging holes for buildings and believing God would fill them with buildings. AND GOD MADE A WAY. But still this is bigger, more complex, more daring . . . yet holds promise to bring more healing to more people than this ministry has ever helped bring before. Still it seemed so impossible for a man to do.

GOD WILL BUILD IT

God said, "I told you that you will not build it, I will build it through you. You have never healed anyone or built anything — I have done the healing and the building." (I knew this was true.)

He said, "I have worked through you as My chosen man. I have also worked through the men and women I have chosen to be your partners. They are chosen as you are chosen. I have spoken in their hearts and they have put in their seed out of their need and I have multiplied it. Through their Seed-Faith I am meeting their needs. It is through their Seed-Faith I am doing great things for them and I am building great things through you for the healing of the people."

I said, "God, but what about my partners concerning the CITY OF FAITH? Will they feel it as I do? Will they see how it will help them?"

He said, "I've been preparing them to launch out into the deep with their *giving and receiving*. Now that I have you ready, I have them ready, each one. You can depend upon them as your partners."

"But how, Lord?" I asked.

"By the Master Plan I have given you. A Master Plan so complete that everyone who reads or hears about it will feel a new spark of hope for their own health — and health for their loved ones."

I said, "But won't it take millions of dollars to build all of this? Won't it take a lot just to start the construction? Even to get the planning underway?"

GET INTO YOUR SPIRIT

God said, "Yes, more than your mind can take in or the mind of your partners. So set aside your mind for a moment and get into your spirit. Your spirit can grasp it, so can the spirit of your partners grasp it. In the Master Plan I give you, I have taken the total cost and reduced it to a perfect number. The number is from $77 to $777. Of course sometimes I may put another amount into the heart of a partner. Each partner must respond only as I lead. All the partners putting their seed together will make a large sum, ENOUGH TO BUILD IT."

I thought: This is the way God has always worked with me and my partners. A seed planted by each of us and all a miracle supply for all our needs. It has been miracle after miracle.

God said, "It is in this way you are to build the CITY OF FAITH — and to open it DEBT-FREE."

"Debt-free, Lord?"

He said, "Yes! I am concerned about the cost of medical care. I want the best medical care given and at a lower cost than the average. I want all kinds of people to be helped. To bring the operating costs down, you will have to build and open it *debt-free!*"

Then I said, "Lord, You will have to give me the greatest miracle I've ever known for building for You. There is just so much I can do."

He said, "*It's your business to plant your seed and obey — it's the business of the partner to plant the seed and obey — then to start building as I have told you. It's My business to do the supplying, to move all the mountains of obstacles.*"

When He said that I felt like shouting. "That's our God, the Source of our total supply! With God all things are possible!"

GOD'S MASTER PLAN FOR RAINING UPON YOUR DESERT

Now I am honored — I count it a privilege — to share with you the Master Plan God gave me for you. He said He had chosen me and chosen you.

If I, and if you, will do exactly what God says, God will give us the greatest healings and miracles of our lives. He will build this Health Care Center through us — the CITY OF FAITH. He will rain upon your desert. You will feel the rain from heaven coming upon you in wondrous ways. Your desert and dry places will explode into miraculous life. I can see these great things happening to you. I can see your Breakthrough from Heaven, and remember God won't be late in '78!

your Breakthrough from Heaven, and remember God won't be late in '78!

First: The Plan deals with an *everlasting seed of faith* I am to plant and you are to plant.

This seed is separate from any other seed you and I are now planting. It it an *everlasting seed of faith*. It is to reproduce itself continually for the rest of your life and for coming generations of your family! It will be the greatest working seed you've ever planted. God impressed me it was to be like the "barrel of meal and cruse of oil that never failed" when the widow of Zarephath planted her seed for feeding the prophet Elijah for the breakthrough she needed *(1 Kings 17:16)*.

Her life had been a "desert" until she did what the prophet Elijah told her, then God rained upon her desert. It was a miracle breakthrough that God multiplied to meet all her spiritual, physical, and financial needs, *a breakthrough that kept on multiplying for her*. It was repeated acts of miracles, not just one, but again and again. That's what God showed me would happen to you through the planting of your everlasting seed of faith — repeated acts of miracles in your life. Now this is important to you. Get yourself in the frame of mind to think of *this seed* as being different. Seed having a *quality* and *quantity* of reproduction that will never, never cease.

It really has to do with your life continually EX-PANDING! I can already feel this happening to you.

Since God said we were to start building in the fall of '77, you are to plant this seed as soon as God directs you.

Second: Since the seed is for physical construction, it is, in this case, to be in the form of money. The Lord will place a specific amount on your heart. And that amount will bring about the fulfillment of His promise of a Breakthrough from Heaven. This seed is to come out of your deepest hurt and need as mine is coming out of my hurt and need. It is to be one of the seeds for the greater part of your Breakthrough from Heaven. It means God won't be late in '78. It also means that God will be on time in '79 . . . and on and on and on. The greater your need the greater your seed for your miracle.

EVELYN AND I AND OUR FAMILY

Evelyn and I and our family have had some terrific breakthroughs but we've also had the deepest hurt of our lives. So our Breakthrough from Heaven started in '77 and is continuing. The seed Evelyn and I planted, and the seed each of our remaining children and their spouses planted during the same time *is a continuing Point of Contact* for our believing AND EXPECTING God to give us our greatest Breakthrough. Each member of my family has been led to plant their own seed. We know it will bring *repeated* acts of God's miracle supply for each of us. And that's what we need. Not just a miracle once, but repeated acts of His miracles for our continuing needs and struggles.

We know exactly what our need is, also what our *desired result* is. That's why we are planting special seed in such expectancy for miracle after miracle to happen to us. *You* are to plant your special seed with the same expectancy for your miracle-after-miracle harvest — a harvest repeated again and again.

It's so clear to me for myself and my family, and for you and yours, that I can feel the "joy of the Lord" flowing in my soul. JOY! JOY! It's such a good seed, a different seed, an everlasting seed. This seed in some strange and beautiful way provides a new link between you and God and us for your greatest breakthrough — and for something better beyond '78. Even beyond '79. YOU WILL BE BLESSED!

Third: As soon as I receive your everlasting seed of faith,
it will immediately be put to work toward the CITY OF
FAITH. Then your letter will be taken to the Prayer
Tower where you and your needs will be prayed over
for 31 consecutive days and nights.

I can't explain why God said 31 days and nights . . .
but there's one thing I know: it's to help you get your
miracle Breakthrough from Heaven. I know yours may
not be complete yet. What is the greatest breakthrough
you need? God has assured me many miracles will be
coming toward you — and you are to receive them. So
look for these miracles . . . and receive them! It is important that you receive them. It is important that you
have repeated acts of miracles!

Fourth:

A BEAUTIFUL POSTER OF THE
HEALING HANDS FOR YOU

The Master Plan God gave me includes the Healing
Hands. As I have already pointed out, God showed me
arms and hands clasped together and standing some 60
feet high, connecting the stream of pure water with the
CITY OF FAITH, symbolizing that all healing comes
from His Hands. (Look again at the colored picture.
You can clearly see the Healing Hands connecting the
stream and the CITY OF FAITH.)

God impressed me to prepare for you a large, one
foot and a half by two feet magnificent color poster of
the Healing Hands. Since I have always used my hands
as an extension of Jesus' hands, I have a deep feeling
this beautiful poster will continually help you think of
God's Hands to touch and heal you. I also feel it will
be an important Point of Contact for your faith. I want
you to have the poster.

Fifth:
REMEMBER THE WORDS OF ST. PAUL

When you send in your everlasting seed of faith, remember the words of St. Paul in Philippians 4:15-19 where he said to his partners in the Lord, "In the . . . gospel, ye only communicated with me concerning giving and receiving. Ye sent again and again to my necessity (for God's great work). Not because I desire a gift, but I desire fruit (a harvest) that will abound to your account (with God). I am full and abound, having received what was sent from you, an odor of a sweet smell (Seed-Faith *giving and receiving* smells sweet to God), a sacrifice acceptable (given out of your need), well pleasing to God (Who is a rewarder of those who please Him) . . . and . . . my God shall supply all your need according to his riches in glory by Christ Jesus."

Remember Verse 19, *My God shall supply all your need,* was said by St. Paul first to those in Philippi who practiced giving AND receiving . . . who gave to Paul's needs for the work of God and received the promise that God would supply . . . and as they had given, they *received.* They received God's supply for all their needs. They got their breakthroughs.

Remember your *everlasting seed of faith* will have a sweet smell to God, it will abound to your miracle account in heaven, and through it God will miraculously supply great needs in your life. So concentrate your hopes and prayers on your Miracle Breakthrough. Think of your *miracle supply happening.* Look for it to happen as I look for mine to happen. There is nothing God cannot do. YOU WILL BE BLESSED!

HERE'S WHAT TO DO

God had spoken so clearly, *"I will rain upon your desert."* He is impressing me to the depths of my soul to obey Him and act — and I am doing it . . . now. I feel God is impressing you to ACT . . . NOW.

Here's what to do:

Mail your everlasting seed of faith. (I am praying even now God will make a way for you to send your $77 or multiples of $77 or the amount He has put into your heart — even when there may seem to be no way. I feel that if you will believe in my prayers, it will happen. You will have the seed to send just as I and my family have sent ours!)

Your letter will immediately be placed with the Abundant Life Prayer Group for 31 days and nights of prayer for your greatest breakthrough.

Your large poster of the Healing Hands will be mailed at once.

Best of all, I know GOD WILL RAIN UPON YOUR DESERT. HE WILL CONTINUE TO RAIN UPON YOUR DESERT.

Expecting to receive your *everlasting seed of faith* during the next 14 days, and expecting you to receive your greatest miracles from God's Healing Hands, I am

                              Your partner always,

                              Oral Roberts

Dear Oral Roberts:

I have learned through this book how to come through my life-and-death struggles. I know there will be more.

I want to share even my little faith. I have learned that by planting a seed I can begin my walk on the water, I can make my leap of faith and come into a closer partnership with God. I can get my greatest breakthrough.

So I am lovingly and cheerfully planting this seed of:

$ 77 ☐

$_____ ☐ (Multiples of $77, such as two $77's, three $77's, etc., on up to $777.)

$777 ☐

$_____ ☐ Other

for the CITY OF FAITH. I'm expecting God's repeatable acts of miracles to help me through all my struggles. I know I will be blessed.

NAME _____

ADDRESS _____

CITY_____ STATE_____ ZIP_____

See next page. ➤

Dear Oral Roberts, my prayer requests are . . .

_____

_____

_____

_____

_____

_____

_____

_____

_____

_____

_____

_____

_____

_____

Name_____

Dear Friend,

My prayer for you is that this book — HOW TO GET
THROUGH YOUR STRUGGLES — will help you learn that
God is greater than any problem you have. But I want to
go beyond that. I want to pray for you personally. So I
invite you to write me and tell me your prayer requests.
I promise I'll pray and I'll write you back. Simply address
your letter:

Oral Roberts
Tulsa, Oklahoma 74171

If you have a special prayer request you are encouraged
to call the Abundant Life Prayer Group at (918) 492-7777.
Call anytime, day or night, and a trained prayer partner
will answer your call and pray with you.

Oral Roberts

FREE AND POSTPAID TO YOU WITHOUT OBLIGATION

Oral Roberts' other books referred to in "How To Get Through Your Struggles"

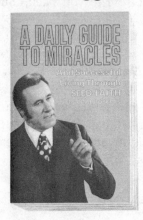

God wants you to have your greatest breakthrough